J.B.S.

The Life and Work of J. B. S. Haldane

J.B.S.

The Life and Work of
J. B. S. Haldane

*

RONALD CLARK

Oxford   New York
OXFORD UNIVERSITY PRESS
1984

Oxford University Press, Walton Street, Oxford OX2 6DP

London Glasgow New York Toronto
Delhi Bombay Calcutta Madras Karachi
Kuala Lumpur Singapore Hong Kong Tokyo
Nairobi Dar es Salaam Cape Town
Melbourne Auckland
and associated companies in
Beirut Berlin Ibadan Mexico City Nicosia

Oxford is a trade mark of Oxford University Press

© Ronald Clark 1968

First published 1968 by Hodder and Stoughton Limited
First issued as an Oxford University Press paperback 1984

All rights reserved. No part of this publication may be reproduced,
stored in a retrieval system, or transmitted, in any form or by any means,
electronic, mechanical, photocopying, recording, or otherwise, without
the prior permission of Oxford University Press

This book is sold subject to the condition that it shall not, by way
of trade or otherwise, be lent, re-sold, hired out or otherwise circulated
without the publisher's prior consent in any form of binding or cover
other than that in which it is published and without a similar condition
including this condition being imposed on the subsequent purchaser

British Library Cataloguing in Publication Data
Clark, Ronald
J.B.S.: The life and work of J. B. S. Haldane.—(Oxford paperbacks)
1. Haldane, John Burdon Sanderson 2. Scientists—
Great Britain—Biography I. Title
509.2′4 Q143.H/
ISBN 0-19-281430-3

Library of Congress Cataloging in Publication Data
Clark, Ronald William
J.B.S., the life and work of J. B. S. Haldane. (Oxford paperbacks)
Reprint. Originally published: London: Hodder and Stoughton, 1968
Bibliography: p. Includes index.
1. Haldane, J. B. S. (John Burdon Sanderson),
1892-1964. 2. Biologists—Great Britain—Biography.
I. Title. II. Title: JBS, the life and work of
J. B. S. Haldane.
QH31.H27C55 1984 575′.0092′4 [B] 83-17216
ISBN 0-19-281430-3 (pbk.)

Printed in Great Britain by
The Guernsey Press Co. Ltd.
Guernsey, Channel Islands

Author's Acknowledgements

M y main and very sincere thanks are due to Dr. Helen Spurway who not only gave me unrestricted access to, and use of, Professor Haldane's papers in Bhubaneswar, but who did so despite the possibility, if not the likelihood, that my assessment of Haldane might differ from hers—an outstanding example of intellectual honesty. Similar thanks are due to Haldane's sister, Naomi Mitchison, who helped in numerous ways although well aware that my views on her brother's politics were different from her own.

The Haldane archives consist of a massive collection which includes family papers; extensive scientific material; files of correspondence accumulated over almost half a century; an unfinished draft autobiography; many autobiographical notes and jottings, some of which were incorporated in later writings with only trivial amendments; and two different sets of Personal Notes for the Royal Society, which appear never to have reached it; as well as Minutes of the meetings of the *Daily Worker* Editorial Board. In handling these I was given great help not only by Dr. Spurway but also by Haldane's three devoted colleagues: Suresh Jayakar, Sri P. Srihari Rao, and Ramaswamy Shastri Mangipudi to all of whom I am immensely grateful.

Dr. Martin Case; Major A. V. M. Chapman, Curator of the Black Watch Museum; Dr. John Godfrey; Professor L. S. Penrose; N. W. Pirie; and Dr. Pamela Lamplugh Robinson, are among those I wish to thank for having read various portions of the manuscript and for having made useful suggestions.

I am also extremely grateful to Haldane's colleagues, acquaintances, students, friends and enemies, who have written to me about him. They have included men who served under him in the First World War, as well as brother-officers; members of the International Brigade; miners who listened to him and those who helped to heckle him, as well as the expected scientists and fellow-workers. They number hundreds, and it would be impossible to thank them all individually here. But I feel that it would be wrong not to record my special thanks to the following: F. G. Balcombe of the Cave Diving Group; Miss Julia Bell; Sir Frederick Brundrett; Professor R. A. M. Case; Professor E. B.

Chain; Professor C. D. Darlington; Professor F. N. David; T. A. Davis; Miss Ann Dear; Professor K. R. Dronamraju; Professor K. W. Donald; Professor Hans Grüneberg; Professor H. Harris; Dr. Gordon Haskell; A. J. Kidwai; Mrs. O. M. Meares; Dr. D. A. Mitchison; Lady O'Malley; Baron Leopold von Plessen; J. M. Rendel; Lord Ritchie-Calder; Miss Brenhilda Schafer; Captain W. O. Shelford, R.N.; Jagjit Singh; Brigadier the Rt. Hon. Sir John Smyth; Henry Rowan Walker; Miss D. de Winton.

In addition, I would like to thank Sir Peter Medawar for contributing the preface, N. W. Pirie for his permission to reproduce the very fine bibliography with which he concluded his Biographical Memoir of Haldane published by the Royal Society, and "The New Statesman and Nation" for permission to reproduce "Cancer's a Funny Thing".

I would like to stress that, while I have received much help and co-operation from Haldane's relatives and friends, responsibility for the facts stated and opinions expressed is solely mine except where the reverse is obvious.

R.W.C.

Preface
by
Sir Peter Medawar

THE lives of academics, considered as Lives, almost always make dull reading. The undergraduate career, full of promise later to be fulfilled; fellowships and chairs and perhaps a manly grappling with administration; honorary degrees, an Order maybe, and grateful letters from high places—these are splendid distinctions, but not of a kind to enthral the reading public. This is understandable enough and there is no reason to lament it. Academics cannot lead lives that are spacious or exciting in a worldly sense. They need laboratories or libraries and the company of other academics. Their work is in no way deepened or made more cogent by privation, distress or wordly buffetings. Close enquiry might show their private lives to be unhappy, strangely mixed up or comic, but not in ways that give one any special insight into the nature or direction of their work.

Yet J. B. S. Haldane's life, as Mr. Ronald Clark recounts it, is fascinating from end to end. Unless one is in the know already, there is no foretelling at one moment what comes next. He could have made a success of any one of half a dozen careers—as mathematician, classical scholar, philosopher, scientist, journalist or imaginative writer. To unequal degrees he was in fact all of these things. On his life's showing he could not have been a politician, administrator (heavens, no!), jurist or, I think, a critic of any kind. In the outcome he became one of the three or four most influential biologists of his generation. In some respects—quickness of grasp, and the power to connect things in his mind in completely unexpected ways—he was the cleverest man I ever knew. He had something new and theoretically illuminating to say on every scientific subject he chose to give his mind to—on the kinetics of enzyme action, on disease as a factor in evolution, on the relationship between antigens and genes, and on the impairment of judgement by prolonged exposure to high concentrations of carbon dioxide. Haldane was the first to describe the genetic phenomenon of linkage in animals generally, and the first to estimate mutation rate in man. His greatest work began in the 1920s, when independently of R. A. Fisher and Sewall Wright he undertook to refound Darwinism upon the concepts of Mendelian genetics. It should have caused a great awakening of Darwinian theory, and in due course it did so, though at the time it did no more than make Darwinism stir uneasily in its sleep. This is "classical work" assimilated into all the standard texts. If he had done nothing else, he would still be classified as a Grand Master of modern evolution theory. Yet Haldane was not a profoundly original thinker. His genius was to enrich the soil, not to bring new land into cultivation. He was not the author of any great biological conception, nor did his ideas arouse the misgivings and resentment so often stirred up by what is revolutionary or entirely new. On the contrary, everything he said was at once recognized as fruitful and illuminating, something to be taken very seriously, something one would have been proud and delighted to have thought of oneself, even if later research should prove it to be mistaken.

What are we to make of Haldane as a human being? The first thing to be said in answer to such a question is that we are under no obligation to make anything of him at all. It makes no difference now. It might have made a difference if Haldane in his lifetime had come to realise the degree to which his work was obstructed by his own perversity. He was so very ignorant of everything to do with administration that he did not even know how to call the authorities' attention to the contempt in which he held them. When he burst into terrible anger over real or imagined grievances it was over the heads of minor functionaries and clerks. Page 198 describes a scene which those who knew him came to regard as typical. On behalf of one of his students Haldane applied for one of the Agricultural Research Council's postgraduate awards. These awards are made provisionally, and are confirmed if the candidate gets an adequate degree. To speed things up, one of the Council's junior officers rang Haldane's secretary up to find out what class of degree the candidate had in fact been given. As it happened, the class lists had not been published, so the reasonable answer would have been "I'm sorry, we can't tell you yet because the results aren't out." Instead Haldane accused the Council of blackmail and an attempt to violate the secrecy of exams: "I refuse to give you the information, and withdraw my request for a grant. I shall pay for her out of my own pocket." If indeed he did so, he inflicted an appropriate punishment on himself. Yet more than once he scored an important victory; over the *Sex Viri*, for example, a sort of *buffo* male voice sextet that tried to deprive him of his Cambridge Readership on the ground of immorality (pp. 75-76). Indeed, the scenes accompanying the divorce that freed Haldane to marry Charlotte read like the libretto of a comic opera—including an adultery, chaste in spite of appearances to the contrary.

We must not take all Haldane's outbursts at their face value. His declaration that he left England to live in India because of the disgrace of Suez was a remarkably effective way of expressing his contempt for the Suez adventure; but it simply wasn't true. I remember Haldane's once going back on a firm promise to chair a public lecture given by a distinguished American scientist on the grounds that it would be too embarrassing for the lecturer: he had once been the victim of a sexual assault by the lecturer's wife. The accusation was utterly ridiculous, and Haldane did not in the least resent my saying so. He simply didn't want to be bothered by the chairmanship, and felt too ashamed to say so in the usual way. But the trouble was that his extravagances became self-defeating. He became a "character", and people began laughing in anticipation of what he would say or be up to next. It is sort of Anglo-Saxon form of liquidation. In the Russia of Haldane's day, as Mr. Clark makes clear, he would have been much more offensive and with very much better reasons, but he would not have lasted long.

Physical bravery, but sometimes moral cowardice; intelligence and folly, reasonableness and obstinacy, vanity and humility, kindness and aggressiveness, generosity and pettiness—it is like a formulary for all mankind: Haldane was a with-knobs-on variant of us all. People who are tired of reading of how lofty thoughts can go with silly opinions, or of how a man may fight for freedom yet sometimes condone the work of its enemies, have a simple remedy: they need read no further. But they will miss a great deal if they don't.

Contents

Illustrations

Acknowledgement of permission to use the photographs listed above is due as follows: 1 and 2, Mrs. Naomi Mitchison; 3, Department of Biochemistry, University of Cambridge; 4, 6 and 7, *Sun*; 5, Keystone Press Agency; 8 and 11, source unknown (prints supplied by the author); 9, Indian Statistical Institute; 10, R. P. Mirsley.

PART

I

TRAINING

I

Life With Father

JOHN BURDON SANDERSON HALDANE was born on November 5th 1892, a Guy Fawkes day link with the dynamiting of authority that never ceased to delight him. On both sides of the family tree his ancestors were vigorous, mentally distinguished, and toughly individualist; from them he was to draw a combination of aristocratic self-assurance, intellectual integrity and almost endearing bloody-mindedness. The dark side was to be represented by an old-womanly fussiness, an irascibility which he took pains to cultivate, and an unpredictable rudeness to juniors and servants, as well as to men of power, which contrasted strongly with his underlying kindliness.

Haldane's ancestors emerge from the mists of Scottish history in the mid-13th century, though he himself frequently boasted that he could trace his line back to Pedro the Cruel, the 14th century King of Castile and Leon. For generations the family occupied what was at first a small fort lying at the foot of Glendevon, and commanding a route from the bleak Highlands to the fair Carse of Perth. "Our main job," J.B.S. once wrote, "was to stop the tribal people of the hills from raiding the cattle of the plainsmen; but perhaps once in a generation we went south to resist an English invasion, and at least two of my direct ancestors were killed while doing so." The tradition persisted, he noted, even after the Union. In the 17th century John Haldane, a direct ancestor in the male line, carried his sword across the North Sea to fight for the Prince of Orange and returned to become Scottish representative with Cromwell's Army during the Civil War. "I am," J.B.S. noted towards the end of a long life, "a man of violence by temperament and training." More recent ancestors echoed more peaceful times— his great-grandfather James who sold much family property to raise money for a Mission in Bengal, and his gentle grandfather Robert Haldane of Cloan. Robert Haldane married Mary Elizabeth Burdon Sanderson, from a well-known Northumberland family—to this day it is possible to find, in the Jesmond

15

area of Newcastle, the neighbouring Burdon, Sanderson and Haldane Terraces—and the second son of the union was John Scott Haldane.

An early member of the Eureka Club, an Edinburgh naturalist group which included Diarmid Paton, D'Arcy Thompson and W. A. Herdman, and which was later to provide seven Fellows of the Royal Society, John Scott Haldane graduated in Medicine at Edinburgh. He worked for a while as demonstrator at University College, Dundee, carrying out there a classic investigation of the air in houses, schools and sewers. He then joined his uncle, Sir John Burdon Sanderson, Waynflete Professor at Oxford University. Kindly, courteous, humanitarian, John Scott Haldane quickly developed into the prototype of the Victorian scientist, dedicated to his laboratory, wedded at first to materialism, keeping one hand stretched out towards God, and moving steadily across the philosophical front so that he could conclude his Donnellan Lectures, "The Philosophical Basis of Biology", by nailing his flag to a new mast. "This is," he concluded, "a spiritual world."

This physiologist who was quietly to revolutionise some of man's theories about the human mechanism, looking in old age rather like an even gentler Einstein, married Louisa Kathleen Trotter, member of a comfortably-equipped south Scottish family which had for years provided its quota of admirals, generals, and gentlemen of leisure. Extraordinarily beautiful in youth, she had a kindliness well laced with discipline. A believer in the white man's burden, she was a passionate feminist, yet in an Oxford steadily moving towards the Left, held the contrary line with a Victoria League whose activities became famous.

From these parents J.B.S. inherited a tendency which never quite left him. Intellectually, there was, it is true, the doubt by which he judged most things. Traditionally, there was one field in which no doubt could be allowed—that when a Haldane made up his mind that it was right to act, then action would follow as a duty, ignoring all obstacles or any suggestion that the proposed course could be anything other than the ideal. Like the aristocrat down the ages, he responded to opposition by not giving a damn for anyone; and his reaction to his upbringing was—like that of his sister, Naomi—a glittering example of Newton's law that every action produces a contrary and equal reaction. J.B.S. would claim in old age that his opinions differed from those of his father "mainly on questions of emphasis and terminology rather than of fact". Yet while

16

John Scott Haldane was able to present the Gifford Lectures, founded to promote ". . . the study of natural theology, in the widest sense of that term, in other words, the knowledge of God", J.B.S. swung contrariwise into the field of dialectical materialism. While his mother thought of India in terms of imperial splendour, her son was to think of it in terms of shackles to be broken.

The details of J. B. S. Haldane's early years which remain, either on record or in reminiscence, fit cleanly together to form a shadow of things to come. His first memory was of sitting in his high chair, of his mother asking why he made such curious faces, and of his explanation that he was trying to imitate various dogs—those with long noses, those with square faces, those with funny eyes. At the age of ten months he screamed so loudly in the same high chair that the result was unilateral infantile hernia—reduced by his mother to whom, as he later put it, he owed his continued existence. At the age of two he was crawling about his father's study floor, watching a complicated game called experiments, whose rules he did not understand but which his father clearly enjoyed. He could read by his third birthday, and before the next he is claimed to have asked, on looking at the blood from his cut forehead: "Is it oxyhaemoglobin or carboxyhaemoglobin?" By the age of five he had been taught German by his nurse, and could already write enough English to leave scattered about the house small notes inscribed "I hate you".

His real education came from his father, to whose example in the scientific approach to facts he owed much of his success. The education began young, and at the age of three the father was taking samples of his son's blood for investigation. A year later both travelled to London where John Scott Haldane was testing the atmosphere on the Metropolitan Underground. "I remember the dirt and smoke vividly," J.B.S. wrote sixty years later. "I even recollect the smell of the latter. [My father] used to open the window and collect air samples in glass bottles from which he sucked the air with a rubber tube . . ." At the age of five the boy was being taught to read the British Association reports in *The Times* while D'Arcy Thompson, visiting the Haldanes at Oxford before J.B.S. could properly walk, was much impressed with the way in which the toddler handled and studied objects "with a precocious and scientific expression".

The young Haldane had a plumpish and misleadingly beatific face that changed only slowly throughout childhood. One feature remained unaltered—the chin that in photographs of J.B.S. at three, four, six years, and on into manhood, appears stubbornly out-thrust however the camera is placed. But podginess eventually developed into toughness; the form that was slightly too well-covered became well-built; the fair hair darkened and the cherubic countenance became that of a youth obviously capable of fighting his own battles. This was as well. An innate shyness forced him to erect his own personal barriers; a brusque rudeness was one way of keeping at arm's length those who might intrude into his privacy; and in such circumstances an ability to take care of oneself was not so much an asset as a qualification for survival. This was particularly necessary for those trained to describe whatever they felt and saw, regardless of the consequences; and objective observation, disinterested description, the logical deduction of one fact from another, and the following of such deductions wherever they might lead, were the common coin of life as it was lived by John Scott Haldane.

J.B.S. learned more than this scientific attitude from his father. John Scott Haldane was one of those very rare men who can train themselves to ignore fear. His son, describing how his father disliked experimenting on animals and "preferred to work on himself or other human beings who were sufficiently interested in the work to ignore pain or fear", explained that his father had achieved a state in which he was almost indifferent to pain. "However," he went on, "his object was not to achieve this state but to achieve knowledge which could save other men's lives. His attitude was much more like that of a good soldier who will risk his life and endure wounds in order to gain victory, than that of an ascetic who deliberately undergoes pain. The soldier does not get himself wounded deliberately, and my father did not seek pain in his work, though he greeted a pain which would have made some people writhe or groan, with laughter." All his life J.B.S. remembered how it was Scott's *Tales of a Grandfather*, those "legends of the war-like exploits of the Scottish nobility", which were most frequently read to him by his father, the man who trained him "in the practice of courage".

This training was part and parcel of the co-operation in his father's scientific work which he enjoyed. By the age of eight he was taking down the numbers which John Scott Haldane called out when he read the burette of his gas analysis apparatus; soon afterwards he was calculating from these numbers the quantities of the gases in each sample. He was promoted to making simple mixtures for his father's use, and to cleaning the delicate apparatus. Before he was ten, his father had explained the rudiments of stereoisomerism so that he ever afterwards "thought in terms of molecules". A few months later his uncle, Sir John Burdon Sanderson, taught him the use of the slide-rule, while only a few years afterwards John Scott Haldane, finding that he had forgotten his log tables on an expedition, is claimed to have commented: "Never mind. Jack will calculate a set for us." Jack, according to the story, sat down and did so. Like many other stories about J.B.S., this one may be apocryphal; but he tried to live up to them.

Intellectual precocity combined with a ferocious memory gave J.B.S. an arrogance which, when questioned, would result in a spectacular loss of temper. This first showed itself when, at the age of six, he began to attend the Oxford Preparatory School, today the Dragon School, and then known as Lynam's after its famous headmaster. Here he was frequently baited, and on one occasion, after being continually tormented during a break, he tore up a complete sapling, roots and all, and attacked his tormentor with it. The assailant dodged the massive sweeps of the weapon until the bell rang for resumption of work. J.B.S. flung down the sapling and stormed into the class-room roaring: "I wish I could kill. I wish I could KILL."

It was fortunate that by this time he was heavily-built and well able to take care of himself. Years later, in fact, he was remembered by Brigadier Smyth as the hero of the best bare-knuckle fight Smyth had ever seen, one of the few fights allowed to take place at Lynam's.

"His antagonist was a Spanish boy called Manuel—quick-tempered, red-haired, a beautifully-built athlete who was as quick of movement as Jack was slow," says Smyth. "What the fight was all about I never discovered. I simply saw a ring of boys and rushed over to join in the fun. Jack was taking a terrible battering. It was just like a bull-fight with Manuel the Matador. But, unlike any other bull-fight I have ever seen, in this one the bull won. Although he had to take three swipes for every one he delivered, that one was a good straight left, with all his weight behind it. And gradually the tide turned, until Manuel, his face swollen and his eyes blackened, fled from the scene." More than half a century later J.B.S. wrote, significantly, that one of his favourite quotations from English verse was:

> Charge once more then and be dumb.
> Let the victors, when they come,

> When the forts of folly fall
> Find thy body by the wall.

The uninhibited pugnacity of the small boy, which was to develop into the grown man's delight in argument for argument's sake, might well have been quenched by a serious accident at the age of eight; so might life itself. J.B.S. was riding on the step of his father's bicycle, the size of the step having been reduced by clips for a luggage carrier. Haldane senior had just turned the corner from the Broad into Parks Road when his son slipped off. This in itself might have caused little damage, but the young Haldane's head hit the stone kerb, and in the infirmary a compound fracture of the base of the skull was diagnosed.

At first the doctor feared that the damage might prove fatal; that the boy would probably be mentally deranged if he recovered; and that he would certainly be deaf in one ear. Since he not only recovered but had good hearing until old age—although being tone deaf—J.B.S. later promised his skull to Sir Arthur Keith should he die first. Keith would then be able to "see how the works of my internal ear were mended".

"We had a desperately anxious time but there were no complications and after about ten days Jack demanded a proper breakfast," his mother wrote many years later. " 'Well, what would you like?' he was asked by the doctor standing with the surgeon at the foot of the bed. I can see them quite plainly exchanging glances, evidently expecting to be asked to allow something very unwholesome. 'Porridge,' said Jack firmly." When the surgeon prescribed a dose from the pharmacopoeia, J.B.S. broke in with: "But you are the mechanical chap. Leave that to the chemical chap."

J.B.S. missed about six weeks of Lynam's. Long afterwards, more than one of his companions believed that it was only after his return that they had first seen a triangle of white hair on his head which seemed unaccountably to have developed round the scar. This was, however, due not to the accident but to a genetic inheritance which did not appear until middle childhood. At least one of his nieces and one of his nephews, were to carry it. Later, at Eton, it was to be remembered in a College rhyme:

> H is for Haldane who has a white spot
> On the back of his head where others have not.

"After the accident," says one of his school-fellows, "Jack blossomed out into a brilliant mathematician and rumour had it that he actually taught the maths master. He went to Eton and again it was rumoured that he was teaching them. All this brilliance was put down by us—and, I believe, by Lynams' masters—as due to the indenting of his skull by the pavement. The fact that his father had a reputation for brilliance may have had something to do with it, but we would have none of that. As far as we were concerned the blow did it."

This brilliance, which quickly developed from that of the exceptionally bright boy into that of the near-prodigy, brought J.B.S. to the top of the School in Latin, translation, arithmetic and geometry before he reached the age of twelve or even entered the top form; only two of the whole school passed him in Greek or Latin Verse. This almost disconcerting success was surpassed the following year, 1904, when he walked off with an armful of prizes including the First Scholarship to Eton. "Haldane kept his form throughout," the examiner wrote of his classical papers, "78 per cent was his worst mark. His work was always interesting and he never lost his head." His maths examiner, who noted that Haldane tackled four questions that no one else attempted, described him as being "in a class by himself".

Such excellence had dangers and it is difficult not to believe that J.B.S., essentially shy and retiring behind the aggressiveness with which he used to keep others at arm's length, was somewhat embarrassed by his own intellectual superiority. He knew that he was brighter, more comprehending, capable of a superior awareness, and he felt, as he was to feel throughout his life, a prickly discomfort about the gap which this created between himself and those who might have been his companions. To a person of Haldane's temperament, the solution was inevitable. He enlarged the gap and rejoiced in it. The impression of one school-fellow, given years later, was that "he regarded most of us, quite rightly, as intellectually sub-human".

Roughly a year before J.B.S. went to Eton, the Haldanes moved from their relatively modest house in North Oxford to "Cherwell", built for John Scott Haldane off the north end of the Banbury Road on a site sloping down to the river, taken on a hundred-year lease from St. John's. Ample and rambling, comfortable and ugly, "Cherwell" was to be the home of the family for sixty years. When erected to John Scott Haldane's specification, no other building was in sight, even the nearest spires of Oxford being hidden by the trees which formed the skyline to the south. To the north, open fields served a farm attached to what was almost a small estate, while to the east the ground dropped gently down towards the water-meadows and the river which rose regularly to cover them at flood-time.

On the wall that faced these fields there was worked in stone the eagle crest of the Haldanes and the single word of the family motto—"Suffer". As a symbol in the life of J.B.S. this was to have the significance of *Citizen Kane's* "rosebud". To suffer and to endure was to seem more a natural part of life to J.B.S. than it did to most men; and when, in old age, he came finally to India, the Hindu cycle of birth and suffering and re-birth was one he recognised.

Inside, "Cherwell" had the rambling inconsequence of an age where both space and servants cost little, and its rooms—between twenty and thirty in number according to definition—varied in size from the almost ballroom proportions of the drawing-room, to the semi-attic quarters below the eaves inhabited by the maids. Of the latest modern conveniences, only one was lacking. As a gas referee, John Scott Haldane had seen enough of the accidents caused by gas or its mismanagement, and he rigorously forbade its presence in the house, although there was a gas fire as well as bunsen burners in his laboratory. His study was on the ground floor, its carpet "hidden under layers of paper, its desk piled high with more papers, chairs laden with reports, notes and sheets of calculations", a description by Kate Terry Gielgud, a frequent visitor, which would later have been accurate of any study occupied by J.B.S. On one occasion Mrs. Haldane asked whether it would be possible for the study to be included in the spring-cleaning and for the carpet to be lifted and beaten. "Yes," she was told, "as long as you don't move any of the papers." On the ground floor there was the laboratory, extended during the First World War for experiments undertaken to help the Services, and containing an airtight chamber, complete with sealable door and observation window through which those inside could be watched. On the ground floor also, the heart of the house as the study was its brain, lay the spacious drawing-room with its cosy hearth and log fire, its book-cases and its cabinets of heirloom china, its well-worn leather sofa and its comfortable chairs, a room next to which was its counterpart, a dining-room from whose walls the ancestors looked down on to a sea of heavy Victorian furniture.

To "Cherwell" there came John Scott Haldane's brother, already a distinguished Q.C. and eventually to become Lord Haldane of Cloan, Secretary of State for War, and then Lord

Chancellor, travelling from the Perthshire estate at Cloan or coming up from his London chambers. Here came his sister, Elizabeth Haldane, social reformer and philosopher, a multiplicity of Trotter relatives, and a constant succession of University notables. They provided the environment in which J.B.S. grew up, an environment which he both loved and hated, and one which created both a base secure from the buffets of the world and an ample incentive to rebellion.

It was from "Cherwell" that J.B.S. went to Eton—with an arm broken in one of the accidents to which he was prone, and still strapped up. Many men, even sensitive men, have come through Eton unscathed; not a few have succeeded in using its somewhat macabre toughening processes for their own benefit. J.B.S. was not so lucky. Yet in one way Eton made him, and made him more decisively than the rigours of a public school can be expected to make boys who are abnormally intelligent or unusually sensitive. It brought out the determined sense of independence and self-sufficiency; at the same time it both enlarged his self-identification with the persecuted minority and developed this into an unreasoning belief that minorities were always more likely to be right than wrong, and always more likely to be persecuted than not. After Eton, Haldane was against—against authority and against the Government, any authority and any Government; if possible in the cause of reason, if not as a matter of principle.

Perhaps Lynam's had been too tolerant. Perhaps there was no escape for a boy of Haldane's intellectual ability; certainly there was none for one of his intellectual arrogance. And in a society where weakness was not tolerated a broken arm was an added handicap. During his first years at Eton J.B.S. was mercilessly bullied, a natural reaction of juvenile demons to a companion who could announce, on being left in a room with three masters, that it was pleasant to find oneself among adults. "The senior boys in College did not like me," he later wrote, although he would probably have made an exception of Julian Huxley, for whom he fagged for a while, and whom he long remembered for giving him an apple, a mark of favour from senior to junior that was considered quite exceptional. During one term he was beaten every night for a week, at least once on the soles of his feet. When Lord Haldane officially visited the school, his nephew was forcibly prevented from meeting him by the drastic process of being pinned down under an upturned table loaded with bags of sand.

The bullying bit deep. Of equal significance was the rift on

23

religion which developed between J.B.S. and authority. His father's spiritual leanings were of a rather orthodox kind while his mother was never a Christian, regarding it as a religion suitable only for servants, and never going to church other than to the New College chapel where she attended, for non-religious reasons, occasional funerals or weddings. Her son had evolved differently. "I developed a mild liking for the Anglican ritual and a complete immunity to religion," he later commented. And at Cloan, on the occasions when he was the eldest male member of the family present, he led family prayers—producing, according to his sister, "some splendid extempore prayers which much edified the cook and butler".

Now, at Eton, he was little affected by the twenty-minute morning Chapel, the ten-minute evening prayers or the two-hour Sunday services. But the efforts of an over-enthusiastic proselytising matron who was, he claimed, "more interested in our souls [from an Anglo-Catholic angle] than our bodies", was a different matter. Her efforts drove him into the ranks of the Rationalist Press Association. By 1908, aged sixteen, he was introducing to one of his companions who had just been confirmed, Haeckel's *Riddle of the Universe* with its reasoning that the Deity is no more than a gaseous vertebrate. Later he began circulating Metchnikoff's *The Nature of Man*, but this was inadvertently left by a companion in the reading-room and taken to the Master in College, A. W. Whitworth. The result, in Haldane's words written at the time, was that Whitworth "tried to get me taken away. Uffer [his father] much amused and rather bored. Mother furious with Whitworth. Hiss [his biology master] furious with me . . . had discredited biology. Tutor a little amused, but said I must be careful."

By this time he was becoming almost non-bullyable owing to size and to a rise in the hierarchy. Although he still had little interest in organised sports, he was a keen if slightly comic "wall" in the Wall Game, and in his last year he rowed on the 4th of June in a kind of honorary boat called the *Monarch*—for now his transformation was complete. He had reached the First Hundred by the age of sixteen and won the Russell Prize —which meant that he was the second mathematician in the school—as well as prizes for physics, biology and chemistry. And he had then, inexorably propelled by ability, become Captain of the School. He also became a member of Pop, which according to his sister he especially enjoyed, "having the power of life and death so to speak, and for a long time he had the rules framed in blue ribbons and pop canes".

He had, as he put it, taken "advantage of chaotic conditions of curriculum to study science better than was possible earlier or later". In practice, this meant that he had switched from one specialisation to another, backed by his father who rejected the accusation of the headmaster, Canon Lyttelton, that his son was becoming a "mere smatterer". The result was that two years of classics had been followed by five terms of chemistry, one term of physics, three terms of history and three terms of biology. This wide base of knowledge meant that Haldane was to leave Eton better equipped than most of his contemporaries. "I could read Latin, Greek, French and German," he later wrote. "I knew enough chemistry to take part in research, enough biology to do unaided research, and I had a fair knowledge of history and contemporary politics. I knew about the Provisions of Oxford and the relation between the German Reichstag and Bundesrath. I have forgotten them all since. On the other hand I knew no economics. I had been forced to read parts of John Stuart Mill's *Principles of Political Economy* and found them ... unintelligible. And I knew practically no psychology or technology."

Thus equipped, J.B.S. went up to New College as expected, on a good mathematical scholarship, leaving Eton with mixed feelings. "From an intellectual point of view the education available at Eton in 1905–11 was good," he wrote twenty-five years later in a draft autobiography. But in one of the two sets of Personal Notes which he prepared for the Royal Society, he commented: "Was far from happy at Eton, nor was I beloved of teachers. My last classical form-master, H. MacNaughton, wrote; 'He is a baffling boy, and I shall be glad to be rid of him'."

This bafflement was probably due to one reason above all others: by the time that J.B.S. left Eton at the age of nineteen he had been forced into a contact with the world outside the schoolroom that was rare for a boy of his class. This was almost entirely due to the actions of his father. It is true that John Scott Haldane was deeply concerned with the spiritual world into which his work was intruding; dedicated in such a way that normal hours or routine ceased to exist; and of an absent-mindedness that became legendary even in Oxford. It was typical that he should comment one evening that he was depressed since he had just spent two hours trying to explain the elements of Christianity to Dean Inge. It was natural that as he rarely went to bed until the small hours, he should arrive at his laboratory at midday, fresh from breakfast, and then work on until the small hours once again. There were times at dinner, according to one colleague of J.B.S., when John Scott Haldane "would hardly notice or address a word to anyone. Then a large, freshly-baked cake would be brought in and as the last course was reached the Professor would pick it up and, comparatively oblivious of his guests, would disappear with it to his laboratory." On one famous day John Scott Haldane's absorption with a problem in physics coincided with an important dinner organised by his wife. He arrived late and after apologising went to dress. On his non-appearance his wife sought him out, only to discover him in bed. "I suddenly found myself taking my clothes off," he explained, "so I thought it must be time for bed."

Yet if John Scott Haldane in some ways represented the popular image of the 19th century scientist, he also typified the 20th century reality. He not only brought his son into the "Cherwell" laboratory as an assistant in his own right, turned to him for mathematical help, and treated him from the age of five as a junior adult. He retained that attitude as his son grew up. By the time J.B.S. went up to Oxford he had therefore been taken down mines where his father was investigating working conditions or the results of explosions, and he had made a forty-foot experimental dive off the Scottish coast. His mother, who according to his sister "didn't hold with us being friendly with shop-keepers or people 'in business', in fact encouraged us to be friends with miners and fishermen". And J.B.S. was thus pushed by his father into close contact with the conditions of difficulty and danger in which thousands of ordinary men earned their livelihood. It was an experience which was to affect his whole life.

It was also while accompanying his father that J.B.S. made his first contact with Indians, a people whose hopes were to impinge with increasing frequency and effort on his own life. This was in the early 1900's when a severe plague in India had induced a number of European countries to experiment with methods of killing rats in ships arriving from the Far East. The French had installed apparatus for doing this with sulphur dioxide, and John Scott Haldane was briefed to report on its effectiveness. Early in October, therefore, he sailed in the Anchor Line's s.s. *Bavaria* from Tilbury to Dunkirk with his wife and son, on the last leg of the ship's voyage from India. The Haldanes were met by a member of the Institut Pasteur, the ship was docked, and the asphyxiating gas was turned on from a neighbouring barge. "On opening the holds," J.B.S. later recalled, "a number of dead rats were seen. The crew, being Muslims, had no reverence for rats, and I joined in their competition as to who could collect most dead rats on entering the forecastle with breath held." The ship was guarded by a very fat gendarme with a sword. J.B.S. eluded him, but was later faced with the gentlemen who expostulated, *"Ventre du diable!"* "These were," says J.B.S., "the first words of French which I heard on French soil. I have liked French and Indians ever since."

John Scott Haldane's main industrial work concerned mines, and to investigate and report on these he was regularly employed by both Government and industry. "My father would go off to any mine disaster wearing his mine clothes and then would send back a telegram, and very often he'd be suffering from carbon monoxide poisoning," his daugher Naomi has said. "And that meant that he'd forget what he'd done, and then there would be a series of telegrams saying 'All Safe' and so on. And we knew that this was a result of the poisoning. This was a very exciting atmosphere to grow up in, and I think my brother set his mind on science and on the kind of science which is likely to help people."

For J.B.S. often accompanied his father, partly as a useful experimental animal whose reactions might be interesting, partly to be taught the facts of life. Thus when father and son were exploring one of the "hot ends" of a Cornish tin mine, the collapse of J.B.S. in the hot moist air suggested to his father a series of experiments which occupied him intermittently for the rest of his life. Teaching his son the rudiments of science was also important, and J.B.S. long remembered a pit in North Staffordshire into which they were lowered not by the usual pit cage but sitting in a large bucket slung on a chain. At the bottom of the shaft, they walked a little way and then, as the roof of the tunnel sank, began to crawl. "After a while," J.B.S. later wrote, "we got to a place where the roof was about eight feet high and a man could stand up. One of the party lifted his safety lamp. It filled with blue flame and went out with a pop. If it had been a candle this would have started an explosion, and we should probably have been killed. But of course the flame of the explosion inside the safety lamp was kept in by the wire gauze. The air near the roof was full of methane, or firedamp, which is a gas lighter than air, so the air on the floor was not dangerous.

"To demonstrate the effects of breathing firedamp, my father told me to stand up and recite Mark Anthony's speech from

Shakespeare's *Julius Caesar*, beginning 'Friends, Romans, countrymen'. I soon began to pant, and somewhere about 'the noble Brutus' my legs gave way and I collapsed on to the floor, where, of course, the air was all right. In this way I learnt that firedamp is lighter than air and not dangerous to breathe."

Such adventures increased his powers of observation and quickened his responses. At the same time they tended to widen the gulf between himself and the schoolboys, and later the undergraduates, with whom he mixed. His brain put him on a different level and the difference was increased when he compared his own experiences with those who tended to be circumscribed by mothers' tea-parties. He, after all, had been able to lecture to the Eton Scientific Society on deep-diving, to demonstrate with a genuine diving suit sent down with an assistant from the manufacturers—and, moreover, to describe his own experiences.

For in 1908 J.B.S. had taken part in experiments which were to transform the whole diving practice of the British Navy. They were the concluding items in a long programme of work in which John Scott Haldane had evolved a system of "stage decompression" for bringing deep-divers to the surface, and were carried out from H.M.S. *Spanker* in the Kyles of Bute off the Arran coast. All the family travelled up to Scotland, and J.B.S. spent a considerable time on H.M.S. *Spanker* during the long programme of dives, undertaken by different members of the crew under varying conditions.

Naturally enough, the young J.B.S., not yet sixteen, eagerly seized the chance of making a trial dive, although the fact was carefully excluded from the long list of experimental figures eventually produced in the official report. Large as he was for his age, he was unable to provide a good fit for the full-scale diving suit available; but with what seems to have been a certain casualness he was kitted out and lowered over the side. The boy had not been submerged for long before water began to seep into his diving dress round the badly-fitting ankle- and wrist-bands. However, he knew how to operate the valves which controlled pressure in the suit, managed to keep the water down to breast height, and remained submerged for the allotted time, at the planned level, before being raised to the surface, dried out, and put into a bunk, warmed by blankets without and a stiff tot of whisky within.

Shortly afterwards there was a sequel when John Scott Haldane was invited to take part in the trial run of a new Admiralty submarine. He needed an assistant and explained to his family that since the ship was on the secret list, his choice was limited. When her husband had become thoroughly worried about the assistant, Mrs. Haldane casually asked: "Why not take Boy?" "Is he old enough?" John Scott Haldane replied, turning to his son to ask: "What's the formula for soda-lime?" J.B.S. rapped out the formula. Shortly afterwards he made his first trip in a submarine.

It was thus an undergraduate more experienced than most who went up to New College in the autumn of 1911. His reputation travelled ahead of him, and it was soon believed that he had entered for a Classical Scholarship, had gone into the wrong room, and triumphantly answered the mathematical paper which faced him. He lived up to the legend, gaining first-class honours in Maths. Mods. within a year.

However, J.B.S. claimed that no one could study mathematics intensively for more than five hours a day and remain sane. This left time in hand, and to occupy it he attended, almost as a relaxation, E. S. Goodrich's finals honours course in Zoology. Goodrich had an unusual record for a Professor of Science, having been trained as an artist at the Slade and only later being drawn into Zoology by Ray Lankester. Half a century later Haldane remembered not only Goodrich's lectures, which he regarded as an inspiration, but also his remarkable blackboard drawings. "He used colours symbolically," he wrote to a colleague. "Sensory and motor nerves would be in a different colour from one another or [from] blood-vessels. And he doubtless distorted shapes so as to represent things not simultaneously visible. But the emotional effect on me was very considerable, partly because he clearly knew his intentions before he started. I venture to call his blackboard drawing, Art." These lectures did more than arouse in Haldane a lasting interest in the mechanism of the living world; they also, indirectly, presented him with the chance of announcing his first discovery in the field that he was to make specially his own, that of genetics.

A decade earlier, in the autumn of 1901, John Scott Haldane had taken his son to an evening conversazione of the Oxford University Junior Scientific Club at which A. D. Darbishire had lectured on the recently re-discovered work of Gregor Mendel. Forty years earlier this Austrian monk had scientifically bred a number of plants, had recorded the results, and had drawn from these results tentative conclusions as to how physical characteristics were handed down from one generation to the next. Only in 1900, with the unearthing of his work, almost simultaneously by three different biologists, did these conclusions appear beneath the floodlight of scientific enquiry. And only in the decade that followed was the basic theory, found difficult but interesting by Haldane as he listened as a boy of eight, developed and expanded in the laboratories of the world. There existed in living organisms, it seemed increasingly evident, minute thread-shaped bodies known as chromosomes, contributed equally by male and female at the moment of conception. On each there existed large numbers of even smaller particulate units, soon known as genes; and these genes controlled, either separately or in conjunction with one another, a multitude of characteristics which differentiated the members of the same species. Knowledge grew throughout the first years of the century, and it was confirmed that this mechanism, first discerned from Mendel's breeding of peas, operated also in the animal world, in mammals and in man himself. As the outlines of this machinery became clearer, so did its complexity; the solution of one problem in this science, quickly seen to be of immense importance to mankind, merely opened the door on fresh riddles, apparently infinite in number. Many, it seemed, could be solved only by men of a mathematical turn of mind: Haldane was to be one of them.

His interest in this subject, vaguely aroused by Darbishire's lecture, was given its first practical outlet seven years later. In 1908 his sister Naomi had suffered a serious fall while riding. She became slightly allergic to ponies, and guinea-pigs were suggested as alternative pets. Within a year or so these provided an unexpected sight for Haldane's undergraduate friends as they turned a corner of "Cherwell", and came to the lawn. "There were no tennis nets or croquet balls," writes one of them. "Instead, behind the wire fencing, were 300 guinea-pigs."

The animals had multiplied, naturally and quietly in guinea-pig fashion, and while Naomi had learned to distinguish their individual voices, her brother was studying them to confirm the laws of inheritance as laid down in Mendel's revolutionary work. He had started by reading all the available literature on the subject, including the latest paper in *Biometrika* of the Darbishire he had listened to as a boy of eight; and he believed he noticed one point which the author himself had missed.

This point concerned "Linkage"—then known as "reduplication"—a subject whose study was to occupy a fair segment of Haldane's working life. One feature of inheritance which had been noted by scientists soon after they had begun investigating it in detail was the way in which the Mendelian theory operated in practice: while many characteristics were passed on from one generation to the next in a simple and predictable way, quite independently of one another, other characteristics appeared to be linked—possibly because the genes governing them lay close together on the same chromosome. This had so far been noted only in plants but Haldane, studying the data in Darbishire's paper, believed that this revealed linkage in mice. He expanded his views on what appeared to be the first specific gene-linkage in vertebrates, gave his paper the pretentious title of *The Comparative Morphology of the Germ-Plasm*, and eventually read it before a seminar organised by Goodrich for his undergraduates in the summer of 1912.

At this stage the paper might well have been published. However, Haldane wrote for advice to R. C. Punnett, a leading geneticist, and was advised to obtain his own data. Mice were therefore added to guinea-pigs. A. D. Sprunt, a colleague of Haldane at New College, was enlisted as co-experimenter and publication was held up until further results had been obtained. "We managed to secure some very odd beasts, including some dwarfs," his sister remembers, "and at St. Giles' Fair, which we always attended if possible, we bought two pink ones who, alas, turned out to be dyed albinos. Still, one had to take a chance." News of experiments spread, and J.B.S. received offers such as: "I understand from Dr. O'Connor that you might care to have my yellow and black cavie, which is, I am sure, the child of two white ones. I should be willing to send it to you for two shillings if you would pay the carriage."

Genetics was not the only subject to which J.B.S. was to make minor contributions soon after his arrival at Oxford. The previous year his father had written to Whitworth, the Eton master, asking if his son could visit London with him on one particular Saturday. "He has," he went on, "been giving me very great help in the mathematical part of a rather important physiological investigation of which I am giving an account at the meeting of the Physiological Society. The paper is in our joint names and Jack's part is a very important one as he has evolved an equation which has thrown light into what was a very dark region. I should like him to be present if possible, partly to fortify me against possible attacks from people who know the higher 'mathematics'."

Now, while less than a year up, J.B.S. was able to read the paper, published in the *Journal of Physiology* for June 1912. While all the necessary experiments, revealing how haemoglobin combined with oxygen, had been carried out by John Scott

31

Haldane and C. G. Douglas, a younger worker in the University's physiological laboratory, the complex mathematical analysis was attributed solely to the younger Haldane.

All this suggested that J.B.S. was now set fair for a purely scientific career. The course ahead for the boy prodigy seemed clear. As was often to be the case, the prodigy veered off, unexpectedly, on a completely different tack. At the end of his first year J.B.S. switched from mathematics and biology to "Greats", from the disciplines of science to the inspirations of the arts.

The switch was supported by his father, but it was in many ways characteristic of the younger Haldane. It showed, according to one's viewpoint, an inability to develop initial work or a protean intellect. At the same time, it brought J.B.S. immense personal pleasure, for the companionship of the Classics was to be a solace in an otherwise aesthetically bleak life. It was to mean that the J.B.S. who swam confidently through the scientific seas for half a century did so without any scientific degree or technical qualification; but there was to be a consolation. In his second and subsequent years at Oxford Haldane learned to write clearly, comprehensibly and with an economy that was to serve him well. He learned the hard way; years later, when a colleague commented that he had a very lucid prose style, he turned on her fiercely: "D'you think I didn't have to work for it?"

Moreover, the isolation of his studies from the world in which he lived encouraged an objectivity, a dispassionate attitude to affairs, which was itself the very stuff of the scientific approach. "The subjects studied," he later commented, "had little relation to modern life, so thought on them was free. The successful Greats Man, with his high capacity for abstraction, makes an excellent Civil Servant, prepared to report as unemotionally on the massacre of millions of African natives as on the constitution of the Channel Islands." This was no bad training for the physiologist contemplating his own reactions to abnormal conditions or the geneticist studying the mysterious linkages of flower-colour. And Haldane, though rarely out of combat with Civil Servants, was to be a successful Greats Man.

At Oxford he was "much happier" than he had been at Eton. He began to make friends more easily—the Gielguds, Aldous Huxley, and his elder brother Trev, Gervas Huxley, and Dick Mitchison who was to marry his sister Naomi. Like his uncle, Lord Haldane, who more than once walked from Cloan to the summit of Ben Lawers and back, a total of seventy-three miles,

J.B.S. was a good go-er over rough country. He showed a marked inability for skilled games, but rowed occasionally. However, he refused to train once he discovered that after several months without exercise he was not only in good health but in good physical form. In those days training was enjoyed, according to his sister, for the sake of its ending—when everyone suddenly got very drunk.

What success Haldane achieved on the river was largely owing to his weight—"fifteen stone in nothing but his hat" as a friend described him—and it was found necessary to have a special oar built for him. This was after a notable occasion on which his "standard" oar had broken at his very first stroke. "Of course we were bumped," says another member of the crew, "and when Haldane waved his broken oar, the cheering of Trinity subsided. We even managed to make a few bumps, notwithstanding our Herculean No. 5, and so went up a few."

He climbed into College like everyone else and invented a number of new routes. Then, when he became a Fellow after the First World War, he had these stopped. "I thought this very unfair," says Naomi, "but he said that it was to make people more inventive. Also, perhaps, to make them braver." He remembered having heard Spooner speak of seeing "through a dark glassly". He appeared a little uncouth, not caring much about his appearance, scolding his friends if they paid more for their clothes than he did, and affecting a disinterest in personal possessions. "I don't want a library of books," he told one friend. "All I need is to know where I can find the knowledge I want. And other books I give away."

His prodigious memory and his love both of the Classics and the English language made him a formidable companion and one friend relates how he, Haldane and Naomi walked from Oxford one evening to see Robert Bridges, quoting poetry all the way, checking each other's knowledge, and concluding that J.B.S. operated on an entirely different level. He had started "capping verses" with his sister some years earlier. "Gradually, I began to read more widely among the moderns, and usually won," she says. "He was very good on Milton whom I couldn't bear. Of course he always won if we had a dead language. I suppose about 1913 we both discovered Housman and then Yeats, the early Yeats of course, where one can play the game of substituting 'bottle' for 'battle' in many lines where Yeats uses it. He knew masses of both by heart, but didn't take to many later poets, not even Graves whom I tried to get him to like. He seemed to stick."

At Oxford Haldane was first drawn into politics, earning a note of commendation from his uncle, joining the University Liberal Club and taking part in debates. However, he was considerably influenced by one contemporary, young Herron—a "syndicalist who had a clear mind and a real passion for justice", who was to be killed in the coming war—and he became a member of the University Co-operative Society, serving behind its counter more than once.

Haldane's entry on to the political stage was to be a portent of things to come. In 1913 Oxford was still served by horse trams whose staff now decided to strike against their wages of less than £1 per week. The strikers' places were taken by blacklegs. "On the first three evenings of the strike, trams were stopped and the horses taken out," Haldane later wrote. "The police made baton charges and finally order was restored. I was unable to participate in these riots, I think because I was in training for a race. On the fourth evening the streets were quiet. I walked up and down Cornmarket St. chanting the Athanasian creed and the hymeneal psalm *Eructavit cor meum* in a loud but unmelodious voice. A large crowd collected. The police ineffectively pushed pious old ladies into the gutter. The trams failed to penetrate the crowd, and their horses were detached and wandered off in an aimless manner. The strike was successful, and as the trams could no longer yield a profit, they were replaced by motor omnibuses, which were capable both of higher speed and higher wages."

For his part in the affair J.B.S. was fined two guineas by the proctors—"the first case for over three centuries when a man was punished in Oxford for publicly professing the principles of the Church of England".

By the middle of 1914 John Scott Haldane was already making plans for the future. He had high hopes of the form his son would show in Greats; when this hurdle had been surmounted J.B.S. was to be switched back to science and after two years he was to be examined in physiology. Then he would begin work under Harrison or Abel in the Oxford Laboratory.

The first part of John Scott Haldane's plans was fulfilled, and on the morning of August 4th 1914, J.B.S. learned he had won a First. The news was, as he put it, "somewhat overshadowed by other events".

2

The Enjoyable Experience

IN the summer of 1914, J.B.S. was in camp with the Oxford University Officers' Training Corps on Hartford Flats near Camberley. He had joined the Signallers, hoping to learn wireless telegraphy, and it was to his unit that there rode up one night a commercial traveller with a satchel of radio devices, and the news that the Archduke Ferdinand had been assassinated at Sarajevo—"the Angel of Death arriving on a motor-bike". A few weeks later, as Britain found herself at war, Haldane volunteered for the Special Reserve of Officers and asked to be attached to a Scottish regiment, if possible the Black Watch whose headquarters were at Perth, a few miles from Cloan. Within a fortnight he had travelled north from Oxford and received his commission in the Third (Special Reserve) Battalion. There followed a four-month spell of training at Nigg, Ross-shire; then, in January 1915, he crossed to France, posted to the First Battalion. The following month J.B.S. became its Bombing Officer.

He was now twenty-two. He was sensitive, apt to hide his shyness by an assumed aggressiveness, a man whose interests were as different from those of his brother-officers as they had been from those of other boys at Lynam's. While he had felt it his duty to enlist, he had little of that ecstatic patriotism which had lifted the early war poets above the mud and blood. Yet, almost unbelievably, Haldane was to enjoy his experiences in France. When he first came under shell-fire his mind slipped back to the occasion, three years previously, when he had been exploring with his father a mine in which there had recently been an explosion, an exploration during which there was danger from poisonous gases, roof-falls, and further explosions.

"One of my first thoughts," he recalled of the Flanders experience, "was 'How my father would enjoy this!'"

He also enjoyed the killing, which he regarded as a respectable if vestigial legacy from primitive times. The feeling left its mark, and the pleasure J.B.S. took from the war worried him for the rest of his life. After killing his first man, he would say, he always felt it cowardly to kill animals. "The second word of the *Gita, dharmak-shetre*," he has explained, "gives an exact description of my feelings when I went to the trenches for the first time in 1915. I was well aware that I might die in these flat, featureless fields, and that a huge waste of human values was going on there. Nevertheless, I found the experience enjoyable, which most of my companions did not. I was supported, as it were, on a great wave of *dharma*."

This was all very well. But for those not lucky enough to be riding such a wave, visits by the young Haldane, whose energy quickly brought promotion to Trench Mortar Officer of the First (Guards) Brigade, were rather discouraged. When J.B.S. arrived, the unit was holding a relatively quiet section of the line near Givenchy, a stretch of country not yet battered by the later huge bombardments of the war, and still recognisable as human habitat. Breaking into the comparative lull would come Lieutenant Haldane with experimental bombs and the first trench mortars—"stove-pipes almost as dangerous to their users as to the enemy", as the Black Watch history describes them— plus an unextinguishable enthusiasm for the use of both.

The task of Haldane's small detachment was to move about the line, firing from different positions, both to harass the enemy and to gain experience in the use of what was a new and frequently unpredictable weapon. "The bombers were not popular in the line," the Black Watch history comments, "since their action invariably drew artillery fire, by way of retaliation, by which time, of course, the mortar-detachment had disappeared." There is a well-authenticated story that Lieutenant Haldane was remonstrated with for walking about "deficient of a Glengarry". He gave as his excuse the fact that the men of a neighbouring regiment had pushed him into a ditch for having fired mortars from their trenches. The military necessity for such alarms and excursions might have been understood and pardoned; what was more difficult to condone was Haldane's grim enthusiasm for the task, his unconventional methods, and the single-mindedness which quickly earned him the long-lasting nickname of Bombo.

Thus psychologically equipped, supported by a Lance-Sergeant Evans from the Coldstream Guards and a dozen or so hand-picked men, J.B.S. commanded a small private army, answerable only to a headquarters further back, and operating its own small workshop where the men put experimental fuses into experimental weapons and undertook minor repairs. Known as the bomb factory, servicing only its thirteen muzzle-loading mortars, it was probably the only such establishment in which smoking has ever been made compulsory.

"I did so on psychological grounds," Haldane has explained, "as I thought it important that we should have absolute confidence in one another and in our weapons. We had no accidents and few casualties."

His small unit enforced no particular discipline, ordered no routine guard-duties. Officers and men lived on one meal a day. For three weeks in April 1915, Haldane did not take off his boots, and it was probably during this period that he was first described by Haig as "the bravest and dirtiest officer in my Army". J.B.S. was proud of his unit—and of the occasion on which a mere eight bombs lobbed on to a suspected machine-gun nest provoked a reply of more than a hundred shells. This April was, as he remembered it, "one of the happiest months" of his life.

The ordering of unpopular bombardments formed only part of Haldane's activities. His brief included the discovery of what the enemy was doing, and in such activities he developed an almost personal interest—perhaps typical of the man who at the age of seventy could write: "I still hope to die in battle at the age of a hundred." Thus while even the most courageous of officers would consider their regular forays into no-man's-land as little more than unpleasant necessities, Haldane appeared to relish them, going out through the barbed wire most nights, lying up close to the enemy lines to hear what he could, and signalling his return with a small torch which alternately shone red and green.

"One night he disappeared into the darkness on his usual errand," says a colleague, "and on this occasion he was gone for a long time. Suddenly there was a bang on the German front, succeeded by a tangle of Very lights and the noise of rifle-fire and machine-guns. Silence then ensued and we waited with some apprehension for the fate of J.B.S. Presently the green and red signal appeared outside our barbed wire, and a very tattered J.B.S. climbed over the parapet. The M.O. was waiting for him and asked him what happened. Haldane replied with his characteristic drawl: 'The Boche was saying unpleasant things about us, so I just tossed a bomb over to them.'" Then, as always, he asked for two favourite tunes on the gramophone —"Where my caravan has rested", and "When we've wound up our watch on the Rhine".

Eventually, the solitary routine was altered. "A superior

officer," J.B.S. later wrote, "insisted on my being accompanied by a private who doubled the noise and halved the speed."

Haldane's own explanation for what was sometimes bravado and frequently brashness, was given almost half a century later when he was advising the Chief Psychologist of the Indian Army on the psychological requirements needed in different military and para-military occupations. An ordinary soldier, he said, might be more efficient if he believed himself to be invulnerable as a result of some magical or religious ceremony—but a company commander, "let alone a general", should avoid such beliefs. "For a junior officer [perhaps for a non-commissioned officer]," he went on, the requirements were "a tendency to 'show off' and, if possible, to excite emulation, with a vivid personal interest in every man under his command. I never achieved the latter, but did achieve the former. For example in 1915, I once bicycled across a gap in full view of the Germans, having foreseen that they would be too surprised to open fire till I was under shelter again. This probably persuaded my less intellectual subordinates that I had luck." "Showing-off" is one description; another is the definition of active courage which Haldane gave years later in writing to his mother of Lord Moran's *Anatomy of Courage*—"taking a novel risk, which you are not ordered to take, and enjoying it".

These exhibitions of audacity tended to make up for the wrath incurred by his bombing activities. And for an officer so different in one way from his brother-officers, so different in others from his men, Haldane was singularly popular. To the first he was "a bawdy old bird in a completely unoffensive way". To the men he was usually "Safety Catch"—so nicknamed during his training days because of his constant reiteration to "remember your safety catch". And across more than half a century one man remembers how during his initial training Haldane took a squad out on a P.T. run one morning. "I dropped out to have a drink at a spring by the side of the road," the one-time private says. "He looked round and came back to me, and lightly touched me on the backside with his stick. So different from the other officers, I thought to myself."

Respected if feared for his bravery—"it seemed hardly natural for a man to be as fearless as that", one of his men once said—admired for his ability to mix with all ranks, and loved for his eccentricities, Haldane was yet set apart from most of his brother-officers by his continuing external interests.

He was, as he later was to boast, the only officer to complete a scientific paper from a forward position of the Black Watch.

This was the final result of the mice experiments, started before the war, with Naomi and A. D. Sprunt who had recently been killed in action. J.B.S. had written to William Bateson, one of the leading British geneticists and director of the John Innes Horticultural Institution at which Haldane was later to work, and told him of the mice experiments, characteristically adding: "If I am killed could you kindly give my sister help if she wants it." Shortly afterwards, working in the trenches, J.B.S. finished the paper. The breeding experiments, continued with the animals on the "Cherwell" lawn, confirmed what he had suspected on reading Darbishire, and the joint paper reporting vertebrate linkage was published by the *Journal of Genetics* later in the year. Haldane long regretted the delay. "Had I been able to publish in 1910," he later wrote in a Personal Note for the Royal Society, "it would have been simultaneous with Morgan's discovery of linkage in *Drosophila*," the first reported linkage outside the plant world.

Haldane's front-line life—"this truly enviable life" as he described it—was to be unexpectedly interrupted in May, but shortly before this he made a brief journey to England, apparently reporting on his trench mortar work to the War Office and certainly calling on his uncle in Queen Anne's Gate. Here he produced "a German bomb which had not exploded", as his father noted without comment; then he returned to the Western Front, expecting to resume what he regarded as a halcyon existence.

However, J.B.S. was now to be caught up in a new application of science to war. On the evening of April 2nd 1915 dense greenish-yellow clouds of gas began to billow out from a number of cylinders in the German lines surrounding Ypres. The two French divisions which received the main brunt of the attack fell back in disorder and the Allied authorities realised that they were now faced with a new weapon against which they had, in spite of warnings, taken no precautions. On hearing the news Lord Kitchener, Secretary of State for War, consulted Lord Haldane, then Lord Chancellor, and Haldane telegraphed his brother in Oxford for advice. The following morning John Scott Haldane arrived in London; the same afternoon he left for France.

Some days later, after a second German gas attack, Haldane learned that 90,000 gas-masks, of a type which he had warned the authorities "could not stop poison gas of any kind", were being distributed. It was clear that emergency measures were needed, and he quickly induced the authorities to do two things: to bring out from Oxford the Professor Douglas with whom he had been working on respiratory problems; and to bring his son out of the line to help in the urgent work that had to be done.

During the first week of May, J.B.S. was ordered to report to Hazebrouck. Here he met his father. Shortly afterwards, together with a handful of volunteers, the two Haldanes and Douglas began work in a converted school. In one room there had been constructed a small glass-fronted cabinet, rather like a miniature greenhouse, and into this known quantities of chlorine gas were pumped.

"We had to compare the effects on ourselves of various quantities, with and without respirators," J.B.S. has explained. "It stung the eyes and produced a tendency to gasp and cough when breathed. For this reason trained physiologists had to be employed. An ordinary soldier would probably restrain his tendency to gasp, cough and throw himself about if he were working a machine-gun in a battle, but could not do so in a laboratory experiment with nothing to take his mind off his own feelings. An experienced physiologist has more self-control. It was also necessary to see if one could run or work hard in the respirators, so we had a wheel of some kind to turn by hand in the gas chamber, not to mention doing fifty-yard sprints in respirators outside. As each of us got sufficiently affected by gas to render his lungs duly irritable, another would take his place. None of us was much the worse for the gas, or in any real danger, as we knew where to stop, but some had to go to bed for a few days, and I was very short of breath and incapable of running for a month or so."

This few days' work saved many thousands of Allied lives and helped blunt the cutting edge of what might have been a decisive German weapon. John Scott Haldane received little credit and attributed this to the campaign which was soon hounding his brother from office. "So far as I could gather, it was considered under the circumstances wiser to leave me out," he wrote privately, "though this was certainly not by the wishes of any of the responsible soldiers." He himself minded little. His son, who believed that his father "had been too frank in his criticism of senior officers", thought differently. The circumstances confirmed all that he suspected of authority. The work, he later wrote, "which was mainly done by civilians, was rewarded by the grant of the Military Cross to the brilliant young officer who used to open the door of the motor-car of the medical General who occasionally visited the experiments. The soldiers who took part in them could, however, for some time be distinguished by the peculiar green colour of their buttons due to the action of the gas."

On May 8th J.B.S. was ordered up to the front, this time for special duties in connection with expected enemy gas attacks. However, on his way up the line, he discovered that the Black Watch was to go into action that afternoon—as part of the Anglo-French attack which became known variously as the battle of Aubers Ridge or of Festubert. To a man of Haldane's temperament the temptation was too strong to be resisted. He decided to rejoin his regiment and, if possible, to take command of his old platoon. But the effect of the chlorine had not yet fully worn off. He moved as fast as he could, but the best he could manage was "a moderate trot worthy of an old gentleman with chronic bronchitis". He was thus well behind the reserve line when the Allied bombardment opened up, and hardly into it when the counter-battery work began.

What happened next is intriguingly unclear. Haldane himself has described in a draft autobiography how he heard an immense explosion and subsequently woke up to find himself covered in mud and blood; how he noted minor wounds in his right arm and left side; how he climbed to the first floor of a building and saw the Black Watch go into action; and how he later found himself walking through the reserve trenches and back to a casualty station. Yet an eye-witness of the action has since filled in details which were wiped from Haldane's memory. The Black Watch reserves, says the onlooker, were mustered behind "the Orchard" by J.B.S. himself.

"We were fully occupied in our sector," he continues, "and casualties were becoming very numerous when I saw J.B.S. and his platoon advancing through the Orchard. Fire was very heavy and the Black Watch was suffering badly. Suddenly Haldane was hit and fell to the ground. He picked himself up and resumed the lead of his depleted command. Racing for the parapet, he and his men passed it, and a short distance into no-man's-land J.B.S. fell again," this time apparently blown down by blast.

The two stories are not mutually exclusive. It seems likely that after being knocked unconscious Haldane carried on with his plan, took command of a platoon until hit again, and eventually walked to the rear with his most recent experiences scrubbed from his mind. There are two curious footnotes to the event. J.B.S. afterwards talked of reading in *The Times* the notice of his own death while "fighting with great gallantry".

No record of this exists. And in 1961 he wrote to Robert Graves saying: "It has always seemed to me plausible that I did not buy a return ticket over the irremeable stream, but have imagined events since 1915. They are now becoming rather outrageous, so perhaps I shall wake up."

As Haldane walked back, passing crowded ambulances, not quite knowing what to do next, a Black Watch officer stopped a passing vehicle and asked for him to be taken to the nearest dressing station. Haldane got in and sat down. The driver was the Prince of Wales who turned to him and commented, "Oh, it's you." They had last met in Oxford, almost exactly a year earlier.

"Somehow I found myself in a hospital in Bethune," J.B.S. later wrote. "The wound in my side was trivial. A splinter had gone through my haversack, bumping me considerably, but only penetrating just under the skin, where it still is." One reason for his escape was that the splinter had lodged in a volume of *Anatole France*. "The wound in my arm was deeper," Haldane continued. "It was probed and roughly disinfected with hydrogen peroxide which was momentarily painful. Then I was put on a bed in a ward full of wounded officers, some in great pain, others delirious. An occasional shell-burst punctuated their groans, but I slept." From Bethune, he was moved to Versailles; then, via London, to his parents' home in Oxford where he was operated on for the removal of an undiscovered shell splinter.

This first experience of war had revealed in Haldane what he knew was a disconcerting enjoyment in its grimmer moments. Yet he knew also that he was an exception and that his enjoyment was wrong. Thus while one part of him was raised to a higher power by the experience, another part could regard war objectively and with severely critical eye. "I was glad," he explained, "that I was an infantryman and not a gunner who might receive orders to shell a town far behind the enemy's line, and thus kill non-combatants, probably our French allies." And kept among his family papers is an official War Office form across which he wrote, possibly in the trenches, the rough draft of a poem that was never finished:

> Thy name is on our foes' lips and on ours,
> Strong in thy name we break and burn and slay.
> And Thy priests tell us in our dying hours
> That 'tis Thy will, and bid its victims pray.
> From this dark pit of desolation

Full of black smoke and shattered limbs of men
Buried in the mud of their damnation
We curse Thee God, and swear that not again . . .

Thus far, the war confirmed what he had learned at Eton: that authority, here represented by the Staff, warranted all the suspicion it drew; and that revealed religion, represented by the chaplains who "generally ran the irreducible minimum of risk", was an object of scorn.

At first it seemed that Haldane was out of the war. "It sounds just the right sort of wound, which will keep him away from the front without doing any permanent damage," a companion wrote to his mother. "Quite frankly, I hope that he will never get within miles of France again—in which I maintain I am much more natural than you. Apart from my own personal feelings I really do feel that if he got smashed by some damned piece of German machinery it would be a loss to the world. That remark would probably make him very angry if you repeated it to him, but still it is true. Any fool can be a Lieutenant or Captain, but you have to go a long way to replace a brain like his. Don't tell him or he'll eat me."

Despite his well-wishers, Haldane recovered quickly. In August he volunteered to organise a bombing school which the authorities were to start at Nigg and here, for the next seven months, he trained some hundreds of officers and N.C.O.'s in the techniques of killing with hand- and rifle-grenades. The grenade was still a primitive and in some ways experimental weapon in the autumn of 1915, and instruction in its use was largely a matter of trial and error. Haldane's methods were as unorthodox as they had been earlier in the year behind the lines.

"I began by lecturing on the anatomy of hand grenades and made each pupil attach a detonator to a fuse with his teeth," he has said. "Should the detonator explode in the mouth, I explained that the mouth would be considerably enlarged, though the victim might be so unfortunate as to survive. Pupils who did not show alacrity when confronted with this and similar tests were returned to duty as unlikely to become efficient instructors."

It seems that this was not the only unorthodox practice at the bombing school. Years later, in a remarkable short story called "The Gold-Makers", Haldane incorporated more than one autobiographical anecdote, and remarked that he was one of the few people to run a bombing school for nine months without casualties. Describing how this was possible, he noted that "among the things which we occasionally did as demonstrations was to catch lighted bombs and throw them back, or more accurately, sideways, out of the trench. I had a one-eyed and rarely quite sober corporal who used to do this, but I sometimes did it myself. I admit that we used to lengthen the time fuse beforehand. Provided you are a good judge of time, it is no more dangerous than crossing the road among motor traffic, but it is more impressive to onlookers. Some idiot asked questions about it in Parliament, and got an army order issued forbidding the practice."

Haldane certainly ran the Nigg Bombing School from August 1915 until March 1916 without serious accident or fatal casualty. In his personal actions, moreover, he was a good example of the fact that knowledge and a clear head stand for survival—if an example that sometimes disturbed his friends. On duty and off, he would carry a pocket of detonators, a quantity of black powder gelignite, and a number of loose matches. At the slightest provocation he would expound on the principles involved in their use, and according to one old friend "those of us who lived in close contact with him regarded his presence in the Mess or Officers' Quarters with some degree of suspicion or fear". This was natural, since Haldane was not above tamping down his glowing pipe with a copper detonator. His idiosyncrasies had their uses and on one occasion, while travelling on leave in a very crowded railway carriage, he produced a mixture from his pocket and gave his fellow-officers a disquisition on the ease with which accidents could happen. The carriage emptied at the next station.

Such incidents illustrated the combination of showmanship and flamboyance which formed an essential part of Haldane's character. But they were also closely linked with his leanings towards pyromania. When he struck a match to light his pipe, he could not bear to blow out the flame when the match had served its purpose; instead, he would let it burn down to the last possible millimetre, often burning his fingers and thumb in the process. He adored bonfires, as well as fireworks, and it seems likely that his devoted study of explosives was a reflection of the same feelings.

Thus running the Nigg Bombing School was at first an interesting task. Then the job began to pall. Haldane was lusting for battle and became dangerously disgruntled when he was sent to an Intelligence post at Scottish Command in Edinburgh in the spring of 1916—"a particularly silly administrative job" as he later called it. Twenty years afterwards he discovered that he had been kept at Nigg after its initial organisation, and then posted to Edinburgh instead of to France, through the intervention of a War Office official who was friendly with Lord Haldane. "If he is still alive and reads this book," wrote J.B.S. grimly at the height of his honeymoon with the Communist Party, "he may repent of his favouritism."

It was in Edinburgh that Haldane received his abiding impressions of wartime Scottish Sundays. "All places of amusement were shut," he wrote. "So were the public houses. Even the churches were open for only a part of the day. On the other hand, the rather numerous prostitutes who were thus protected from an unfair competition enhanced their other blandishments by the offer of whisky."

This reference to what J.B.S. sometimes called feminine blandishments, and sometimes described more bluntly, was a trait that developed as he grew older. In the Second World War he was travelling one Sunday on a Glasgow bus laden with church-goers. As the vehicle stopped, he nodded down a street and commented to his colleague: "That's the place where I came to fornicate as a boy." Such utterances, issued in all companies, under all circumstances, had by the 1940's become part of the Haldane image. They were partly the result of a mischievous and rather clown-like desire to shock. They were partly the outcome of a genuine belief that the facts of nature must be spoken about naturally. But they were, perhaps even more, the result of two other things. One was a shyness with women which he never overcame, an inferiority complex which he tried to disguise by a simulated but open bawdiness. The other was his failure to become a father. In later life he would boast both of his mistresses and of his sexual prowess, creating the picture of a man forever popping in and out of bed. The truth was very different. The charade is not unfamiliar, but with Haldane, a man who throughout life desperately felt the need for a son, the result was tragic.

All this lay in the future as, in the autumn of 1916, Haldane finally succeeded in prising himself loose from Edinburgh and, in October, sailed for the Middle East to join the Second Black Watch in Mesopotamia. They rounded the Cape, reached Basra in December, and then travelled slowly by barge up the Tigris to the long line of trenches which some miles to the north ran from the river to Lake Serwaikiyeh.

The Black Watch held a four-mile stretch of the river. Across it, 400 yards away, lay the Turks; and with the Turks Haldane now started his own personal battle. He had been appointed second-in-command of a company but had also been put in charge of the battalion snipers. With these, as with his mortar-unit back in France, he operated as though with his own personal force. They devised their own versions of telescopic sights; they elaborated on the well-known ruses for making the enemy reveal himself just enough to get killed; and their success soon brought a roving commission to operate on a longer stretch of the river. War here was as different from the Western Front as the Western Desert of the Second World War was different from Normandy. Here were no civilians to confuse the issue. Here were relatively few impersonal artillery barrages. Here, as Haldane put it, men were "pitted against individual enemies with similar weapons, trench mortars or rifles with telescopic sights, each with a small team helping him. This was war as the great poets have sung it. I am lucky to have experienced it."

No doubt. Yet it was typical of Haldane's character that while he could see war as a great game, played for the stakes of life or death, he deplored its limitation by artificial rules. Thus he long remembered an occasion on this Mesopotamian front after a Turkish airman had developed considerable flair for shooting down British observation balloons. A British officer raised a balloon loaded with gun-cotton which blew up and destroyed the Turk. "For this deed," Haldane wrote indignantly, "he was severely reprimanded by the local officer commanding R.F.A. for unsportsmanlike conduct. This gentleman doubtless felt little objection to bombing, for example, Transport columns consisting mainly of non-combatants and animals, incapable of retaliating. [One may remark that between wounds and thirst perhaps 30,000 Turkish animals perished during our final victory in Palestine.] But he objected to airmen being killed except by other airmen. I, fighting in the mud beneath them, and exposed to the bombs of both sides [I was severely wounded by one of our own], felt differently."

Before this wounding by a British bomb, which was to remove Haldane from active service for the rest of the war, he made a second contact with Indian troops. His first had been in France where he had compared an Indian unit under bombardment with the Scots Guards who swore with fluency, dodged round traverses and were rarely hit. "The Indians," J.B.S. noted, "stood and waited to be killed, which they were. They apparently thought that the bombs were devils and could not be dodged." Now he received a complaint that the Bhopal

46

Rifles, on a neighbouring sector, were being killed by Turkish snipers. "These wretched Indians were completely and utterly fed up," he wrote. "They hated the war, and did not want to kill the Turks, their fellow-Muslims. They hated life and allowed the Turks to kill them. By a judicious display of helmets on sticks we drew the Turks' fire and located them. We returned their fire and got our gunners to give them a few rounds of shrapnel. The Turks, who had no desire to die for their country, but couldn't resist the opportunity to kill the Indians, who were no more dangerous than rabbits, went away to a safer place."

Compared with the Western Front, even the sniping was of a desultory kind and Haldane found himself behind the lines with time on his hands. He practised marching on bearings with a prismatic compass. He played a good deal of bridge, winning about a pound a month. Life had begun to slacken off. Then, in the New Year, the Allies crossed the Tigris. But Haldane's battalion attacked almost abandoned trenches, and then advanced past them a considerable way with very little loss. He himself, moreover, had been left behind with a small unit to reconstitute the battalion should it be wiped out. "Fate, however, decided quite firmly," as Haldane put it, "that the intentions of my guardian in the War Office should be frustrated . . ."

On the evening of the advance, one of the large tents, which served as hangars for the aerodrome attached to the camp, was seen to be on fire. With other officers and troops Haldane succeeded in driving some of the lorries from the burning tent. However, these did not represent the main danger, for the Royal Flying Corps had somewhat imprudently stacked their bombs beside petrol cans. The result was spectacular but unfortunate. As a stack of petrol flared up, a bomb would explode with the heat; the blast from the bomb would blow out the petrol fire; but enough sparks would be strewn round to re-ignite the petrol, and the process would then be repeated.

Haldane was running towards the fire when one particularly big explosion occurred. At first he thought that his throat had been blown away. Then he realised that he had been hit in the leg. He was put in an ambulance, taken to a field dressing station and placed with another officer who succeeded in setting the tent on fire in trying to light a cigarette. Then, at the next stage back, a Casualty Clearing Station, a chaplain enquired about his religion. On being told "None", the chaplain entered "C. of E." on the necessary form. Haldane had already done his best to avoid being given a label, going "the round of permitted religions, ending up as a Jew, after making sure that there was no rabbi in the neighbourhood". Now he protested, as he was to protest vehemently, at the slightest provocation, for the rest of his life, at the fact "that clergymen should be allowed to insult wounded soldiers . . . by labelling them as members of a religion to which they do not adhere".

He was loaded on to a hospital ship—and noted that while he was reading Helland and Tait's *Introduction to Quaternions*, the officer on his right was engrossed in Lamb's *Infinitesimal Calculus*. Some while later he landed at Bombay.

Haldane's stay in India, from the summer of 1917 until the autumn of the following year, greatly affected his life. It was, however, merely one item in a long train of random events, scientific interests and personal prejudices which eventually drew him to India for his final years. Scattered through his massive collection of printed papers, private letters, and unpublished notes and memoranda lie innumerable references to these events—to the contempt for Imperial rule fostered by his mother's Victoria League; to his chance meeting with the Indians on the s.s. *Bavaria*; to his friendship with more than one Indian scientist; to the movement of his interests towards the form of biological enquiry for which India presents so fine a field; and to his India experiences of 1917 and 1918—all events which start to wear a spurious air of predestination, as though they led inevitably towards a shaded verandah in Orissa.

In 1917 Haldane went first to Poona, where he learnt Urdu while in hospital. Thence he was sent to the summer capital of Simla, to recuperate in a convalescent home and then to serve at Army headquarters. Naturally enough, as a matter of principle, he refused to conform. He travelled as widely as possible, took few of the precautions expected of him, drank unboiled water and chewed betel-nut, bought food at road-side booths and, as he agreed, generally behaved in an un-English manner. He excluded himself, as far as possible, from the official hierarchy, no doubt regarding them, as he had regarded his companions at Lynam's, as "intellectually sub-human". Yet he was also cut off from the majority of Indians, since he could only become intimate with anyone on a basis of equality. "So long as I am a member of a 'ruling race', such equality is impossible," he later wrote. "When an Indian and I are both genuinely trying to be polite to one another he suspects that I am being condescending and I suspect that he is being servile.

The Indians with whom I got on best were Indian army officers holding King's [as opposed to Viceroy's] commissions, with some of whom I used to play chess." That he found points of contact at this level—and that he unbent so far as to appear as "Time" in the Grand Variety Entertainment organised by Her Highness the Rani Sahiba of Kapurtha—is not so surprising as might at first appear. "The key to India was snobbery," he wrote. "The Hindu caste system is the greatest glorification of snobbery that the world has ever known."

Reading this today, it may seem strange that it was towards Hinduism and its interlocking layers of existence that Haldane was eventually drawn. Yet beneath his outwardly socialist principles there flowed a persistent streak of what was often interpreted as snobbery. Certainly he appreciated that human beings are born on a biological pyramid—"How surprised they'll be when they find that they are not all born equal" he remarked in the early 1920's of the Communist Revolution. Certainly he was a snob about courage, both the physical kind and the kind that refuses to "truckle"; he had good justification for being so. "He was also," writes a friend, "a snob about the degree to which a man could pour out his energy, emotion and ingenuity into his work. I have seen him be extraordinarily patient with not very clever people who were obviously in love with their work, and have heard him be devastating to far far more able men who were being pretentious, or bluffing. Certainly he recognised that all men were not born with an equal share of brains or artistic ability, but he always, it seemed to me, respected courage, a kind of obstinate pride, and attachment to some kind of work." It is true, also, that towards the end of his life, after he had emigrated to India, he revealed an instinctive liking for some aspects of the caste system. He had a sneaking sympathy for the Brahmans, and claimed that he saw a certain kinship between the exclusive university education systems of which he had been part and the old Brahmanical villages of Orissa, the state in which he finally settled.

In 1917 at Army Headquarters Haldane revised the guidebooks to areas in which military operations were likely. He wrote reports of recent minor campaigns on the frontier, and he carried out a good deal of other miscellaneous work which left him, as he was pleased to note, considerable time to investigate the India that lay outside the compound. He attended the Legislative Council. He studied Indian architecture. And, curiously in the light of his future history, he came to the con-

49

clusion that he was a potential Muslim but not a potential Hindu.

"An act of faith admits one to Islam," he commented in his draft autobiography. "Hindus are born, not made. And Islam is a religion of universal brotherhood, whilst Hinduism perpetrates a complex hierarchy of classes. Further, I am sufficiently prudish to find the human sexual organs unsuitable as religious symbols." And at Pryag, the holy spot outside Allahabad where the Ganges, the Jumna and an invisible river called the Sarasvati all meet, Haldane attended the Magh Mela, the only white person in a gathering of a million and a half. Here he watched the fantastic pageant of elephants carrying solid gold idols in solid silver howdahs, of gorgeously clothed holy men, and religiously-inspired thousands over whom great gusts of emotion swept like wind over standing corn.

For Haldane, the leisurely life ended in February 1918 when he was posted to the Bombing School at Mhow in Central Provinces. Here he lectured on British, French and German weapons and on the explosives that filled them. And here his clinical approach to danger saved more than one life. There was, for instance, the day when a squad was being trained to fire Mills bombs from rifles. A cup was fixed to the rifle, which had a slot to hold the lever after the pin had been removed. Firing was carried out behind a wall of sandbags with Haldane watching the operation. One corporal failed to fit the lever correctly but nevertheless withdrew the pin. As Haldane saw the error he jumped down to the man, grabbed the rifle and threw it over the sandbag wall, a few seconds before the grenade exploded. This personal lack of fear had disadvantages. On one occasion he was teaching a squad how to demolish a lorry with gun-cotton. He demonstrated how to fix the explosive, how to fuse it, and how to detonate it. When all was ready, he lit the safety fuse and walked back. He then looked at his watch and commented that the explosion should take place in four seconds. When nothing happened after about a minute, he advanced towards the vehicle. Suddenly the voice of the Commandant boomed out across the ground—"Where do you think you're going, you bloody fool?" Haldane halted. Seconds later the lorry was blown apart.

Haldane had mixed feeling for this Commandant. In his typically boisterous way he claimed that the officer had "illegally constituted himself Mess President, and insisted on a meat diet in the hot weather, instead of the vegetarian or nearly vegetarian diet of the country which sensible Englishmen adopt".

But he admitted that the Commandant had probably saved his life by indirectly preventing his return to the Western Front. For now—mainly as a result of the meat, so he always claimed— J.B.S. developed jaundice; was invalided once again up to the foothills of the Himalayas; and when fit was sent back to London where, on November 11th 1918, he was still attached to Military Intelligence.

Haldane's wartime experiences had confirmed and consolidated his isolation from his fellow-men. They underlined the fact that his colleagues not only respected him but felt for him an affection which they found it difficult to explain. "He was," as one of his fellow-officers put it, "far too clever for his contemporaries and had little in common with them apart from soldiering." But he was remembered as kindly and as perpetually cheerful in places where there was little cause for cheerfulness.

More important, the war fixed for ever in Haldane's mind the virtue of courage, the comradeship of men living and dying for a common cause, the deficiencies of "a civilisation in which people take refuge in war from the worries of everyday life in peace". Much of his activity, much of his political belief and much of his superficially contradictory attitudes can be traced back to the experiences in the front line that he actually enjoyed.

"My own liking for war goes somewhat deeper," he wrote. "I get a definitely enhanced sense of life when my life is in moderate danger. On the other hand I do not get thrills, in the sense of automatic excitation causing goose-flesh and erection of the hairs. I get these from motoring, when I have 'narrow shaves' . . . I also find happiness in practising the virtue of courage. I am not a particularly brave man. I have not got the requisite courage to dive head first into water, and I am frightened by flying in bumpy weather, and by several other things. However, I was taught courage by my father, and am sufficiently self-conscious not to pretend that I am doing something else on the rare occasions when I am being brave. I believe that this attitude is far commoner in France than in Britain, where the best people do not even admit their virtues.

"Finally, I enjoy the comradeship of war. Men like war because it is the only socialised activity in which they have ever taken part. The soldier is working with comrades for a great cause [or so at least he believes]. In peace-time he is working for his own profit or someone else's. If I live to see an England in which socialism has made the occupation of a grocer as honourable as that of a soldier, I shall die happy."

In January 1919, after a week in Ireland where the reserve battalion of the Black Watch was stationed, Haldane once more became a civilian. Now he had a double aim in life: one was to give service to science; the other was to make honourable grocers.

PART

II

TESTING TIME

3

The Mathematics of Evolution

BEFORE the end of the war Haldane had accepted a Fellowship at New College. The election did not take effect until October 1919, and on demobilisation early in the year he faced eight months as a post-graduate student. Like many other officers in their late twenties, he settled down well enough to the academic routine which he might have started in 1915, relieved that the stresses of battle were over although, in Haldane's case, vaguely missing them; thankful to be alive yet inwardly aggrieved by the wasted years. In addition, J.B.S. felt himself out of tune with the university hierarchy, largely composed of men who had missed the war and were out of touch with post-war life. "The motivations of, say, an ambitious 18th century English landowner are highly foreign to our minds," he wrote nearly thirty years later. "But such people existed. I saw a remnant of such life in the Oxford colleges, where unmarried fellows lived in an atmosphere in which the main satisfaction was 'cultured' conversation, but it was not thought good to be perceptibly more brilliant than one's neighbour."

Haldane's reaction was an aggressive outspokenness; to the detailed discussion of battles long ago he would respond with the number of segments into which a man might be blown by high explosive; while the High Table would talk quietly of entrées, he would boom on about entrails. Those who continued to live in the past should not be allowed to forget the debt they owed to the present.

This immediate post-war period reinforced his instinctive move to the political left. He made, as he put it, his "last appearance as a Liberal", sitting behind Mr. Asquith at Oxford and then, apparently shortly afterwards, supporting a meeting addressed by George Lansbury and Austin Harrison, held to protest against the original version of the Treaty of Versailles whose terms had just been made public. Haldane attended in the role of thrower-out.

"The interruptors, who were the sort of people who now hail

Hitler," he wrote in the late 1930's, "threw tomatoes. I had my tactical scheme prepared. I approached one of the smaller ones from behind, placed a finger in each nostril, and dragged him backwards, hooked and struggling like a salmon, and too agitated to hit me in a vital spot. The rest followed, but before they rescued him they were half-way to the door." According to Haldane's version of events, "there was some rather half-hearted fighting with chairs before we cleared the Corn-Exchange". Then, on his way home, the opposition counter-attacked, and he took refuge in a jeweller's doorway, a tactically strong position between plate-glass windows. His enemies dispersed on the approach of a policeman who, as J.B.S. saw it, "scented danger to Property".

This version must be taken with caution, and not only because it was written almost twenty years later and at the height of Haldane's Communist enthusiasm, which insisted on the policeman only arriving to save the jewellers. When it came to discussion of physical combat, or of sex, J.B.S. insisted on appearing larger than life. His conversation gave a vivid impression of how he would have behaved in really tight corners or if presented, *ex gratia*, with the most voluptuous woman in the world. In fact, outside war he disliked hurting people or things, and he remained shy with women; to help disguise this his fights and conquests tended in retrospect to be given an heroic quality that sometimes seemed hardly warranted.

It is not clear that such suspicions were justified. "Certainly Haldane spent a lot of the time showing off, but with a twinkle in his eye as a rule," says one old friend. "Partly he showed off much as other people might make polite conversation, partly to keep himself in practice in a kind of ingenuity and memory-retrieval game, partly as a contribution to the drama which was needed, in his case, to keep life properly gingered up. One result was that this caused people to disbelieve some of the things he says about himself which I suspect were probably true."

During this immediate post-war period Haldane spent much of his time helping to revive college and university life, becoming Vice-President of the Union under Hore-Belisha and bringing the New College Essay Society back into existence—with an essay which was to have a strange and vital influence on his life. He also made the pilgrimage, natural to a nonconformist of left-wing views, to the Garsington Manor of Lady Ottoline Morrell. Here there already sparkled such stars of the post-war literary firmament as Vanessa Bell. Katherine

56

Mansfield and Lytton Strachey; here also shone Aldous Huxley, an old friend from Eton days who was to use John Scott Haldane as the prototype for Lord Tantamount in *Point Counter Point* and was to pillory J.B.S. as the Shearwater of *Antic Hay*, the biologist forever wrapped in his physiological experiments while friends took his wife to bed.

"Shearwater," J.B.S. later commented, "is given a charming, but neither faithful nor intelligent wife called Rosie. I was not married when the book was written. My present wife avenged Rosie by reviewing *Brave New World* in *Nature* under the title 'Dr. Arnold and Mr. Huxley', the suggestion being that the souls of Aldous Huxley's ancestors, Dr. Arnold [headmaster of Rugby] and Prof. T. H. Huxley, fought like Jekyll and Hyde for the possession of his pen. Shearwater is further endowed with a hopeless passion for a not really inaccessible lady. Now in 1919 Aldous Huxley observed me making advances, which he doubtless considered rather cumbrous, to a lady of his acquaintance. So many of the 'highbrows' of that day boasted of their amorous conquests, real or imagined, that he regarded such behaviour as universal. It is not. Indeed, had the lady in question not been dead for many years, I should not even now venture to suggest that Shearwater may have known when to hold his tongue"—an entry in Haldane's draft autobiography quite as revealing of himself as it is of Huxley.

At Oxford J.B.S. now decided to teach physiology, a decision which would have been recklessness in a lesser man, since he had neither degree nor other qualification in the subject. In fact Haldane, Fellow of the Royal Society and the author of more than three hundred scientific papers, never did hold any scientific degree, thus following his father who never took a course in engineering but became President of the Institution of Mining Engineers.

However, J.B.S. was already well versed in one smallish part of physiology, that concerned with breathing. He knew nothing of the rest and began learning the subject "with about six weeks' start on my future pupils". He managed to keep the lead. The future Lord Brain, and the future Dame Janet Vaughan were among the six of his students who from sixty in the University were to gain Firsts. "Forty years ago," he wrote wistfully during his last years in India, "I could teach."

J.B.S. was an impressive tutor; tall, heavily-built and with a voice that easily carried across the largest lecture-theatre. He was already unconventional and uninhibited, and forty years on one former student still remembers how he presented himself nervously at Haldane's door for his first tutorial. He knocked once, twice and then, after what appeared a strangely long interval, heard footsteps on the other side. A voice boomed: "Come in, come in." The door was opened to introduce the student to his tutor, who was seen to be holding a chamber pot in his left hand.

"He completed his natural need as he told me to sit down," the student recalls, "and after this unconventional meeting became a good friend to me."

One reason for Haldane's success as a don was his fierce energy. Of his weekly thirty hours teaching duties, ten were usually after dinner, and of the rest nearly half were concentrated in a single day. "So," he has said, "I get some time for research and reading." Another reason for success was his catholic view of the part which science, or any particular department of science, should play in a man's education. He belonged to a committee which met regularly in the Robinson Tower and tried to hammer out a degree course which would combine unified science and philosophy. Professor Lindemann, later Lord Cherwell, was also a member, and Haldane's comments on him, written years later to Charles Snow, are revealing.

"I was generally on Lindemann's side, but [in my opinion] he wrecked the scheme by being unduly critical of the philosophers," he said. "He gave the impression that he thought he knew the answers to various very broad questions, and did not hide his contempt for those who found these answers unsatisfying . . . I suspect that he was happy not only when risking his own life in the air, but when risking all our lives—and losing a great many—by impracticable schemes. Some such people take to rock climbing."

Haldane's interest in a unified science course reflected his own ability to take up a new subject and worry his way quickly into its essentials—an ability comparable to that of a barrister who may have to master a new subject with each fresh brief. With physiology, to which he quickly devoted himself, he had the aid of environment, since he had been brought up surrounded by the rules of the discipline. Now, during the years that followed the Armistice, his father came to his aid in a more specific way. John Scott Haldane had discovered that it was carbon dioxide in the human blood stream which enabled the muscles to regulate breathing under different conditions. But it was not known whether the carbon dioxide did so by making the blood more acid, as was suspected, or by some other

58

method. Haldane therefore taught his son the technique of gas analysis developed by himself, a technique by which very small amounts of gas can be accurately measured. Then he gave him, together with Peter Davies, a young worker in the physiological laboratory, the task of finding exactly how carbon dioxide did this particular job. The experiments which followed enabled J.B.S. to make a number of useful discoveries and they encouraged him in the practice of self-experimentation for which he was to become famous.

He and his colleague argued that if acidity of the blood was the vital factor, then an increase in the amount of alkaline sodium bicarbonate in the blood would slow down breathing—since such slowing-down would help to retain more carbon dioxide and thereby retain the normal balance. The first task was therefore to discover the amount of sodium bicarbonate already in a normal person's blood. This was not easy. In fact it was three months before Haldane and Davies got their different estimates to agree, and the experience was one which provided Haldane with a guide-line for much of his life. "Our three months of failure taught us a lot," he wrote. "We scientists have a moral lesson to teach the world, because we are up against Nature and Nature may be defined as That which does not accept excuses. Never before in my life had I been in a situation where there was no one to whom I could give some plausible reason when I failed."

Once Haldane and Davies had finished this first part of their work, they began to use themselves as guinea-pigs—for one reason which Haldane was always fond of emphasising: neither a dog nor a rabbit, nor any experimental animal other than man can "tell you if he has a headache, or an upset of his sensators of smell, both of which I obtained as symptoms during these experiments".

They wanted to see if John Scott Haldane's theory about breathing was correct, but they wanted to give a quantitative answer—to be able to state, for instance, how much more one would breathe if the alkaline reserve in the blood was increased by a stated amount. And they wanted to find out if any symptoms of certain diseases could be put down to changes in the alkalinity of the blood.

The first part of the work was fairly easy. Haldane and Davies each ate about an ounce and a half of bicarbonate of soda—and each, as expected, found that his breathing was slowed and that the carbon dioxide in the blood rose to balance the bicarbonate. Here Haldane followed what was to be his universal rule. When reporting experiments on himself he would rarely, if ever, note "I felt . . ." or "I began to pant . . ." Scientific thinking was objective thinking, and the records were couched in the impersonal form of "J.H. panting . . ." or "J.H. finding difficulty in breathing." Explaining this, J.B.S. once wrote: "In fact, I try to think of myself as I would of anyone else. This is the essence of justice."

Getting acid into the blood was more difficult than getting it out. To start with, Haldane began by drinking hydrocholoric acid; if neat, this would have been fatal so he had to dilute it— but he diluted it so much that it failed to have much effect. He then worked out a number of chemical tricks to smuggle the hydrochloric acid into his blood disguised as something else. One method was to drink a solution of ammonium chloride. At the first attempt he dissolved five grams in a hundred c.c. of water—and on drinking the solution was violently sick. He then diluted it still further and tried again; this time the trick worked, although he had to drink less than the carefully-calculated amount which he estimated would kill him. The ammonium chloride, absorbed from the intestine, went to the liver where it was turned into urea, leaving the acid behind. One or two ounces of it, J.B.S. found, was sufficient to make him very short of breath, and after some of the experiments he panted for several days.

It had seemed unlikely that any practical results would spring from this work, However, as Appleton found when radar grew from his ionospheric research, the "purest" experiments can produce the most utilitarian results. So it was with this work on the acidity of the blood. Soon afterwards, a Continental doctor discovered that one particular kind of fit, from which some babies suffered and a few died, was caused by the extreme alkalinity of the blood. The ammonium chloride treatment was successfully used by the doctor to cure the condition. "Since then," J.B.S. said during the last war, "a better cure has been found, but probably he saved a few lives and a good deal of suffering."

Many similar experiments followed during the next few years, some in the Oxford physiological laboratory, some in John Scott Haldane's own private laboratory at "Cherwell". There was a thirteen-day experiment during which J.B.S. drank eighty-five grammes of calcium chloride dissolved in water, and produced "intense diarrhoea, followed by constipation due to the formation of a large hard faecal mass. There was great general discomfort, pains in the head, limbs and back, and disturbed nights". To discover the change in the pressure of carbon dioxide in the lungs after violent exercise, he ran five times up and down thirty-foot stairs, repeated the sequence nineteen times, and had samples of his breath taken after each. In the gas chamber of the "Cherwell" laboratory he recorded his own and other people's reactions in various concentrations of gas. And at "Cherwell", also, he drank quantities of hydrochloric acid, reporting afterwards that walking at three miles an hour caused severe panting, and that cycling was impossible. "There were occasional slight headaches. A certain exhilaration and irritability of temper were noticed at times by myself and others, but there was no mental confusion, and the experiment was not unpleasant." In the case of the more dangerous carbon monoxide, the symptoms of poisoning were, he wrote, "the same as alcoholic poisoning, except that carbon monoxide goes a bit further. One is that you cannot walk straight or talk straight, although you feel you are perfectly all right. If you go into a mine full of this gas with a bird in a cage, the bird gets drunk first, and then comes off its perch, and you yourself will probably feel full of beans. That is the great danger, for you tumble over, get unconscious, and die".

These experiments, which had to be tied in with Haldane's quota of teaching, were frequently uncomfortable, frequently unpleasant, and sometimes both. "If you like to use an ancient Indian word," he once told an Indian audience of the occasions on which he had eaten large amounts of sodium chloride, or common salt, "they were *tapas*, intended to achieve knowledge not obtainable by other means. I remember that at the end of one of them I was so thirsty that when the hour which I had fixed beforehand struck, and I allowed myself to drink a litre of water, I grabbed so violently for the measuring cylinder that I knocked it over and broke it." On this occasion Haldane unexpectedly found that about half of the salt had been put away under his skin so that when he started drinking his ankles swelled up as they do with dropsy. But a little more information had been acquired about the way the human body works, a satisfactory conclusion for a man who could say, as Haldane did, that "you cannot be a good human physiologist unless you regard your own body, and that of your colleagues, with the same sort of respect with which you regard the starry sky, and yet as something to be used and, if need be, used up".

However useful it was, and of that there can be no doubt, there was a trace of exhibitionism about the way he spoke of such work, a flamboyance epitomised by his comment that the only way to test a chemical's reaction was to take ten times the dose listed as fatal in the British Pharmacopoeia. Despite such remarks, he had a good case for making even the more esoteric of his experiments; as in other fields, he sometimes made the worst of it.

Many of Haldane's colleagues looked upon this self-experimentation with amusement as well as admiration—as when G. I. Taylor, seeing him waiting for a London train with a small bag, asked whether it contained sulphuric acid for his lunch.

"No," came the reply from J.B.S. "My dress clothes. I'm going to town."

Since it was the height of the Opera season Taylor asked whether the occasion was *Götterdämmerung* then being performed at Covent Garden.

"No," replied J.B.S., "but something very like it—the Annual Dinner of the Rationalist Press Association."

Haldane's belief that he might actually be living through the twilight of the Gods was by this time firmly fixed. It was, after all, natural that he should swing to atheism. The wisdom of the move had been confirmed in his eyes both by Eton, where he found the authorities apparently afraid of free discussion, and by the First World War where he found that the Protestant chaplains "very rarely took the opportunities offered them to promote the cause of religion by risking their lives". This attitude was further confirmed by his work. "When I set up an experiment I assume that no god, angel or devil is going to interfere with its course," he wrote; "and this assumption has been justified by such success as I have achieved in my professional career. I should therefore be intellectually dishonest if I were not also atheistic in theory, at least to the extent of disbelieving in supernatural interference in the affairs of the world. And I should be a coward if I did not state my theoretical views in public."

For Haldane, "public" meant not only readers of his popular articles but also the converted members of the Rationalist Press Association. He had become a member in 1924, and was a regular contributor to the *Rationalist Annual* from 1927 onwards. He also attended the dinner of the Rationalist Press Association held in 1925 to mark the centenary of T. H. Huxley's birth. It is claimed that towards the end of the dinner the chairman, a Mr. Whale, proposed the toast: "Let us eat, drink and be merry for tomorrow we die", and it is certain that he dropped dead from a heart attack during the dinner.

In the appalled silence, Haldane's bellowing whisper came from the end of the table—"The Whale's been harpooned."

.   .   .

By 1925 Haldane had already made the first of his leaps into a fresh discipline. In the early 1920's it might have been safe to predict that he would continue to work as a physiologist, probably in Oxford with its family links, its familiar backgrounds. It was typical of Haldane that he should turn biochemist and move to Cambridge in the process, although the switch is not as strange as might at first appear. "We all move around," comments Norman Pirie who knew Haldane for some thirty years. "Not perhaps so much as we used to, but the distinction between physiology, biochemistry and the more chemical aspects of pathology, botany and zoology, is so slight as to be negligible. The only surprising thing would have been if he had moved into geology or astronomy, and either would have been possible."

Biochemistry is the chemistry of living things, or physiologic chemistry, and when Haldane had spent the Long Vacation of 1921 at Edinburgh Royal Infirmary, it was as a biochemist that he had done so—although delay in completing the laboratory meant that he spent most of his time walking the wards with the medical students. Much of the subject is concerned with the chemical mechanism producing the physiological results which Haldane had been studying. And it was also pertinent to genetics, although less so than today, since Haldane already appreciated the biochemical nature of the gene itself. Even if these links had not existed, the move would have been less surprising than it might appear today, as well as less surprising for Haldane than for most men. Specialisation had not reached its later importance, an importance of which J.B.S. was always sceptical. He always believed in the unity of science, welcomed the return of the deductive method to the biological sciences as a sign of this, and in one of his last papers outlined his belief that there might be "only one science, of which physics, biology and psychology are different aspects".

In 1921 Gowland Hopkins, whose seminal paper on vitamins had been published in the *Journal of Physiology* nine years earlier, had become Sir William Dunn Professor at Cambridge. A Readership in Biochemistry was created shortly afterwards, and Hopkins wrote to Haldane offering him the post, in effect that of second-in-command in the Department. Haldane accepted, went to Cambridge in 1923, and was to stay there for a decade.

"Although I did some research and some teaching," he later wrote, "my most important duty was the supervision of research work carried on by others on a great variety of subjects, including the chemistry of men, animals, higher plants, and bacteria. My salary was £600 per year, and Trinity College gave me bed, board, and amenities, such as newspapers, at an extremely cheap rate. This was a great advance on New College, which gave me £150 per year, rising to £250, free rooms, and a subsidy towards my evening meal."

Haldane's work during his decade under Hopkins lay in two distinct but related fields. One was that of enzymes, the complex substances produced in living organisms and largely responsible for the processes of metabolism. Forty years ago it was known that these mysterious substances existed; it was sensed, if not precisely known, that they played vital parts in the complicated process by which most living organisms continue to live. What was not known was the range, number and extent of these substances, the exact functions that they performed or the ways in which they performed them. It was to these problems that Haldane turned his mind during the mid-1920's and early 1930's. With a colleague he produced what is still called the Briggs-Haldane Relationship, a proof that reactions produced by enzymes obey the known laws of thermodynamics. He calculated, with some plausible assumptions and some elegant mathematics, the rates at which various enzyme reactions took place. And in *Enzymes*—a book largely drawn from his Cambridge lectures—he helped to provide an overall picture of how these substances did their job. "My own most important discovery," he has written of his work at Cambridge, "was perhaps that a substance, for which carbon monoxide competes with oxygen, now called cytochrome oxidase, was found in plant seedlings, moths and rats. The most remarkable thing about this discovery was that I was able to find out a good deal about a substance in the brains of moths without cutting them up, much less killing them."

Of comparable significance to Haldane's work on enzymes, and probably of more lasting importance, was his work in genetics. As he read some of Muller's papers before the war, he had experienced "all the satisfaction of reading a first-rate detective story, much enhanced by the fact that the story was true". In Delhi, he had continued to study the latest developments reported in the scientific journals and had "done a little rather second-rate theoretical work on genetics, working on results obtained by Morgan and his colleagues in New York". During his brief post-war stay in Oxford he had begun to probe the use of mathematics in genetics, and now, at Cambridge, he threw a great deal of his intellectual effort into this branch of the developing science.

Much genetical research consists of two closely-linked parts. There is the breeding and examination of large numbers of experimental "animals", the most famous of which is the *Drosophila* fly whose short life-cycle combines with other factors to make it ideal for the purpose. And there is secondly the mathematical analysis of the various characteristics found in the flies or other animals which have been bred, and the interpretation of the results. It was in the second kind of work that Haldane excelled. Rather like the great Rutherford—and to an extent which some of his friends are loath to admit—he was clumsy with his hands. This may sound strange of a man whose life had often depended on the correct handling of a grenade or a mortar; yet the care required in the trenches is of a totally different order from that demanded in the laboratory, and there is no doubt that Haldane was unhappy and uncertain in the handling of delicate laboratory specimens. "There is a legend," it has been written, "that he learned the basic rudiments of *Drosophila* genetics from Jack Schultz during a visit to Cal. Tech. But his occasional attempts to manipulate a few flies under a low-power binocular were a source of much amusement to his associates." J.B.S. was perfectly aware that he was poor at laboratory manipulation, the sole exception being the delicate operation of the Haldane gas-analysis apparatus, which had become second nature to him through work with his father. If his students included females he would delight in confessing this ineptitude—so that he could add as a rider, "but I do claim to be an accomplished exponent of the use of the paternal apparatus".

It was no doubt partly owing to ham-handedness as well as to his formidable stature as a mathematician, that most of Haldane's work in the field of genetics was theoretical. However, the word is used in a special sense. Few men had a keener eye than Haldane for the practical implications of the work he did. His calculations, slightly esoteric except to mathematicians of his own calibre, might be concerned with the fortunes of specific genes down the generations, with the interplay of one factor of heredity on another, or with the position of a specific gene on the chromosome. Haldane rarely failed to extrapolate these calculations into terms of practical application; his ultimate concern was their effect on the living world in general and on human beings in particular.

Two other attitudes run through much of his genetics. One was an approach to Nature which considered it entirely in terms of atoms and molecules, an attitude common today but much rarer in the 1920's, and one which permeated much of his work. Secondly, there was his continual desire to provide a statistical framework for his experiments and his arguments. He believed that "if you are faced by a difficulty or a controversy in science, an ounce of algebra is worth a ton of verbal argument". This belief he carried far beyond his own specialist fields, and in commenting on various proposals for Death Rays, which he considered while on a government defence committee of the 1920's, he remarked that "the great majority can be rejected at once because their authors have clearly not thought in numbers, but in words or pictures".

There is also a third attitude which is not so constantly or so readily seen, an attitude which Haldane himself would sometimes try to conceal. This was the fascination of his personal struggle with the continuing mysteries of science. In many ways he was among the last of the "string-and-sealing-wax" scientists, the men who could achieve results by themselves, without the aid of a committee, and who could, without the help of another committee, see how their discoveries fitted into the larger pattern of scientific knowledge. This individual engagement with science gave to his work some of the features of a personal encounter; he would write "J. B. S. Haldane" instead of "I" in his reports but it was in some ways a leaning over backwards, an attempt to disentangle himself from the solitary struggle in which he so strongly felt himself to be engaged. It is difficult not to feel that he was somehow embarrassed by this engagement; as though he was forever trying to stifle the romantic in his own nature, the imaginative potential one can discern in some of his writings and which continued to bob to the surface however hard he tried.

Haldane's first genetical work after his return from the war had consisted of papers which outlined the best way of estimating linkage, and in which he provided a formula which related the amount of linkage to the distance between particular genes on the chromosome. He also showed, with a clarity which had not previously been shown with vertebrates, that the linkage of at least certain factors varies considerably with age. In this case the animals concerned were chickens, the factors involved being the barring of feathers and the substitution of silver for golden hackles. These factors were clearly seen to be linked when the chickens were mated at the age of one year; but if they were mated a year later the linkage was found to be half as strong again, and after another year it had once again increased by almost a half. In itself, the fact might have no significance. But the same differential linkage might be true for other genes affecting weight, tenderness, breeding ability, or any of the various factors of importance to man in the creatures which he domesticates. In any case, it threw fresh light on one more part of the machinery which moves the natural world.

Another part which Haldane first illuminated, largely through his facility for seeing the implications between apparently unrelated facts, was that covered by what is still known as Haldane's Law. Based on forty-eight agreements and one exception, this deals with the fact, noted by laymen and scientists alike, that the crossing of several animal species produces an offspring, one sex of which is rare or absent—and, if present, is sterile—while in occasional cases the missing sex is represented by intermediate forms. Haldane analysed all possible cases where such animals had been bred in captivity, where more than ten offspring had been raised and in which one sex was absent, sterile, or with sex ratios more than two to one. In all cases, he found, the sex which was absent, sterile or rare, was that which had a pair of dissimilar chromosomes, and and he went on to give an explanation of the facts which still holds good, in spite of the exceptions to Haldane's Law which have been found.

Shortly after its exposition, J.B.S. began to produce what he, and some of his colleagues, consider his most important work. This consisted of ten papers—"Mathematical Contributions to the Theory of Natural Selection"—published in the *Proceedings* and *Transactions* of the Cambridge Philosophical Society between 1924 and 1934, and later summarised as an appendix in Haldane's *The Causes of Evolution*. Written on a plane or which even mathematicians can lose their way and which the layman will regard as highly esoteric, their importance is indicated by the title of the book in which they were summarised.

By the 1920's the fact of evolution, as postulated by Darwin, was generally accepted; it was realised that one species did evolve from another and that, although there were still gaps in the record, the history of living things could be regarded as one composite whole, infinitely inter-connected, infinitely complex

67

yet infinitely rational in its development, and explicable according to natural laws. It had also become increasingly realised during the preceding two decades that the machinery of inheritance used chromosomes and genes to transmit specific characteristics from one generation to the next. But how exactly did this machinery work so that the genetic differences of successive generations finally produced not different individuals of the same species but members of different species? How, in fact, did evolution work?

It was these questions which Haldane set out to answer in his series of papers which were to become known as "The Mathematical Theory". "I am still publishing what could have been sections of it," he wrote forty years later. "I am not, however, ashamed of it." Other men were also providing a mathematical framework for Darwinism, notably R. A. Fisher whose theories had some similarity to Haldane's, and Professor Sewall Wright, who has described "The Mathematical Theory" as Haldane's outstanding contribution to genetics. Thus it would be wrong to consider his work in isolation to theirs; he was not unique; but he was one of the three men whose evidence showed not only that Darwin's theory of evolution could work but exactly how it could work. What he did was to produce a formula which gave a numerical indication of how Mendelian genetics would work if Darwin's theory of natural selection was correct. In other words, he removed the either/or choice from the Darwinian—Mendelian argument that was developing. He estimated how quickly the frequency of dominant and recessive genes would change under various types of selection; he estimated the effects of selection on a characteristic which was itself produced by the presence or absence of a number of genes; and he suggested that it might be possible to estimate the rate at which certain genes with known harmful effects, were produced in living bodies by the process of mutation.

All of this was theoretical and much of it was to remain unproven for years. Yet there has been one almost startling illustration of how correct Haldane's views in fact were. In the first of his papers he used his calculations to estimate the selective advantage given to the darker form of the "Peppered Moth" by the gene which produces grey wings rather than the whitish wings of the variety prevalent in England a century ago. It was clear that industrialisation, which had killed off or darkened the light lichen on which the lighter moth was less visible to birds, had made life safer to the darker variety. But just how much safer? Haldane used his calculations to estimate that the single wing-darkening gene, transmitted down the generations, conferred a selective advantage of about 50 per cent on those who had it. This figure was in the early 1920's considered almost impossibly high. Roughly thirty years later Richard Kettlewell, carrying out studies in the field, arrived at a similar one.

This work in the mathematical stratosphere, the research into enzymes, and the physiological investigations which he continued, were together insufficent to satisfy Haldane's protean mind. He began his questionings into cosmology which were to culminate in "The Origin of Life", a lengthy article in *The Rationalist Annual* which described a plausible mechanism for the synthesis of organic matter which Darwin had merely assumed to have taken place. He joined General Ashmore's Cabinet sub-committee on Air Defence, and served on it until the early 1930's. He began, moreover, to write the first of that long collection of brilliant popular essays which are one of his main claims to fame. Their subjects ranged from "Darwinism Today" to "Cancer Research", from "Food Poisoning" to "On Being One's Own Rabbit"; they appeared in the *Manchester Guardian* and the *Daily Mail, Discovery* and the *Graphic*, while in America they were published in the *Atlantic Monthly, Harper's Magazine* and the *New Republic*.

This explanation of science to the layman, a field in which Haldane was the direct successor to T. H. Huxley, brought down a good deal of criticism from his scientific colleagues. Many of them already disliked him for the booming voice which would be carried up to High Table describing the most intimate details of life. Many felt that a considered policy of shocking one's companions formed no part of the academic scene. Many took offence at the calculated rudeness with which this fundamentally shy man was apt to keep the world at arm's length. All this was bad enough. That he should stretch out and touch the world of common men was unforgiveable.

Haldane himself had once thought in a similar way on this last point. When he and his friend Julian Huxley had both been dons at Oxford a few years previously, Huxley had written his first popular article—largely to explain and modify the sensational press accounts of an experiment he had recently finished. A highly distracted Haldane had immediately called upon Huxley and his young wife to protest that this was not the task of serious scientists. Now he himself was to take up the task —and to excel at it.

While still an undergraduate, Haldane had written a lengthy essay dealing with the future of science. He had tucked it away among his papers on joining the Black Watch and had only pulled it out nine years later when suddenly called upon by the New College Essay Society to produce a paper at three days' notice. He remembered "The Future of Science", re-furbished it in the light of wartime experience and the scientific advances made since 1912, and successfully read it. A few years later, called upon to address the Heretics in Cambridge, the utilitarian essay was once more brought up to date.

This time it was called *Daedalus, or Science and the Future*; and this time there sat among the audience C. K. Ogden, the creator of Basic English and until the previous year editor of *The Cambridge Magazine*. As a "scout" for Kegan Paul, Ogden urged publication of *Daedalus* in *Today and Tomorrow*, a series which the firm was about to launch. Haldane agreed and *Daedalus* appeared in 1924, a slim octavo volume of about one hundred pages which sold for what was then considered the excessively high price of 2s. 6d. Within twelve months, it had passed through five impressions and sold about 15,000 copies. Years later Haldane boasted that it had brought him £800.

Daedalus concentrated on future biological discoveries and enlarged on the possibilities of ectogenesis, or birth outside the human body. This subject, taken up a decade later by Aldous Huxley in *Brave New World*, was one on which Haldane would frequently expound loudly and at length, quickly clearing tea-shops of the more susceptible ladies present. In *Daedalus* it led on to discussion of a variety of scientific fields. Haldane produced numerous Aunt Sallies, demolished them entertainingly, and generally exhibited a proficiency as a writer which was either slight or non-existent among most contemporary scientists. The short book also revealed two other traits which later hardened into essentials of Haldane's character. One was his tendency to write and speak in what would now be called "quotes of the week". The other was his emphasis on the fact that the sciences and the humanities are but interlinked parts of the complete life. "I am absolutely convinced," he wrote, "that science is vastly more stimulating to the imagination than are the classics, but the products of this stimulus do not normally see the light because scientific men as a class are devoid of any perception or literary form. When they can express themselves we get a Butler or a Norman Douglas. Not until our poets are once more drawn from the educated classes [I speak as a scientist] will they appeal to the average man by showing him the beauty in his own life as Homer and Virgil appealed to the street urchins who scrawled their verses on the walls of Pompeii."

Daedalus, with its suggestions of test-tube babies, may have upset those for whom it was not intended. Yet it had, in fact, merely suggested that humanity might extend its ideas into the future; it had not attempted to dynamite sacred beliefs. This task, at which Haldane was to become such a master-operator, was undertaken with logic and some success, in a second volume in the *Today and Tomorrow* series, published in 1925 as *Callinicus, A Defence of Chemical Warfare*.

This subject, which was to become one of Haldane's hobby-horses, was still enveloped in a swathe of emotion produced by the gas casualties of less than a decade previously. J.B.S. saw the removal of this wrapping as one of his duties, although his belief that gas was among the less inhumane of weapons was equalled by fear that it might be used with success were the public not properly prepared. He had no hesitation in driving home the lessons he wanted to teach and was long remembered by the people of Auchterarder, a few miles from the family home of Cloan, for a lecture he once gave in the Church Hall. Here he explained that one of the gases suggested to the War Office during the last war was produced by the heating of cayenne pepper. It would not kill and therefore, Haldane went on, the authorities turned it down. However, he added, it would have been useful enough. He then produced a spirit-lamp and a spoonful of pepper. Holding the spoon over the lamp without warning he suddenly vaporised the pepper; within a few seconds almost the entire audience was coughing and rubbing their smarting eyes.

Haldane was unconcerned. "If that upsets you," he remarked, "how would you like a deluge of poison gas from an air fleet in real war?"

Callinicus, titled after the inventor of Greek fire, had started life like *Daedalus* as a lecture, being given at Murren for Sir Henry Lunn in August 1924. Lunn had been one of the first travel agent tycoons to lard the business of holiday-making with the lectures of experts, and he no doubt found that Haldane on chemical warfare was tough meat. For the speaker trod, as *The Times* put it in a leading article on the little book, "lightly but perceptibly on the toes of politicians, military authorities, officials, pacifists, journalists and newspaper proprietors". Haldane blandly suggested that everyone in Britain might with good result be fitted with gas-masks—not a popular idea in the 1920's—since this would lessen the chance of surprise attack. He castigated the inefficiency of the authorities. And he came to the nub of his unpopular argument with the propositions that the use of gas was not ethically different from the use of other weapons and—even less susceptible to rational argument—that it was probably more humane. His first proposition rested on one claim: "If it is right for me to fight my enemy with a sword, it is right for me to fight him with mustard gas; if the one is wrong, so is the other." The second was supported not only by a list of possibly unpalatable facts but also by personal experience. "Besides being wounded, I have been buried alive, and on several occasions in peacetime I have been asphyxiated to the point of unconsciousness," he said. "The pain and discomfort arising from the other experiences were utterly negligible compared with those produced by a good septic shell-wound."

These two brief books, on the future of science and on chemical warfare, helped to bring Haldane into the harsh and critical public limelight, an illumination about which he would unceasingly protest but which he rarely failed to enjoy. More important, the first brought him into contact with the young woman who was to become the first Mrs. J. B. S. Haldane.

4

A Geneticist in the Headlines

By the mid 1920's Haldane had become a public figure. The nephew of the former Lord Chancellor and War Minister, an unconventional don, a man who at the drop of a question would produce answers that were provocative but just substantial enough to arouse opposition, he was decidedly newsworthy, a man whom any journalist could rely upon to produce quotable comments on any subject or situation. In person he was tall, commanding, and as physically impressive as intellectually formidable; thickish sandy moustache and head almost innocent of hair had already begun to give him the air of a playfully alert walrus.

In some ways he was ambivalent. To children he was warm and kind hearted, with a warmth that was later pathetic if one knew how much he desired his own. Yet there was another side to his nature well epitomised by the description of Mr. Codling, the central figure of Ronald Fraser's *The Flying Draper*, a novel in whose first edition J.B.S. could be identified. "Possibly libellous statements were expunged (not at my request) in later ones," he noted. Fraser's Codling was not only a man of genius, but one who at times seemed to be set apart from the rest of mankind, a man whose friends sometimes "realised with force what one was apt to forget after a few days of his society—Codling's unhumanness. It was like being friends with a fish, or a bird, or a half-human god."

On a summer afternoon in 1924 Haldane was sought out in his rooms at Trinity by a young woman reporter of the *Daily Express*. She had been born in London as Charlotte Franken. Married before the end of the war, Mrs. Burghes, as she had become, was already planning her first novel, *Man's World*, in which the human race would be able to choose the sex of its children, and she wanted to ensure that the scientific basis of her story was credible. She had read an abridged version of *Daedalus* which had been published in the American *Century*. And she had immediately thought "This is my man". Her editor, J. B. Wilson, agreed that Haldane would be worth an interview. And it was thus with a double objective that Mrs. Burghes wrote to J.B.S. She waited for a fortnight but received no reply. Then, prepared to wait no longer, she visited Cambridge and ascended the narrow stairway of Nevile Court to the white door beside which Haldane's name was painted.

Mrs. Burghes explained that she "wanted information, references to books, to biological sources", for a novel which she was writing. The great man was helpful. He loaded her with advice, with references, and with books, and learned only as he was escorting her to the bus that she was a newspaper reporter as well as novelist. He made a few pungent comments on the daily Press but added that he had that very day taken 10 c.c. of his own blood for experimental purposes. "To my astonishment," he later wrote, "the resulting paragraph in the *Daily Express* not only kept to the facts, but, as had been stipulated, did not mention my name. For this, and other reasons, I fell in love with the reporter and my love was reciprocated."

This last sentence was presentation of the problem rather than its solution. In the 1920's desertion was no ground for divorce. Adultery had to be committed—and proven in court with the necessary tribal details. Divorce, moreover, still involved a social slur. It was a solution to a human problem which still carried built-in disadvantages, and it was a solution avoided wherever possible by professional men. Bateson, still running the John Innes, commented on hearing of the case in which Haldane was to be involved: "I am not a prude, but I don't approve of a man running about the streets like a dog." Both Mrs. Burghes and Haldane were alive to such possible reactions —particularly Haldane who was well aware of the likely repercussions in a small University city which relished its own priste gossip.

"I informed the Vice-Chancellor of Cambridge University," he later wrote, "that I was about to commit this act, to which he replied: 'Oh!'"

In February 1925, preparations were complete and Haldane and his future wife arrived at an hotel. Mrs. Burghes disliked its appearance and suggested that they move elsewhere. This presented a problem since it was essential that the enquiry agent, whom both knew to be following, did not lose the trail. However, the future Mrs. Haldane had not been a reporter for nothing and had already marked down as the detective a rather nondescript man in the hotel lounge. "I asked him to accompany us to the other hotel, which he did, carrying one of our suitcases," J.B.S. has explained. "The next morning he appeared in our bedroom with the morning papers. Save for one moment when I had feared that we might lose sight of the detective, everything had passed off without a hitch."

Haldane's account of the incident, written in his draft autobiography, is revealing but selective. This is natural enough. For after Mr. Burghes had in due course filed the expected petition against his wife, an extraordinary development occurred. Having taken great care to ensure that they were followed to the hotel and that the available evidence was suitably compromising, Haldane and his future wife now filed answers, and he denied the charge of adultery against him. The truth seemed clear to those who knew Haldane well: he had not committed adultery, and he felt obliged to say so. His defence to the charge was struck out, and when the case was heard in October, Lord Merrivale granted a decree to Mr. Burghes. He also awarded £1,000 damages against Haldane.

However, J.B.S. and Charlotte were free to marry. Before they did so, a small cloud arose on the horizon. It came in the form of the Sex Viri—"meaning the Six Men, not the Sex Weary", as Haldane remarked. Under the University Statutes this body was able to deprive any Cambridge University Reader of his post if he were found by them guilty of gross or habitual immorality. It might be questioned whether, even in the distant days of 1925, one act of adultery with a woman whom a man was obviously intent on marrying could fairly warrant the description of gross or habitual immorality. The authorities were in no doubt, and they were probably supported by a considerable fraction in the University which had long been disturbed by the faintly irritating consistency with which Haldane had refused to conform. Now, they felt, he had rashly delivered himself into their hands. Here, surely, was an opportunity to get rid of him. Professors or Readers so accused invariably resigned without protest or second thoughts, and Haldane himself later reflected that had he been asked to do so on first raising the matter with the Vice-Chancellor, he might well have complied. The Vice-Chancellor's "Oh!" induced him to fight.

On the morning of December 13th he received a letter informing him that the Sex Viri had "unanimously decided to authorise me to inform you that judgement of deprivation will be given in the event of notice of resignation of the Readership held by you not being received by me, as Vice-Chancellor, before noon on Saturday, December 19". The weakness of the University's position was revealed in a final sentence. "I cannot refrain from adding that I hope you will see fit to tender your resignation and so avoid publication of the judgement."

Haldane did not see fit. Instead, he appeared before the Sex Viri, consisting of heads of Colleges and Professors of law and apparently led by the Rev. Dr. Pearce. He produced a cutting from *The Times* describing the divorce case, and added documentary evidence showing that he had not broken up a home since there had been no home to break up. He then offered to call witnesses and suggested that he might be legally represented. Both these suggestions were refused—refusals which were tactical if not legal errors by the body concerned. For when, shortly afterward, notice of deprivation was served, the case was not closed. Haldane was deprived of his Readership—although he still lived in College and gave his lectures—but under the University Statutes he had the right of appeal to a tribunal of five to be appointed by the Council of the Cambridge Senate.

Haldane appealed. In doing so he raised the stakes, since loss at the higher level would certainly increase his difficulty in getting another academic appointment. He was helped by the support of Hopkins who refused to appoint another Reader and who thus openly took Haldane's side in the argument which was splitting University loyalties. In addition, there was backing from the National Union of Scientific Workers, as it then was; if the appeal failed, Haldane planned to stand for re-election to the empty Readership, and the Union agreed that its members would be advised not to apply. "As my Chief wanted me back, this would have created a situation of some interest," Haldane himself noted. To these advantages of principle were added those of finance. J.B.S. had only recently received a legacy which had helped to buttress his divorce costs and now enabled him to prepare for the appeal.

The five members of the tribunal were appointed by the University in February 1926, under the Presidency of Mr. Justice Avory, and in March Haldane appeared before them at the London Law Courts. Represented by Stuart Bevan, later to become Conservative M.P. for Holborn, he called as witnesses both Hopkins and his father as well as his sister Naomi. It would be difficult to think of two men more likely to influence the judgement of such a court. Hopkins was at the height of his fame, recently knighted, and within a few years of becoming

President of the Royal Society, a Nobel Prize winner and a Member of the Order of Merit. John Scott Haldane was almost equally the paradigm of the objective scientific man, and one whose judgement of his son's case would be unaffected by personal feeling.

Whether or not due to such witnesses, the Court gave a majority verdict in Haldane's favour, deciding that "in view of all the circumstances of the case, which have been more fully before us than they were before the Vice-Chancellor and the Sex Viri, the appeal should be allowed". However, this was not to be interpreted as condonation of licence. "This decision," the judges added, "is not to be taken as any expression of opinion that adultery may not be gross immorality within the meaning of the statute."

Haldane was not sure, he later wrote, "whether Mr. Justice Avory was more horrified by my conduct or by the fact that the Sex Viri, like the jury in Alice in Wonderland, had delivered their verdict before hearing the evidence." Perhaps that point, the failure to hear evidence at an earlier stage, was the vital one; certainly much of Cambridge believed that the Sex Viri had been hoist with their own legal petard. Whatever the internal causes, Haldane was re-instated. He had, in fact, won not his own case alone, but that of others. University staff have not since been threatened because of their private lives. The Sex Viri, moreover, changed its name—a prudent step now that the "sex weary" of J.B.S. could so easily be murmured under the breath.

A new era in Haldane's life now began. He moved from his bachelor rooms in Nevile Court to Roebuck House, facing the Cam at Old Chesterton on the north-eastern outskirts of Cambridge, and here created with his wife a centre to which the more left-wing and non-conformist dons and undergraduates were inevitably drawn. Over the years more than one young research student came to live for a while with the Haldanes. One in particular, Martin Case, was to play an important part in J.B.S.'s life during the Second World War.

Roebuck House was large and rambling, and much converted, approached through a single wooden gate and standing in the middle of largish grounds which sloped down to the river near the "Horse Grind", a cumbersome and primitive flat-bottomed ferry worked by rotating a handle that picked up a chain. During the summer, ferry-users would frequently see J.B.S. swimming in his slow deliberate style while puffing away at his pipe. In term-time he would cycle into the city every day

77

on his tall upstanding bicycle, wearing an open-necked shirt in all weathers, a formidable example of academic non-conformity.

His habits were simple and comparatively spartan. He would breakfast on porridge and milk, drink coffee in the middle of the day, take a few slices of bread and jam with his afternoon tea and cycle home for the large evening meal which he visibly enjoyed. He was a strong supporter of Movements, particularly anti-clerical ones, and of The Cambridge University Benskin Society.

This society was inaugurated in the middle twenties, and was a somewhat extroverted and uninhibited institution devoted to the enjoyment of beer (not necessarily Benskin's, though that brew was highly esteemed originally) and of bawdy and ribald verse and song. "It was in no sense a degenerate or reprehensible 'Hell-Fire Club', but more a channel for periodical blowing-off of steam on the part of really rather serious and academically-minded undergraduates and recent graduates," writes Martin Case. "It was part of the constitution of the Society that there should only be one designated Member; everyone else had to hold the title of some office, from Chancellor or Vice-Chancellor downwards. The Society used to meet several times a term in various members' rooms in this or that College; but the meetings always became exceedingly uproarious, and eventually one culminated in the emptying of a full jerry from an upper window over the heads of the police and the University Proctors who had arrived simultaneously to investigate the hullabaloo. Considerable ill-feeling ensued, and the Society was proscribed and forbidden to hold meetings in any College of the University.

"When Haldane heard of the antipathetic attitude of the Proctors and the restrictive measures taken, he immediately suggested Roebuck House as the future meeting-place; his proposition was accepted with alacrity. Charlotte and J.B.S. were forthwith elected to the Society, the former in the capacity of Matron and the latter in that of Patron and Sanitary Inspector, which title he insisted on having amended to that of Insanitary Spectre. It must be recorded that the Society's ribald repertoire was significantly expanded by contributions from J.B.S., quite a number of them original and *ad hoc*. In view of his uneasiness over the gulf between himself and the common herd, it is worth emphasising the very real and perhaps almost pathetic delight that Haldane felt and very obviously showed in his acceptance and assimilation at this rather unintellectual level."

As a teacher J.B.S. became known for the encouragement he gave to originality, and for the independence of his judgement; the graduate who gained only a poor degree and was encouraged

78

by Haldane to go on to work which led to a Nobel Prize was not exceptional. He cultivated a reputation for bad temper but had a sense of humour as well as wit, and no student was ever certain what his reaction would be.

There was, for instance, the occasion when he was demonstrating the gas-analysis apparatus devised by his father. Several students had spilt the mercury through mishandling, and J.B.S. made it quite clear that mercury was an expensive material that should not be wasted. The exercise involved the analysis of Haldane's own breath, and one of the students inadvertently backed up the mercury into his instructor's mouth. J.B.S. was unable to say anything until he had spat it out. The students expected an explosion. Instead, Haldane merely took a deep breath, looked at the student keenly, and commented: "I am not syphilitic yet."

For years he had been a casual writer of light verse and at Cambridge he helped fill the pages of *Brighter Biochemistry*, the comic journal of the Department. Typical of his contributions was the rhymed "Report to the Secretary of the Sir William Dunn Institute for the Year 1924-1925", consisting of more than 150 lines and including the following:

> Miss Robinson and R. McCance
> Have made a notable advance
> In dealing with tyrosinase,
> And the queer laws which it obeys.
> Aided by Anderson and others
> Our saccharologist Carruthers
> Attacked the problem of rotation
> Of glucose during activation.

Contributions like this formed part and parcel of Haldane's enjoyment in less intellectual clowning. He loved demonstrating to children his ability to put a lighted match into his mouth and withdraw it still burning. And to adult visitors he would apologise profusely as a large white cat jumped down from a door-top on to their shoulders as they entered the room—having been trained by J.B.S. to do so.

The English love "characters", and it was as a "character" that Haldane worked himself slowly into the heart of Cambridge. Only by some of the University authorities was he still regarded as one to be treated with respectful caution rather than friendship. Those who rejoiced in the discomfiture of the Sex Viri did not, necessarily, rejoice in the triumph of Haldane, while among many there lingered a regret that his wife was a writer for the popular newspapers. "When they entered a room," a contemporary has said of the Haldanes, "people were apt to stop speaking about their work and go on to subjects that could not possibly be of news value." J.B.S. was well aware of this; he cared about it as little as he cared about other unreasonable prejudices.

"Our marriage was happy for some years, which, given man's mortality, is something," J.B.S. later wrote. But over it there fell the lengthening shadow of Haldane's failure to father a son. "I was passionately eager to have more children," Charlotte has written. "The deepest and strongest bond J.B.S. and I had in common was this philoprogenitiveness." Yet while Haldane watched his step-son, Ronnie, playing in the grounds and growing up into a son of the sort he himself wanted, he failed to father a child of his own. "How I wish," he said to an old friend years later as he watched her young son cavorting round the London Zoo ". . . how I wish I had a son like that." The failure did more than move him strongly. To warp is to "bend, curve or twist an object out of shape", and Haldane's childlessness tended to warp his character out of shape. For a man of his potential, this was a tragedy not only for himself but for the society in which he lived.

Except for this dark area of disappointment, the years that followed Haldane's re-instatement under Hopkins were among the best of his life. He was happily engaged in what he knew to be important work, helping to found biochemistry as the science which it has become today. His anguish for the world had not yet pushed him into the ranks of the Communists, so that he was not yet riven by the stress and uncertainties of political combat. He formed part of a community in which he could encourage young men of promise and enterprise; and if the elder members of University society tended to steer clear of him they yet provided that slight irritant, that cause for genuine complaint, without which Haldane could never be really happy.

The loyalty which he engendered among both students and colleagues, the alarm which he aroused among more conventional members of the University, and much of his own individual eccentricity, were all revealed after one of the students living at Roebuck House had been charged with dangerous driving. The chief prosecution witness was a night watchman most of whose daytime hours were known to be spent in one particular public house. "If you care to leave this to me," said Haldane on hearing the details, "I think I see a possible course of action that *might* just . . ." Nothing more was said.

"My case," says the student concerned, "was the first to be heard on the afternoon of the momentous day. The customary mumbo-jumbo was enacted, and in due course the prosecution called their chief witness. A shambling, bleary scarecrow stumbled into the box, and a kind of *frisson* that I imagine was experienced by everyone in the court proclaimed that there was some sort of unusual element in this situation.

"With fantastic difficulty he was processed through the routine of the oath, identification and so on. Then, when requested to give his version of the incident under enquiry, he goggled wildly around him, mouthing tremulously and soundlessly. The question was repeated. He made a gigantic effort, clutched the front of the box, and blurted out: 'Ecumuptheillikefuckinell-anwentarseovertip.' That was the exact word, as it came out, all in one gobbling splurge. It impressed itself indelibly on my memory at the time, and I have never forgotten it.

"An official said sternly: 'You cannot say that sort of thing here. Kindly tell us what happened in a way that the Court can accept as evidence.'

"This seemed to incense the witness, in so far as it was possible for anything to make any kind of impression on him. He belched violently, retched, and repeated in precisely the same manner, except that this time it was several times as loud: 'Ecumuptheillikefuckinellanwentarseovertip. I'vetoldyeronce-avent'tI?'

"He then sank to the floor of the witness-box, from which he had to be extricated like a winkle. The remains were shovelled as expeditiously as possible out of the door of the court-room. Everybody was too incredulous and flabbergasted even to laugh. The case was dismissed, and so was I.

"I didn't see J.B.S. until that evening at home. He had gone to the lab in the afternoon, had not bothered to attend the judicial proceedings, and was curious to know how they had gone on. After I had finished telling him he looked a trifle dissatisfied, and said in a rather disappointed voice: 'Oh dear, he managed to get to the court, did he?'"

Haldane then haltingly recounted how he had gone at opening time to the public-house, taking the morning off from the lab to do so; had identified that most regular and reliable of the pub's customers, the night watchman; had got into conversation with him, proffered refreshment and been gratefully accepted as god-sent mug and providential perpetual host for the entire bibulous session. He had plied his victim relentlessly with booze for nearly three hours, being (he confessed rather ruefully) "compelled himself to indulge somewhat more profusely than was his wont on an ordinary week-day morning"; and had finally quitted the premises about an hour before they were due to shut, leaving behind him in the Public Bar a carcase which he felt would be incapable of performing any act of its own volition for several hours to come.

"I was speechless with admiration and with gratitude," says Martin Case, the student concerned. "However, Haldane wasn't Haldane and Scottish for nothing. 'Don't be *too* effusive in your thanks,' he said, 'until this little corollary has been adjusted!' and he produced from his pocket a tattered old envelope on which he had meticulously entered, item by item as they mounted up, every expense incurred on behalf of both parties to the morning's orgy.

"It was a fairly staggering total, but even so not to be compared with the fine that would doubtless have been incurred, to say nothing of the odium attaching to a conviction."

It was during this period of the early 1930's that J.B.S. began to savour the pleasures of the English countryside, and of English history. "He always used to enjoy Highland scenery," says his sister, "but it certainly made a difference to him that he was aware all the time of the underlying geology, just as it makes a difference to me going through any kind of country that I look on it partly from the point of view of a farmer, and also, when I am among recognisable flora, as a field botanist."

In many ways he led an aesthetically arid life. He was so tone-deaf that he recognised the National Anthem only because everyone stood up for it. The visual arts passed him by, while a colleague remembered how when Haldane later drove up to London from Merton, while working at the John Innes Institution, he would choose "the dirty route" through Tooting and Balham instead of the finer road across Wimbledon Common whose trees and prospects he failed to notice.

Aesthetically it was only the classics—Lucretius in whom he found the principles of genetics, and Dante in whom he discovered the application of genetics to human affairs—and English poetry which came to the rescue. With these he was happy and, now that he began to look beyond the laboratory more frequently, with the splendours of the past and the patchwork pattern of the English countryside.

He bought a small and unassuming car which he drove with a mixture of fearless abandon, little skill and old-world courtesy, "talking like an angel as he went up the Tooting Road missing bollards, policemen etc. by a hair's breadth", as one companion

82

remembers. "I used to avoid telling him I was going up to town as I was frightened for my life to accept a lift."

In his car J.B.S. visited a good deal of England. One of his oldest friends, René Wurmser, always remembered two visits. On one Haldane took his friend and wife to Avebury and Stonehenge, those two great monuments to the country's prehistory; on the other, they went by road to Scotland, and on this second occasion it was the turn of Norwich and Lincoln cathedrals. On both occasions the scientist dissolved into the man of many parts, as able to summon up the scrub-covered Wiltshire landscape of 4,000 years ago as the scurrying activity of the medieval builders.

Haldane himself once said that he had come to love England mainly as the result of owning a motor-car, and in describing that England to a Danish audience he revealed a man very different from the image.

"When I say I love England I do not mean that I love the soul of England, whatever that may be, or the English race, which is, I believe, a statistical abstraction, like the average man or the probability that I shall live till the age of seventy," he said. "I am speaking about the country, which has played a large part in making the people, and in turn has been moulded by them. I do not mean that I merely love the beautiful spots such as the upper Thames valley or the Lake District. I get a considerable satisfaction from some of the ugly ones, such as Burton, where we make our best beer, or Stoke, the great smoky pottery town of which Arnold Bennett wrote." In less than 7,000 words he went on to give his audience a picture of England that would have been a splendid achievement for a geographer, meteorologist, a geologist, or a social historian. Coming from a scientist, it was an illustration of what one friend called "the vast erudition which made Haldane an incomparable companion".

Throughout these first years of marriage Haldane consolidated his position as a popular writer, discoursing upon any scientific or sociological subject that an editor suggested. He wrote at home, stretched in a deck-chair on the Roebuck lawn, during the broken periods between meetings or lectures; on railway journeys; making use of the miscellaneous odd moments that most men would discard. During these he would produce one of his long series of hard-backed exercise books and with a pencil continue the thread of the argument where he had left it hours or days previously. "He was very good at doing two things at once including, naturally, reading and writing," says his sister. "I have seen him do two equations at once, but I am inclined to think that this must have been showing off."

Much of his more serious writing was interspersed with trivia, so that the first few pages of a book might contain the draft of an article for a popular Sunday paper and the last few, filled in after the book had been turned upside down, the mathematical formulae for a learned journal. No time was wasted, and one of his younger colleagues, Cyril Darlington, still remembers that when he travelled with Haldane from Oxford to Cambridge he had, almost unthinkably, to buy a First Class ticket. "I always travel first on journeys like this," insisted J.B.S. "Enables me to get some work done." So it did. The exercise book came out and he scribbled away for the whole journey.

Almost all his work showed the professional touch. He had, it is true, written *Daedalus*, and a number of other pieces, before meeting Charlotte; yet she not only acted as secretary and agent but also smoothed his way into writing for the more popular markets where he was to make a second literary reputation. Articles for the *Atlantic Monthly* or, later, for the *Daily Worker*, might contain much the same material, but they had to be tailor-made for very different markets.

Whatever the exact extent of Charlotte's tutoring for the world of popular journalism, there is no doubt that she set Haldane's writing on a good financial keel, using her experience to sell in the most profitable markets, and ensuring that the minimum of "material" was wasted. He himself took much the same canny line and when colleagues pointed out that election to the Royal Society entailed entrance fee and subscription, he replied: "Have no illusions; I have been writing articles for five guineas—now it will be fifteen."

However, it would be totally wrong to imply that hard cash was the driving force behind Haldane's long series of articles ceaselessly written for journals and newspapers—some of which he was subsequently to upbraid for alleged inaccuracies and distortions. Until the Communist Party swept him up with its proselytising fervour there was only one real motive for his writing. "Many scientific workers believe that they should confine their publications to learned journals," he wrote in his preface to *Possible Worlds*, his first collection of articles and essays. "I think, however, that the public has a right to know what is going on inside the laboratories, for some of which it pays. And it seems to me vitally important that the scientific point of view should be applied, so far as is possible, to politics and religion." Later there became implicit in his writings what one critic called "the doctrine that the duty of the scientist is not to explain the world but to alter the world". This, however, was still seven or eight years away.

The task that Haldane was at this time setting out to perform was that of instruction and explanation. He carried it out with a curious combination of scientific detachment and artistic brilliance. The first of these attributes was represented by the careful, clinical, almost laboratory-style method of his approach, the formula for which he described in a paper on "How to Write a Popular Scientific Article". The writer should, he pointed out, start from a known fact, such as a bomb explosion, a bird's song or a piece of cheese. "This will enable you to illustrate some scientific principle," he said. "But here again take a familiar analogy. Compare the production of hot gas in the bomb to that of steam in a kettle, the changes that occur in the bird each year to those which take place in men once in a lifetime at puberty, the precipitation of casein by calcium salts to the formation of soap suds." By far the greatest number of his articles utilised this method whether they were discussing the world of the future, the prospects of peace, or the latest discovery in biology. This was a good start for a difficult operation. Yet Haldane was enabled to carry on with it by his facility for using the penetrating phrase. He wrote, quite naturally, of Einstein as being "the greatest Jew since Jesus"; and of Darwinism he noted in *The Causes of Evolution* that "the few really pertinent attacks were lost amid a jabber of ecclesiastical bombinations". He also had a constitutional inability to pull his literary punches which made him a delight to more than one newspaper editor. Thus he could write of psychology, eugenics and criminology that: "The small and cautious army of scientific men and women working in these fields is surrounded by such a horde of vociferous quacks that I can sympathise with the snipers like Beachcomber, who are fighting a rearguard action against the advance of science."

The surprising thing about him was not so much the volume as the variety of his output. Like his contemporary Aldous Huxley, who could produce fashion trivia for *Vogue*, articles for the popular papers of the "Do Mothers make Good Wives?" type, and at the same time confound the intellectuals with *Antic Hay* and *Point Counter Point*, J.B.S. could turn his hand to almost any task that required the handling of words. With Julian Huxley he produced a popular volume on *Animal Biology* which greatly amused the elder Mrs. Haldane since one of the two deep sea angler fish in the frontispiece was skinny and fierce-looking like Huxley while the other was round and angry-looking like Haldane. He wrote "The Gold-Makers", a long short story of remarkable quality whose possibilities as a potential film were being considered when he died. He continued, moreover, to produce a continuous stream of scientific papers. Most of these were the result of his biochemical, genetic or physiological work at Cambridge or in the "Cherwell" laboratory; others, however, dealt with such subjects as the scientific point of view and the place of science in western civilisation— both published in the ill-fated *Realist*—and with cosmology and the origins of life.

This latter subject attracted Haldane for almost half a century. It also intrigued his Russian contemporary, A. I. Oparin, and Haldane and Oparin's postulation of the same theory, built up without contact between the two men, has a similarity to the story of Darwin and Wallace. Haldane's most important conclusions were presented in a short article for the *Rationalist Annual*. In this he suggested a method by which life could have been synthesised from the simple carbon compounds and minerals of the prebiotic earth; and he outlined the essentials in two sentences which well convey his style. "When ultra-violet light acts on a mixture of water, carbon dioxide and ammonia," he said, "a vast variety of organic substances are made, including sugars, and apparently some of the materials from which proteins are built up. Before the origin of life they must have accumulated until the primitive oceans reached the consistency of hot, dilute, soup." Haldane's "hot dilute soup", theory was novel. But over the years it gained general acceptance—so much so, Haldane himself later commented, that his mistrust of orthodoxy made him doubt whether it could be correct.

His ability to discuss the origin of life as well as the question "Is History a Fraud?"; to write on genetics as well as the drift of civilisation and the challenge of our times, was the measure of his breadth of interests. "To me," one younger colleague once said, "he seemed to be the last man who might know all there was to be known." Whenever a controversy involving science or sex, war or religion, loomed up on the horizon, the figure of J.B.S. would almost certainly be present, asking awkward questions, undermining accepted opinions, epitomising his own view that the whole point of education was to make people think.

Haldane fought the good fight not only as a matter of principle but also to keep in practice, and he eagerly picked up the opportunity offered in 1930 by the ageing F. E. Smith, first Lord Birkenhead, former Lord Chancellor, former Secretary of

State for India, and now failing under the weight of work, worry and extravagance. In the spring there appeared, under Birkenhead's name, *The World in 2030*. Written by a "ghost", a mere minor item in the profusion of projects with which Birkenhead surrounded himself even in his last years, the book might have passed almost unnoticed had not a copy found its way into Haldane's hands. In more ways than one, Birkenhead's luck was running out. Discussing the book in the *Weekend Review* under "Lord Birkenhead Improves His Mind", Haldane said that as he read it a strange feeling began to oppress him. "Certain of the phrases seemed unduly familiar. Where had I seen them before? Finally I solved the mystery. They were my own." A total of no less than forty-four similarities between Birkenhead's book and *Daedalus* had been noted, he said. He then listed three of them, printing his own version and Birkenhead's side by side and pointing out that the first pair of extracts came from essays supposed to have been written by undergraduates in 1930, and the second from essays fictionally supposed to have been written in 1978. Ruling out "I will not say . . . plagiarism, but . . . a certain lack of originality . . . because it carries with it corollaries which I find unthinkable", Haldane suggested, tongue-in-cheek, that both he and Birkenhead must have seen the same originals—including, of course, the one written forty-eight years hence—or been controlled by the same discarnate intelligence.

Birkenhead—or rather his "ghost"—had said in his preface that he was following "*longum post intervallum* in the footsteps of Jules Verne, Bellamy, Wells and Haldane". A man of his ingenuity could therefore have admitted his failure to give sufficient acknowledgment to others, could have pleaded ill-health and the press of other matters and could probably have avoided public humiliation. This was not Birkenhead's way. Instead, he waited three weeks and then drew a ripe red herring across the trail, attacking Haldane in the *Daily Express*, a paper of gigantic circulation but one with few readers who were likely to have seen Haldane's book, Haldane's review, or Birkenhead's book.

Haldane replied in the columns of the *Weekend Review*, countering Birkenhead's assertion that he had not even a smattering of historical knowledge with the retort that his smattering of ancient history had afforded him a first in *Litterae Humaniores*. As to the claim that Birkenhead was following in other men's footsteps, Haldane noted that he had no objection to this. "I object to them stealing my boots to do so, and I am amused when they do not know how to put the boots on," he added. This was telling, as far as it went. Yet Birkenhead's reply had not been without effect, since it drew from Haldane a point-by-point answer in the *Express* which dealt not with plagiarism of which there could be no doubt but with personalities and opinions. "The red herring," notes Birkenhead's son, "had served its purpose, and Birkenhead, with a sigh of relief, let the matter drop."

J.B.S. had enjoyed the argument. He enjoyed all argument. And it was natural that he should be drawn into the vivisection controversy even though his position here was radically more qualified than was publicly realised. He felt bound to hit out at the extravagances of the Anti-vivisection lobby which often spoilt its case by overstatement, and it was inevitable that he should react when, in the spring of 1927, a petition was circulated by the National Canine Defence League in support of the Dogs' Protection Bill then before Parliament. "The dog has of late years been specially selected by vivisectors for extensive and peculiarly revolting and painful experiments" it was claimed, "and also for demonstrations of a prolonged and agonising nature before classes of students." Haldane publicly offered to pay the League the sum of £100 if they could produce the name of any demonstrator who had performed "a painful experiment on a dog before a class of students in Great Britain and Ireland within the last ten years". He added what was to become a familiar if casuistic argument. "I have seen many experiments on dogs and other animals," he said, "but none which, so far as pain is concerned, I should object to having performed on myself. On the contrary, experiments have frequently been performed on me for scientific purposes without anaesthetic, which the authorities will not allow to be performed on dogs, although they are no more painful than having a tooth stopped."

Yet in spite of this apparent conformity with the vivisectionist cause, Haldane saw humans and the other animals as being part of the same natural world; he felt that the profit and loss account of suffering must be carefully calculated, and as he grew older he swung towards an attitude which finally induced him to tell Gandhians that they should "avoid causing suffering to others unless they volunteer for it. That is why," he added, "I do not recommend you to experiment on dogs and rats." And in Britain, where foxes, hares and deer are torn to pieces in the name of sport, he commented: "I have never known a physiologist who went in for shooting animals; physiologists know too much of the process which occurs to a wounded beast or bird that creeps away to die." Haldane, the plain man's idea of the scientist, had to be an outspoken, newsworthy critic of the anti-vivisectionists. Beneath the skin, he felt limitations and qualifications.

These qualifications provided one reason for the heartiness with which he used himself as an experimental animal. Another was that in many experiments the human animal was the ideal guinea-pig. In addition, one cannot entirely discount his instinctive flair for the newsworthy act. He always claimed that newspapers misquoted him; most of them, during his Communist days, were "capitalist lackeys", and in his mid-sixties he cheerfully helped throw a reporter down the stairs of his Calcutta flat. Nevertheless, he had a facility for getting into the news as strong as Lawrence of Arabia's for backing into the limelight.

From the time of his marriage in 1926 to Charlotte, Haldane travelled quite extensively. He spent his honeymoon in Switzerland where both of them lectured for Sir Henry Lunn's travel organisation, and then travelled on with his wife to Stockholm where the Physiological Congress was being held. Here he lectured and gave a demonstration of the typical symptoms of tetany caused by overbreathing. "The spectacle was terrifying," says René Wurmser, whose life-long friendship with J.B.S. began at the Congress. The following year the Haldanes attended the International Congress on Genetics—remembered by Nirmal Bose as the occasion on which J.B.S. taught him the art and significance of limericks—and later in the year they visited Russia.

This last visit was of great importance to Haldane's future in two different ways. It gave him a first-hand view of the tremendous impact which the Revolution would have on science, and thus coloured much of his later thinking. It also brought him into close contact with Nikolai Vavilov—who was in fact responsible for his invitation to Russia. This was the same Vavilov who was later to be chopped down by the rise of Lysenkoism, and Haldane's casual abandonment of Vavilov's cause in the interests of the Party was to leave a nasty taste in the mouth—even for many who could defend much of Haldane's attitude in this crucial controversy.

Vavilov, then the President of the Academy of Agricultural Sciences which had been set up by Lenin a few years earlier, arranged for J.B.S. to lecture to geneticists in both Leningrad and Moscow. He had been trained under Bateson in England; he correctly regarded Haldane as in the vanguard of British work; and he ensured that the Haldanes got the maximum benefit from the powerful position that he then occupied in

Russian science. Both J.B.S. and his wife were impressed with what they saw in the U.S.S.R., particularly J.B.S. who sympathised with the difficulties of a country then lifting itself up by its boot-straps. He returned converted—not to Communism which he still regarded as a threat from the east comparable to the threat of Americanisation from the west, but to the way in which the State was supporting science and scientists.

On his return to England Haldane spoke extensively of his experiences—and in discussing scientific man at the Central London Fabian Society, experienced his first brush with Bernard Shaw. When the subject was thrown open to discussion after Haldane's lecture, Shaw rose to ask what the description "scientific man" really meant.

"Am I, for instance, a scientific man?" he asked.

"Mr. Shaw," J.B.S. replied, "you are a great and famous playwright. One cannot be *everything* in this life." In Shaw's later words, "he dismissed the notion that I could be a man of science as a bad joke, exactly as he must have wagged his ankle if I had clipped him across the knee."

By 1930, when he became the Royal Institution's Fullerian Professor of Physiology in succession to Julian Huxley, Haldane was firmly established. He could be relied upon to fill a lecture hall, to respond to an editor's request for an article on almost any conceivable subject. In truly scientific fields he had already elucidated a number of physiological problems, had carried out a good deal of basic work on enzyme mechanisms, and was still adding to his mathematical theory of natural and artificial selection. In typical fashion, he now decided to change scientific horses in mid-stream, to relinquish his academic work on biochemistry and to switch, wholetime, to genetics.

The move came at the end of 1932, a vintage year for J.B.S. in which he was elected a Fellow of the Royal Society, published no less than fifteen scientific papers, as well as two of his most important books, and toured the United States. In the States he worked for some weeks at Cal. Tech., and visited the famous "fly room" at Columbia. Even in America, however, he was to be remembered as much for his unexpected actions and wit as for the scientific virtues. Thus at Columbia he arrived breathless in Professor Hecht's thirteenth floor laboratory and gasped out that he had just run up the twelve flights of stairs in so many seconds flat as the lift took so long to arrive. And during a blackboard discussion he symbolised the gender of various geneticists by drawing the accepted scientific symbols—some male, some female; to some he appended both symbols.

The two books of 1932 were very different. *The Inequality of Man*, a collection of essays and miscellaneous writings—including "The Gold-Makers"—confirmed his position as a writer about science who could make himself intelligible to the layman, an ability then enjoyed by Julian Huxley but by few others. The second book, *The Causes of Evolution* was more important. It was based on a series of lectures given the previous year at the Prifysgol Cymru, Aberystwyth, under the title "A Re-Examination of Darwinism", and above the introductory chapter Haldane put the epigraph " 'Darwinism is dead'—Any Sermon". He then proceeded, by looking at the latest information on heredity and variation in the light of Darwin's theory, to prove that Darwinism was very much alive. He reviewed the implications of his own mathematical theory and of the others being put forward by Fisher and Sewall Wright; and he showed that while the advances of the last few decades might have modified Darwin's theory of evolution, they had been far more important in explaining its mechanism—in buttressing the whole edifice which *The Origin of Species* had built. His pride in the book was somewhat qualified by the fact that he was unable to correct the proofs adequately. One result was that his sixteen bibliographical entries were credited not to him but to his wife.

The Causes of Evolution provided a milestone in the story of man's understanding of evolution, and in the appendix, which included a synopsis of the Mathematical Theory, J.B.S. wrote: "The permeation of biology by mathematics is only beginning, but unless the history of science is an inadequate guide, it will continue, and the investigations here summarised represent the beginning of a new branch of applied mathematics." This was important. Quite as interesting was the light which the book threw on Haldane's metaphysical thinking. He wrote of "that inexhaustible queerness which is the main characteristic of the universe that has impressed itself on my mind during twenty-five years of scientific work", and he hinted at the facts which limited human scientific enquiry. "The world is full of mysteries," he said. "Life is one. The curious limitations of finite minds are another. It is not the business of an evolutionary theory to explain these mysteries."

Here was more than a hint of interests which were to grow. Meanwhile, Haldane prepared for another move. In August, 1932 he left Cambridge, having resigned his Readership. The resignation took effect at the end of the year, and was announced early in 1933.

5

"The Prof" of U.C.

IN the spring of 1933 Haldane moved from Cambridge to University College, London, where he was to work for almost a quarter of a century. He was to create his own department, to impress his own character and beliefs on a distinctive corner of University College, to become almost an institution. Yet the move from Cambridge was not entirely happy. It was not that he had stepped down in status—rather the reverse; it was not entirely that the qualities of Cambridge appealed to him more than the gregariousness of London. And although he had moved of his own free will there remained some suggestion that Cambridge men still felt him to be an outsider rather than one of them. Yet there was another side to the coin. "I believe that he was very lonely and would have been a lot happier at Cambridge in a society in which he could have found a niche," says James Rendel, one of his research students who later became a colleague. "In his London days he never had one. Of course, we did in time form an esoteric group of which he was the centre but it did not give him what I believe he would have liked—a background against which he could relax; it was always more of a working than a social group."

Haldane's initial post in London was that of Professor of Genetics, the Chair having been created following a reorganisation of the Department of Applied Statistics. This department had evolved from the biometric work originated by Karl Pearson's course of lectures on the mathematical theory of statistics in 1895, and from the eugenics laboratory which Galton had started in the College in 1904. After Galton's death, a Laboratory of National Eugenics and a Chair of Eugenics had been founded; Pearson held the Chair, and under his reign eugenics, statistics and biometry were all taught in the Department of Applied Statistics. He retired in 1933 and the separate Chair of Genetics was created in the subsequent upheaval. One indication of the way in which Haldane was expected to direct its work came in a statement from University College which said that his "great knowledge of Biochemistry will enable him to introduce into Genetics, which has heretofore been purely morphological in nature, those physiological conceptions which alone can lead to an understanding of the mode of action of the genes on which the hereditary transmission of structure rests".

There were some remarkable resemblances between Haldane and Pearson, the man on whose foundations he was to build. Both had as young men shown a facility for non-scientific work, Pearson as a barrister and Haldane as the writer of non-scientific, or at least only quasi-scientific, magazine-articles. Both had eventually produced a huge mass of purely scientific work. And both—perhaps allowing controversy to become the sole outlet for emotion, as Pearson's biographer for the Royal Society suggests of his subject—had drifted into a position where their arguments were apt to be remembered as long as their achievements. Pearson, who could write that "the paper by Messrs. X and Y does not seem actuated by a desire to reach the truth of an important problem," was to be equalled by Haldane, apt to feel that those who disagreed with him must inevitably be doing so for the worst of reasons.

Haldane's duties at University College can very roughly be put under three headings. He had to administer a department. He had to teach students. And he was expected to carry out at least a minimum of research. In the first of these duties he was lamentably inadequate. Years later he would complain that he had only been able to carry on his department because Hitler had provided him with staff—the refugee scientists for whom he found posts—and the Rockefeller Foundation had provided him with money. This was almost true. But it was also true that a good deal more money would have been forthcoming had Haldane only applied for it by using what was anathema to him, the "proper channels". He would, and did, dig down into his own pocket over the years for materials and salaries, for equipment and out-of-pocket expenses, on occasions when no U.C. money was forthcoming; but there is ample proof in the tangled records that in many if not most of these cases the cash would have been forthcoming had Haldane been prepared to argue out his case, apply where requested, sign on the dotted line, and agree at least nominally to the conditions that authority demand. The huge sea-lion-like "Ouff" of protest was no substitute for this.

One result was that a research student might live virtually hand-to-mouth, wondering how the future could be faced. Eventually he would be told by Haldane: "Oh, by the way, I've managed to get your grant of £50 from X"—and he would be able to see ahead for another three months.

If Haldane left his own anarchic imprint on the department's administration—*après moi la déluge* he said to a colleague on preparing to leave in 1957—the marks which he left on students, and on the department's research, were different, if equally individual. He was now forty, big, bushy-browed, and with a head which in some ways resembled that of the *Drosophila* fly which was the raw material for much of his work. The first contact with him was apt to be unforgettable, as it was for one zoology student when the Professor of Genetics walked unannounced into an unattended class and looked at the students with their miscellaneous vertebrate bones strewn across the tables. Haldane, huge and clumsy, carefully picked up one bone after another. They were far from straightforward, including various difficult reptiles and the skull of a manatee. Haldane stuttered out the names without a fault, pointed out the diagnostic features of each, and after ten minutes walked out without further comment.

He exhibited, or, more accurately, appeared to have cultivated, an irascibility which would easily collapse. Those who knocked at his door would probably hear an exasperated "Yes?" On entry, they would be told by Haldane that he was often asked why he didn't write a book; the reason, he went on, was that so many people came knocking at his door for help with their own work that he couldn't get on with his own. This was the Haldane defence mechanism at work, always available for action against the polite curiosity of people who tended to visit him for little purpose. But if the visitor then backed out with apologies, Haldane was apt to go after him, to call him back, and then give him a full morning's discussion. His training in both cultures helped. Thus an Indian student who called to discuss the history of science in relation to the Greek miracle, had a good reception. "After I had posed the question, he asked me if I had read the plays of Aristophanes," he says. "Hearing my reply in the negative, he said he had thought so, and asked me to study particularly *The Clouds*." Then he lent the young man his own copy, carefully writing inside the cover before handing it over: "This book belongs to J. B. S. Haldane."

When it came to teaching, Haldane had his own ideas. He more than once said that the whole business of University education was to teach people to think; the corollary was that the more they were personally controlled in their studies, the less individual thinking they were likely to do. One outcome was

94

that he often appeared unable to direct properly the work either of students or of his research colleagues.

"When I joined him as a research student," says James Rendel, "he said I could have a room and if I hadn't thought of what I wanted to do in six months I was to let him know. This was all the direction we got, until we had collected some data. Then it was a different story."

Scientific discoveries came, after all, from noting facts that no one had noted before, and for Haldane such discoveries were the stuff of life. Thus, he said, he failed to understand one of C. P. Snow's early novels, *The Search*. How, asked Haldane, could a man who had once tasted the joy of scientific discovery be persuaded to give it up in consequence of so trifling a thing as a setback to his own personal ambition?

He succeeded in transmitting much of this personal enthusiasm to his students. You were either transformed by it, became a devoted Haldane supporter, and continued to look on him, despite his eccentricities, as one of the really great men; or the Haldane image failed to impress and you stayed outside the small group of students and colleagues which gathered round him during the later 1930's. The resulting impressions of J.B.S. during this period are strikingly different even when smoothed out by retrospect.

"When I started at U.C.," says one of his women students who graduated to become a colleague, "I went one evening to one of the little workmen's cafés in the Euston Road. I noticed a big hunched figure at one of the tables and recognised it immediately." Haldane rose, swept off his dirty green beret with his normal affected courtesy, and asked the student to join him. For the next hour or more he ranged across the classics and science, the mysteries of the Universe and the fascinations of research. "The next thing I remember noticing," she says, "was that the staff were stacking up the chairs because the café was being shut."

Yet in spite of this intermittent ability to spark off lasting friendships, as this one was, J.B.S. gave the impression of being lonely, of an inability to be accepted. The barrier was perhaps epitomised in the research students' difficulty in knowing what to call him. "Professor Haldane" was too formal. "Jack" was ruled out since Haldane always maintained that he was called Jack by his family and by people he didn't like. "J.B.S." might have done but the initials seemed in those days more suited to commerce than to learning. Eventually he became "Prof"; natural enough, maybe, but ironic when one considers that this was also the name for Lindemann, later Lord Cherwell, a man for whom Haldane had less than sympathy.

In one matter, however, Haldane and Lindemann saw eye to eye. Both worked hard for the Academic Assistance Council which enabled Jewish scientists endangered by Hitler to take up research in England. And while Lindemann was touring Europe in his Rolls Royce, deftly organising to England such men as Simon, Kurti, Mendelssohn and Kuhn, Haldane was continuing the activities he had begun at the very start of the Nazi régime.

On January 30th 1933, Adolf Hitler was created Chancellor of Germany. In the afternoon Boris Chain, then a young biochemist of twenty-seven, left the country, arriving in England the following day with only a few pounds in his pocket. Soon he was seeking out J.B.S. at University College. Chain had already published a number of papers. Haldane had read these, had realised their importance, and now arranged for the bright little genius to work at University College under Sir Charles Harington. "A few months later he got me a more permanent post under Hopkins at Cambridge," says Chain, "and from there I went on to work with Florey at Oxford. In fact the whole of my career in England is really due to Haldane." J.B.S. himself later described his intuitive response to Chain, the first of many refugees whom he was to help, as "what posterity may regard as the best and most important action of my life . . ." For Florey and Chain later isolated penicillin. "Perhaps all my discoveries will be forgotten," J.B.S. mused, "and I shall only be remembered in the words of the ancient Greek poet Pindar: 'He once nourished the contriver of painlessness, the gentle limb-guardian Asklepios (Dhanvantari), the heroic conqueror of manifold diseases'."

Chain was the first of many refugees from Hitler who found their way to University College during the next few years. Less than six months after his arrival, Haldane was writing a typical letter to Hans Grüneberg, a geneticist in Cologne. "I am informed that you are out of work," he said. "Have you considered the possibility of a position in England?" He went on to outline the work which was going on in his department, suggested current problems that Grüneberg might be willing to tackle, and subsequently suggested that although the pay was small, Grüneberg would "have a reasonable amount of money left over for music, books and beer (the latter is very expensive here!)". Following Grüneberg there came Dr. Ursula Philip and then Hans Kalmus, a Czech.

J.B.S. at the age of three

J.B.S. as a boy

J.B.S. in Gowland Hopkins' laboratory at Cambridge

J.B.S. addressing a 'United Front' meeting in Trafalgar Square, January 1937

J.B.S. fishing for eels with members of the unemployed workers movement in the uncompleted A.R.P. trenches on Primrose Hill, Regent's Park, February 1939

The rise of the Nazis, of which the coming of the refugees was an ominous sign, strongly affected Haldane's politics, as we shall see, but during his first years at University College he was not unduly Left-wing, and was at times heard to mutter under his breath that the place was "as full of bloody Communists as Cambridge". He would also claim that while his department was full of Communists he was a Marxist, although he always liked one of them more than the rest—Groucho, whose jokes he knew by heart and would repeat with great gusto. Haldane enjoyed verbal jokes and puns, described men and women from the wrong intellectual drawer in the printers' term of "wrong fount", and when it came to personal letters would end by writing that he would be glad "2CU2". Such enthusiasms overflowed into a schoolboy clownishness, so that he was unable to leave the notices in the gentlemen's lavatory as they were; users found themselves requested not to leave their goats or cats.

He took more care than most scientists to explain his work to laymen—and not only by the popular articles which he was by this time producing in great numbers. His attitude is illustrated by one typical reply to a letter received after he had mentioned his immunity to bed-bugs, with which he had been experimenting. "I do not think that [this] is anything to do with my moral attitude to them as fleas and mosquitoes make me swell up and I did not know about bed bugs until I tried," he wrote. "It is difficult to practice non-violence to such animals consistently, since some of them feed on nothing but human beings, and if you did not give them grub fairly frequently they would starve, a death which is very probably less pleasant than being suddenly squashed or drowned in the laundry. However, you certainly find out more about them if you regard them as interesting rather than repulsive."

His work persistently brought him up against the feelings of the anti-vivisectionists but even by the 1930's he would, as a matter of principle, use an alternative to a "violent" experiment if one were possible. This is, of course, no answer whatever to the anti-vivisectionist. Yet it is true that even at this date Haldane actively disliked hurting animals. He would not allow the cobwebs in his rooms to be removed—because, it was widely believed, he harboured a dislike for disturbing the spiders; certainly he would not allow sprays to be used on them, pointing out that this would be dangerous in a *Drosophila* laboratory. He was quick to defend himself and when accused of torturing mice, following an article in the press, he replied: "I am actually engaged in studying congenital defects, such as deafness which afflicts all waltzing mice; if I am a torturer, so is every breeder of these charming little animals. Actually, my animals are kept under such hygienic conditions that my colleagues are able to study diseases of normal old age in them. For example, some races of mice are particularly prone to kidney disease, others to cataract. I may add that no amount of torture will originate a hereditary disease, and hence if these accusations were true, I should be futile as well as cruel."

Haldane added to such laboratory stocks as the need arose. He had been doing so when he arrived at the College by car one evening. A student, who had just tried unsuccessfully to recover some books, explained that the College was locked up. "At this Haldane became very anxious," he remembers. "He explained that he had just come from America, where he had collected some mice whose genetic constitution would be entirely different from those in Europe. It was a cold evening. The mice were getting cold in the car and unless they could be got indoors they would die. His journey to America would thus have been wasted." There was a certain grotesqueness about the situation—the huge man locked from his laboratory and the wretched mice dragged half-way round the world. Haldane knew what to do. "Together," says the student, "we forced a window and the professor and his mice were soon inside in the warm."

The breeding stocks—of mice, of rats and of *Drosophila* flies —formed the main stock-in-trade of Haldane's department. When he had been asked, on arrival at University College, what he wanted, he had at first said: "A study." Later he had elaborated, adding that a good supply of writing pads and pencils was also needed—and it is true that the picture of J.B.S. pulling out a pad at unlikely moments and getting down to mathematical problems soon became a familiar sight. His understatement of requirements was a typical Haldane exaggeration; like most of the others, it contained a substance of truth. While other workers might require apparatus of varying degrees of complexity and expense, Haldane required little more than generation upon generation of laboratory animals, the simple equipment with which to observe simple characteristics, and the pencil and paper to record these and to calculate their significance. This final part of his work would be carried out in a big leather armchair which rose rock-like in the middle of his study, surrounded by the desert of books and papers which spread around on chairs, tables and floor, some covered with dust, some containing reference-markers. At times they formed almost geological strata, each stratum representing a paper or thesis on which he was at work. Occasionally an item would arrive which he did not like or which he wished to forget. This he would invariably stuff down into one of the crevices of his chair where it would lie conveniently forgotten until it became ancient history.

Much of the work on mice, rats and *Drosophila* was shared by Haldane's colleagues. He himself continued his research on linkage-problems, using for raw material, as we shall see, the plants bred at the John Innes Horticultural Research Institution. But he also gave increased study to the problems of linkage in man, and began to apply to this awkward animal the lessons of his earlier mathematical studies on evolution. At the same time, and with a disconcertingly broad appraisal, he ranged out over a wider field, writing in 1934 and 1935 alone on quantum mechanics as a basis for philosophy, on anthropology and human biology, on human biology and politics, human genetics and human ideals, and on various problems of mathematical biology. Haldane—*"ce n'est pas un homme, c'est une force de la Nature"* said Boris Ephrussi—was already beginning to consolidate his belief that all science was one; already he was perceiving in the inter-relationships of science and politics, of politics and philosophy, and of philosophy and science, a unity which he had often suspected.

Now, in 1936, there came two events which were greatly to affect his life. The first was the death of his father.

By this time seventy-five, still working, a Companion of Honour, and widely recognised as a pioneer who had taken physiology into entirely fresh country, John Scott Haldane had in his later years devoted increasing thought to the philosophical basis of science. Even before the First World War he had delivered four lectures to students at Guys Hospital which had concluded with the affirmation: "Personality is the great central fact of the universe. This world, with all that lies within it, is a spiritual world." In 1932 he had given the Donellan Lectures in Dublin, published as *The Philosophical Basis of Biology*, and vigorously attacked by such scientists as Joseph Needham who commented on the failure of Haldane, both exact biologist and idealist philosopher, "to differentiate between the two constituents of this dual personality". Yet the simplest picture of his beliefs was given not in his published works but in a letter to his daughter Naomi, written after his publication of *The Sciences and Philosophy* in 1929. "I don't think we can ever know in detail which is God's way, but we can be confident that it is the way of a realist," he wrote, "and this brings us, or ought to bring us, peace of mind, courage to fight on with our job, and Christian charity, since God is not outside ourselves or those around us. The supposed realities of science, or knowledge of any kind, are only the tools God works with."

J.B.S. had no such faith. He already firmly believed that if God existed, which he considered unlikely, He was certainly not cast in any such mould. In addition, father and son took diametrically opposed views of the lines along which their disciplines were developing. "The new physiology is biological physiology," said John Scott Haldane, "not biophysics or biochemistry. The attempt to analyse living organisms into physical and chemical mechanism is probably the most colossal failure in the whole history of modern science." Only a decade later J.B.S. was reminding readers that unless a geneticist was a pupil of Hopkins, "he may sometimes forget that the only precise account of the most fundamental phenomena which he studies must ultimately be a biochemical account".

These differences of view between father and son, combined with the similarity of initials, was a recurring source of dismay to J.B.S. He would open a letter ostensibly addressed to himself, would begin to read, and would then drop the letter on the desk before him, holding head in hand and emitting his walrus-like "Ouff!" He took care to point out on a public platform that Professor J. S. Haldane was one person and Professor J. B. S. Haldane was another. And when asked, on more than one occasion: "Are you related to Professor J. B. S. Haldane?" he would reply: "That depends on whether identity is a relationship."

This meticulous desire that neither should be saddled with the other's opinions was a sign only of scientific rectitude. Deep attachment between father and son continued unbroken, and in 1932 in his preface to *The Inequality of Man*, J.B.S. felt it necessary to state his annoyance at claims that he had become alienated from his father. "We agree to differ on some points," he wrote. "The only one on which we ever had a serious dispute was a question about thermodynamics."

When the elder Haldane fell ill at Oxford in the middle of March 1936, his son immediately left London to be by his side; and he insisted on personally giving blood for transfusion. His father died at midnight on March 14th—after confiding to his son: "I've had a telegram that Priestley is dying too, but I *think* it was an imaginary telegram."

· · ·

In 1936 Haldane's professional life was also to suffer a change, not to say upheaval, almost as great as his personal life. During the summer he was offered, and in the autumn he took up, the duties of the first Weldon Professor of Biometry in University College. The appointment was important in itself, but it was more important in that it fortuitously saved him from a private rebuff which he himself, with his love of a public fight, might have turned into a public humiliation.

Since 1927, J.B.S. had been engaged on what was technically part-time work for the John Innes Horticultural Research Institution; in practice, he had not only carried out much valuable research there but had pulled the Institution through a serious internal crisis. But there had been troubles, as there so often were with J.B.S., and according to a special committee set up by the Council of the Institution at the end of 1936, the Weldon appointment had one result; it removed the objectionable necessity of sacking Haldane from John Innes. The story of his relationship with the Institution has some elements of tragedy since the break with it in early 1937 confirmed once again his views about authority and may well have encouraged—some of his friends would put it more strongly—his movement into the Communist Party.

"John Innes" had been set up in the early years of the century "for the promotion of horticultural instruction, experiment and research". Under Bateson, Director from 1910 until his death in 1926, it had been transformed into a nursery for the growing science of genetics, but with Bateson's death it faced two dangers. One arose from the fact that many of its ablest young workers had, on maturity, left the nursery. The second arose from the constitution of the governing body. In 1926 the John Innes might easily have been heading for disaster. It was saved by two things.

One was the appointment as Director of Sir Daniel Hall, former Director of Rothamsted and chief scientific adviser to the Ministry of Agriculture. Hall, already in his sixties, an able administrator, had only one failing so far as the directorship was concerned: he knew relatively little of genetics. He did, however, know his own weakness, and he turned for advice to Julian Huxley, then Professor of Zoology at King's College, London. Huxley recommended that Haldane be brought in as geneticist, and in March 1927 Haldane was engaged— to visit the Institution fortnightly for a day and a night during the Cambridge terms, to spend one month at the Institution at Easter and another during the Long Vacation.

and to be free for work there during the Christmas Vacation.

Bateson's work was thus thrust into Haldane's capable care. Cyril Darlington, then a colleague of Haldane's at the Institution and later its Director, has stressed that this was the salvation of the John Innes. "For ten years Haldane came half the year at a modest salary, toiling away with those Mendelian ratios which he had described in his first letter to Bateson," he says: "He sat at the next desk to me. I was drawing chromosomes. He was doing sums. No microscopes for him. No calculating machines, no slide rules, no logarithms even. All long division sums based upon data collected and recorded by Bateson's assistants from plants grown by Bateson's gardeners. The sheets would pile up. And then there would be a break for lunch. Bread and cheese, and the fruits of the garden and coffee and talk. He was not a great talker but he was a good talker. Not quick or sparkling; naturally, for every statement which was not outrageously speculative [in the style of *Daedalus*] had to be related to fundamental assumptions about the nature of life or belief and thoroughly purged of emotion or rhetoric. But philosophical thoughts might be interrupted by a probably perfect quotation from a lesser-known Latin author absorbed and preserved at interminable length by his unquenchable verbal appetite. The meaning was irrelevant and the sound was monotonous—for speaking on both an inward and an outward breath he could not easily control either the pitch of his voice or the rhythm of his sentences. But we listened patiently for he always listened patiently to us."

For ten years Haldane managed to hold together the genetical work of the Institution, partly by sheer force of personality, by the impression which his towering figure created as he stood arguing a point like an articulate Rock of Gibraltar; but partly, also, by the work which he carried out during this decade. He was already deep in his studies of enzymes. He was intrigued by the links between chemical cause and physiological effect in human beings, and he now became increasingly intrigued by the links between chemical cause and genetic result which could be investigated in flowers. Shortly after joining John Innes he suggested that joint work should be started by the Institution and Hopkins' laboratory on variation in flower colours and later he claimed that this was his most important contribution to genetics. The person chosen for the research was a Miss Rose Scott-Moncrieff; and among the results was the discovery that in certain plants a total of thirty-five genes were concerned in the production of the anthocyanin pigments—the principal blue, purple and red pigments. There were two results of such work. "By crossing plants with known chemical characteristics we can now combine and rearrange these qualities in their progeny just as surely as we can mix chemicals together in the laboratory," as Miss Scott-Moncrieff put it; "and when these controlled biological reactions diverge from the expected, we obtain important evidence of other unknown processes which must also be involved." In a wider field, more became known of the general principles linking chemical composition and genetic inheritance.

Here at John Innes, with the help of an Institution worker, Miss Dorothea de Winton, Haldane also worked on linkage. As experimental material he chose the ornamental plant *Primula sinensis* which is found in forms having twice, three times, and four times the normal number of chromosomes. First, he developed a complicated theory of how linkage would operate in the case of such polyploids. Then he and Miss de Winton carried out a long series of experiments involving three linked genes in the plant. The cross-over percentages were found to be closely similar in the varieties having two and the varieties having four sets of chromosomes—as forecast in Haldane's mathematical theory.

While this work helped to keep John Innes on the scientific map, Haldane's personal position in the Institution steadily became undermined, partly owing to the logic of events, partly to his constitutional inability to let sleeping dogs lie. Some of his eccentricities were loved, as when he acknowledged a box of sugar lumps from the lunch club on his November 5th birthday with the following lines on a postcard:

> Rockets that might have graced a duke rose
> To celebrate your box of sucrose
> And my delight at every cracker owes
> Much to your timely gift of saccharose.
> Between each bang I went and sucked aside
> A lump of glucose—fructoside.

His instructions were apt to be unexpected, as when he sent a note to his secretary, headed "Wanted" and listing "1. Insignia of order of Holy Ghost. 2. Mr. Ford's bank balance. 3. Clara Bow. 4. Information on all trains between 11 a.m. & 5 p.m. from London-Paris. 5. £5 [cheque cashed]. 6. 4 safety razor blades [Star or ever-ready] from Woolworth. 7. If you can manage, a max of botches. 8. Karl Marx's *Kapital* [Everyman's Library]."

The other side of the coin was a pernickety rudeness, for which the later very real excuse of constant pain could hardly be argued, an irritability that went beyond failure to suffer fools gladly, and a facility for pursuing an argument to the bitter end. "When I was young, I thought he was the greatest man I was ever likely to meet," says one young graduate who worked at a bench at John Innes during this period, "but with time I modified this view—feeling that no man who could behave so intolerably with his inferiors could be really great."

In addition, John Innes was, first and foremost, a horticultural Institution. For a while Haldane certainly gave his recreation in *Who's Who* as "gardening", but his friends felt that this was more an act of faith than a comment on work done. Just as he was almost perversely unhandy with a microscope, and all thumbs with many delicate instruments—although finely perceptive when touching living things—so it was clear that spade, fork or pruning knife were not for him. Thus there was no chance that irascibility would be pardoned by common interest, or an outburst of bad temper be overlooked because the culprit had been born with such green fingers.

These little irritations were put into shadow by the growing unhappiness of relations between Haldane and the Director. Here Haldane no doubt had a genuine grievance; he nursed it carefully. When Sir Daniel had written to the Chairman of the Council in 1926, proposing that a full-time geneticist should be employed, he had added: "He should be a man also of general capacity who could be expected to succeed to the Directorship." Haldane himself has claimed that he "went to Merton with the promise that Sir D.H. would retire in 1932", and it was taken for granted by many of the staff that the succession would take place fairly soon. In 1929 Sir Daniel reached the age of sixty-five—but saw no reason for retiring. It has been stated, perhaps with more truth than charity, that Lady Hall had no wish to be succeeded by Mrs. Haldane at the pleasant home which went with the John Innes directorship. Whatever the reason, Sir Daniel hung on. In 1934, he passed the age of seventy; but he still gave no sign of retiring, a situation which, it was stated two years later, precipitated a number of "unhappy incidents". Just what these incidents were it is difficult to disentangle from the silence of Sir Daniel and the vituperative comments which Haldane committed to his Royal Society Notes and his correspondence. The least of the charges was that Hall "messed up my work very badly about 1935 by using my genetical material to test a compost which happened to kill off the weaker stocks".

The truth was very different. What happened was that one year the *Primula sinensis*, which was the main winter crop, picked up a hitherto unknown fungus which caused a collar rot and led to great losses. The curator of the garden, J. W. C. Lawrence, consulted a firm which gave him the formula for their sterilised compost. The following season the *P. sinensis* seeds were sown in this, and the remedy was worse than the disease; *P. sinensis* proved to be very sensitive to the excess nitrogen which arose from the method the firm used at the time, and the majority of the seeds failed to germinate. Lawrence then took the problem apart, and developed the now famous "John Innes Compost". The formula did the trick and there was no further trouble. Hall had nothing to do with the incident except for the concern he naturally felt for any trouble arising in the gardens.

In June 1935, he made a sincere attempt to hold the ship together. "As you prefer a written constitution and as I desire to guard against any suggestion that I don't hold to my word," he wrote to Haldane, "here are the conditions of our collaboration in the control of the Institution." These conditions covered employment of staff and programmes of work. They did not cover everything but Sir Daniel hoped they would be seen as "evidence that I want to work in complete agreement with you and to give you every opportunity of joining with me in the responsibility for the work of the Institution . . . I want your confidence and will give you mine".

It was not exactly confidence that Haldane wanted; he would have preferred the Directorship. The unhappy situation grew unhappier, and in the summer of 1936 a committee was set up to enquire into the organisation of the Institution and the conditions of appointment of the staff. The members of the committee had, they later reported, "considered the question of terminating Mr. Haldane's services by giving him formal notice". Then, out of the blue, there came news that J.B.S. was to be offered the Weldon Chair. By the autumn of 1937 he would be fully occupied at University College—or, as the committee put it, "fortunately, circumstances have arisen which, quite apart from the relations now existing between him and the Director, should lead to his early resignation".

It is implied in the committee's report that the switch from the Chair of Genetics to the Chair of Biometry would involve J.B.S. in so much additional work that the John Innes task would automatically be ruled out. This was probably a polite euphemism, for Haldane had, in fact, been interviewed by the

Committee before he had accepted the Weldon Chair and was "not left in any doubt" of its decision to appoint a full-time geneticist. Thus when he accepted the new appointment in London he already knew that the running of John Innes, on which he had set so much, had escaped him.

The crucial period was between the end of November 1936 and the end of the following February. It has been suggested that had Haldane been offered the Directorship he would have found it more difficult to vacillate over the great Lysenko controversy which was just raising its head, that he would have had less time and less inclination to espouse the Communist cause. This is possible but appears unlikely. Haldane was already a firm non-Establishment man; personal events were already driving him to Spain, and if he had become Director of John Innes he might well have tried to tie it to the tail of Lysenko's comet.

．　　．　　．

As Weldon Professor, Haldane now began work as a biometrician, concerned "in an attempt to substitute mathematical expressions for such useful, if slightly vague, biological expressions as race, type, heredity and variation". Founded by a bequest from the widow of Walter Weldon, who had helped to create the science of biometry at the end of the 19th century, the Weldon Chair was the first of its kind in any British university, and Haldane accepted it in the hope of great things to come. He was to be disappointed. He never got a building for his own use, and in 1957 claimed he would never have accepted the chair had he not been promised accommodation. "Owing to the war, and for other reasons, this promise was not kept," he complained. "I have been unable to carry out the duties of the Chair adequately." However, Haldane had accepted, and he began his first course of ten lectures in October.

By this time he had been joined by one junior colleague who was to play a significant part in his life. Her name was Helen Spurway and in 1934, at the age of nineteen, she had attended Haldane's elementary genetics lectures. Four years later she took her Ph.D. but long before this had become a semi-permanent feature of Haldane's Department, helping where she could, learning what she could, and quickly becoming a member of the small group over whom J.B.S. exercised his own personal attraction. From the first, he liked her. She made no bones about her feelings and was widely reported to have said that two of her current aims in life were to take a degree and to marry

Professor Haldane. The outspokenness was typical. In the 1930's Helen Spurway was a trim dark-haired young woman of considerable attraction and irrepressible energy. However, these were not her most remarkable qualities, which were three-fold and very different. One was an ability to expound her views at great length, at top pitch and with a ferocity not easily quenched. With this, went a combination of honesty and moral courage which frequently meant, in practice, speaking the unpalatable truth as she saw it. Less obvious, and only to be revealed during the War, was a physical courage, supported by the scientist's clinical attitude no doubt, but of a quality rarely seen in men and rarely looked for in women. These were not accommodating qualities. But it is easy to understand Haldane's instinctive reaction to them; honesty and courage are awkward virtues, but J.B.S. was never a man who looked for the easy options. Throughout the two decades of work at University College which followed Haldane's Weldon Professorship. Helen Spurway was to become an increasingly essential part of his life.

The kind of research on which he was to be engaged for these years is shown by the report of his first year's work. "My colleagues, Philip, Spurway, and Street and I have investigated natural populations of the house mouse, two insects and one plant, with a view to a causal analysis of their variation," this went. "The results have been, or will shortly be, published. I have also published an analysis, by modern methods, of a large group of the late Professor Pearson's data on human inheritance. With characteristic scientific integrity he had presented them in such a form that workers who did not share all his theoretical opinions could make the fullest possible use of his observations. I have made several contributions to statistical theory. My colleague Dr. Grüneberg is opening a new chapter in pathology by his investigations of hereditary disease in animals." Much of this, as was typical with Haldane, involved the study and analysis of other workers' results. He himself carried out little practical research, and it seems likely that his work did suffer from this, as is often claimed. Thus his colleague Professor Penrose has noted that many of his speculations on sex-linkage have been proved to be not valid, and that "his errors here were the result of accepting published medical records uncritically".

During these years immediately preceding the outbreak of the Second World War, Haldane devoted an increasing amount of his time to human genetics. A good deal of this work concerned the problem of mutation, that process by which a gene is mysteriously transformed. Evolution largely takes place, it was already being realised in the 1930's, by the natural selection of mutations, the majority of which have a harmful effect on an organism; and, even before the question of mutations caused by nuclear fission became a political issue as well as a scientific problem, it was appreciated that greater knowledge of these transformations would provide a valuable instrument for the study of genetics.

Haldane made two important contributions to the subject. One, published in *Nature* in 1936, provided the first estimate of the mutation rate in man—the number of mutations which could be expected to take place naturally in any number of generations. The second, published in the *American Naturalist* two years later under the title "The effect of variation on fitness", has become of increasing interest during the last twenty years as the effects of nuclear explosions have come under discussion. For what Haldane showed in convincing detail was that the effect on a population of recurrent harmful mutations depends not on the harmfulness of the newly-mutated genes so much as on the rate at which the mutations take place over the generations. It is, in fact, as though the degree of drunkenness were more affected by the speed of drinking than by the alcohol content of the drink.

As a result of his earlier interest in linkage problems, Haldane now began to study the position of specific genes on the human X-chromosome—for technical reasons the only human chromosome into which investigations could practicably take place. In other words, he started building up a map showing where on the chromosome lay genes having specific effects—in much the same way that a railway map shows where various stations lie along the line. This had already been done for certain laboratory-bred animals—notably by Sturtevant in the United States, working on *Drosophila*. The problem presented by humans was infinitely more difficult—partly because the numbers of humans with requisite traits are likely to be less numerous than experimental animals, partly because their pedigrees are, in the required sense, less detailed. A further point is that map-positions can be deduced only when more than one identifiable gene is handed down at a time, and with humans this is unusual. Despite these problems, Haldane succeeded in 1935 in preparing a provisional map of the X-chromosome, showing the positions on it of the genes causing colour-blindness, severe light-sensitivity of the skin, night blindness, a particular skin disease, and two varieties of eye peculiarity.

The following year he began, with a colleague, Dr. Julia Bell, to investigate how close was the link between the gene which caused colour-blindness and that which caused haemophilia. Behind this work there lay, as there lay behind much that Haldane did, a feeling for practical utility. Haemophilia can, as it happens, be detected more easily than colour-blindness. But to discover how such linkages could be accurately measured might have important results. If, "to take a possible example," Haldane and Bell later wrote, "an equally close linkage were found between the genes determining blood group" and that "determining Huntington's chorea, we should be able, in many cases, to predict which children of an affected person would develop this disease and to advise on the desirability or otherwise of their marriage." For the traceable member of two genes might suggest the existence of another, potentially lethal, which would otherwise have remained concealed until its effects became evident in some luckless human being.

It first became necessary for Haldane and Bell to track down as large a number of haemophiliacs as possible, to reconstruct their family pedigrees and to discover which members of the families, if any, also suffered from colour-blindness. At first there were difficulties in tracing sufficient families; then they tried St. Bartholomew's Hospital where a particularly famous dentist was practising. He was the man to whom haemophiliacs were often sent when teeth had to be extracted, and in Barts there was a long list of haemophiliacs which could be used as a starting-point. Not all were willing to co-operate readily, and Dr. Bell long remembered how she and Haldane gathered together a particularly large family; one member was expected to be "difficult" but an explanation by Haldane of what science was and of what it might be able to do, brought him successfully round to full co-operation. And the complete investigation of one group was stopped by a family quarrel when a member wrote: "Though I bear at present the name of X, I consider myself of no blood relationship to that family and no useful purpose would be served by visiting me."

Eventually the pedigrees were as complete as was possible. In one, all the four living haemophiliacs were colour-blind while four non-haemophiliac brothers and one non-haemophiliac son of a haemophiliac's sister were not colour-blind—"thus," said Haldane and Bell, "in this case the family linkage between haemophilia and colour-blindness has been complete." Other examples were less than perfect. But the results ruled out any theory of a physiological connection between the two diseases, and the probability that the findings were due to a run of luck was estimated at about one in a million. "It is, moreover," they added, "difficult to frame any hypothesis other than linkage which will account for the results."

In six of the pedigrees collected during this investigation, haemophilia had fairly clearly been produced by mutation; in other words in these cases the gene normally concerned in the clotting of blood had been transformed, by a process of which little is even now known, into the inactive gene whose visible effect was non-clotting, or haemophilia. Mutation of such genes was, as Haldane pointed out later, one reason for the continuance of the disease. For haemophiliacs frequently die young and, on average, beget about a quarter as many children as normal people. In fact, to account for those living in Britain in the 1930's, Haldane calculated, it would have been necessary for the whole population to have been haemophiliac 1,000 years previously—had it not been for the process of mutation, which, he estimated, occurred once for every 50,000 people per generation.

For J.B.S. haemophilia had the double attraction of a subject of both scientific value and sociological impact. For Queen Victoria had been a transmitter of the disease which had appeared by mutation, most probably "in the nucleus of a cell in one of the testicles of Edward, Duke of Kent, in the year 1818". And, through its effects on the Tsarevitch Alexis, and the heir apparent to Alfonso XIII at the time of the Revolution in 1931. "Queen Victoria played a minor, but not insignificant part in bringing about the Russian and Spanish Revolutions", as Haldane said in a long and intriguing article on "A Study of Haemophilia in the Royal Families of Europe".

Much of his work had a more direct and less esoteric relation to human problems. He spent some time testing a calculation of the proportion of colour-blind daughters to be expected from a colour-blind man who married a first cousin. He showed mathematically that some genes which were dangerous or lethal if received from both parents must carry some advantage if they were received from one parent only—a theory which alone, he showed, could explain their continuing numbers. Years later the theory was found to be true of sickle-cell anaemia, produced by a double-dose of genes, a single dose of which not only fails to produce sickle-cell but also produces an increased resistance to malaria.

Haldane liked to stress that science was directly involved in human problems and in *Heredity and Politics*, published in

1938, he examined "certain suggested applications of biology to political science". The first part of the book was a simple exposition of human genetics, and was followed by chapters dealing with the inequality of man, sterilisation of the unfit, differential birth-rates and the effects of so-called racial differences. In it Haldane was able to indulge in his favourite pastime of puncturing illusions, and pointed out that sterilisation of the unfit was both ethically questionable and practically ineffective. His statistical background enabled him to wonder whether "the death-rate among potters from bronchitis is still eight times that of the general population", and to ask whether, if so, "it would not be unreasonable if a certain proportion of the funds devoted to pottery research at Stoke-on-Trent were spent on research on potters rather than pots". He was, despite his reputation, a kind man, and the whole trend of his arguments as put forward in this book was exemplified by his questions as to why sound people should be taxed to support the unsound. "The answer to this is not a matter of biology," he said. "In most human societies it is regarded as a duty to help our weak or unfortunate fellows. This may be a fallacy. I do not think that it is, but I clearly cannot argue the matter here."

Throughout the mid-1930's Haldane became almost a British institution. He stood in the fashionable way for the Rectorship of Glasgow University—coming bottom of the poll with 220 votes against Churchill's 281, the Scottish nationalist's 364 and the Peace Pledge Union's Dick Sheppard with 538. He took on Arnold Lunn in a long series of letters which provided blow and counter-blow in an argument published as *Science and the Supernatural*. Even the most charitably disposed towards religion probably agreed with *Nature*'s verdict that Lunn "although a clever controversialist, is not in· the religious sphere the equivalent of Professor Haldane in the scientific sphere". Though neither opponent achieved a knock-out, J.B.S. won on points.

In spite of the book, J.B.S. had an undogmatic approach to inexplicable experiences and once described how he went into his home and saw himself sitting in his own chair smoking his favourite pipe. "Irregular" was his word for the phenomenon, "indigestion" his explanation. He walked across the room and sat down on his own image. Of such fringe phenomena as e.s.p. he was open-minded and he once said of telepathy: "I daresay it does happen, but it's still a damned intrusion on one's privacy."

He gave such extensive evidence to the Archbishop of Canterbury's Commission on the prohibitions of marriage on the grounds of kindred and affinity that it was printed as an appendix. And when he made a second visit to the United States he not only lectured on biological problems at Columbia University but spoke on two successive days to the Book and Play Club in Chicago on "Science and Human Life", and to the city's Council on Foreign Relations on "Is There a Chosen Race?"

Moreover, he continued to write. Here, as in science, his interests and his output were too large and too various to be accommodated by the channels which would have satisfied most men. In the trenches, two decades earlier, he had produced not merely a scientific paper but the bulk of a full-length novel whose characters had deplored the war in bitter terms. Now, as he supplied editors with articles, papers and essays on genetics, sociology and cosmology, keeping all the subjects in play like the multi-coloured balls of a juggler's act, he also found time to write *My Friend, Mr. Leakey*, a unique example of how science—and much more—can be made both intelligible and entertaining to children.

All this would have provided enough work for most men. But by the late 1930's J.B.S. had been drawn deep into politics.

PART
III

INTO BATTLE

6

Really Facing the Dictators

B Y 1937 Haldane was a dedicated Marxist and an open supporter of the Communist Party, although not yet a member of
it. Like many other men he had been driven into the Party's
arms by the combined efforts of Hitler, General Franco, and
the Chamberlain Government. "Perhaps my final conversion,"
he wrote, "dates from Mr. Eden's signature of a pact of friendship with Mussolini when Italian bombers were sinking British
ships."

Only a few years earlier he had been, if he could be cate-
gorised at all, a pinkish Liberal. "I had a nice academic job
which I supplemented by writing essays that were a little advanced without being troublesome to anyone of importance,"
as he put it. "I was a mild socialist in the sense that I thought
it would be a good thing if the state took over some of our more
grossly monopolistic industries. But I did not take politics very
seriously." Indeed, where his glance turned towards that subject he revealed a distinctly non-Marxist vein. In *The Causes
of Evolution* he had noted that "with regard to the doctrines of
Darwin's great contemporary, Marx, it is possible to adopt
socialism but not historical materialism". Similarly, writing in
1931, one of the articles for the popular newspapers he was later
to deride, he pointed out that Europe was "threatened by two
types of civilisation on its east and west, namely Communism
and Americanism, which claim to be improvements on it. Both
of these interest me enormously, and I think that we could copy
some features of each with advantage. I should like London to
have as good operas as New York and as good biological teaching for the average person as Moscow. But I do not desire that
London should adopt either of their standards of personal
liberty . . . I cannot accept the American and Communist
ideals, because both are too exclusively economic." Even four
years later, speaking to students in 1935, he warned that Marxists believed that the transition in society which he himself saw
as inevitable could only come about with considerable blood-

shed. "It is up to you to prove that the Communists are wrong by seeing that a peaceful transition is possible," he said. "The more people believe it to be possible, the more likely it is that the Communists are wrong."

That Haldane moved from this position to the far left in a matter of years was largely a result of the logic of history—he did not move so much as was pushed. Yet this was not the only explanation. There were others, and their complexities helped to qualify Haldane's communism, however much he sought, out of loyalty to a cause, to conceal such qualifications from the public gaze. One attraction of the Communist Party's red banners was that the majority of Haldane's friends were shocked by them. He had an inborn puckishness which pushed him on to the unpopular side in any argument, and St. John Ervine's comment is only just too exaggerated to be literally true. "Roughly speaking," he says, "Haldane may be said to be a Conservative when he is in the company of Socialists, and a Socialist when he is in the company of Conservatives. To a Primrose Leaguer he talks like a Bolshevist; to a Bolshevist he talks like a Rotarian." He might have added that in a Communist State he would, almost inevitably, have drifted into the position of an underground Right-wing leader.

However, Haldane was predisposed to Communism by far more than bloody-mindedness or personal frustration. The party stressed the ineptness of the higher military commanders during the First World War, a subject on which J.B.S. was always pleased to produce ample supporting evidence. Its members had crusaded against the conception of God in a way of which he wholly approved. They had, moreover, been among the first to see science as a utilitarian subject directed towards the needs of the many rather than as a philosophical discipline understood by the few—an attitude which appealed to more than one side of Haldane's character.

His own tendency to consider science almost exclusively in the light of human problems—in one way a reflection of his father's work in the Dundee slums—had become the subject of controversy long before J.B.S. entered the Communist fold. Thus in December 1933 Professor A. V. Hill, considering the status of scientists in a world of acute political tension, had commented in *Nature* that "If scientific people are to be accorded the privileges of immunity and tolerance by civilised societies, however, they must observe the rules." Haldane, justifying the second half of his later description as a cuddly cactus, thought the cap fitted him and questioned whether Hill had "done a service to science by penning a sentence which might be interpreted as meaning that his profession should only be tolerated in so far as it is muzzled". Any doubt about the personal overtones of the argument were dispelled by Hill's reply: "Of course," he said, "I should not condemn men for studying human diet, but the motive should be the discovery of scientific facts, not the demonstration that the British working class is underfed . . . A reputation gained by scientific achievement, and the immunity accorded to scientific pursuits, should not be lightly used to extort consideration in other respects."

By the mid-1930's, J.B.S. was already seeing, quite naturally, the political overtones of almost any scientific development or discovery. To this extent he was certainly not "conned" into the Party; the legend of Haldane as the simple scientist bemused by the political complexities of a world he did not understand may be satisfying but is remote from reality. He came of his own free will and he might more than once have spoken out in open criticism of the Party—as he more than once threatened to speak—had it not been for his belief that Communism was the best instrument for the drastic surgical operation on affairs which he felt was necessary. "Your point about constructive and destructive activities is all right," he once wrote to his sister Naomi. "But you (and the Labour Party) will have to realise that construction . . . can't start till the necessary destruction is done. I used to want to be constructive, but for at least four years I have realised that the work was idle . . . Why worry, you are in good company. Your study of Christianity should have taught you that J.C. *inter alia* is reported to have said: 'For this cause came I into the world that I might *destroy* the works of the devil.' I think in your recent book you hardly emphasised the destructive or revolutionary element in the primitive church. The constructive element, loving your neighbour and all that, will only work after destroying the works of the devil, such as class society, and then it will probably be fairly automatic. Till then it is only fully effective in small revolutionary organisations such as you described."

Haldane thus supported Communism for the good which he felt would come from it. Yet his attitude, to its theory as well as to its practice, changed throughout the years. What is confusing is that the attitude which he showed to the world was at all times incomplete and was sometimes misleading. Thus up to 1948, the date which marked the watershed of the Lysenko argument, his public and almost ignominious acceptance of all that the Communists said and did was privately qualified by a host of disagreements, limitations, and suggestions. After 1948, when in the popular mind Haldane almost became a Johnny-come-lately ex-Communist, his faith in Marxism remained unshattered even though he could no longer stomach some of its practical applications under Stalin.

All these are overtones to the fact that in the mid-1930's Haldane moved into the Communist camp. The movement had begun in a leisurely way as he realised what was happening to German science under Adolf Hitler. "I began to realise," he later wrote, "that even if professors leave politics alone, politics won't leave professors alone." He soon found himself, moreover, appealing on platforms not only for money which would help refugees but for funds to help victims of Hitler in general.

"Sometimes," he has written, "I found myself speaking with a Mr. Harry Pollitt, and discovered that he talked sense, which rather surprised me, for he was a Communist." Most of those who had previously put him off Communism, he added, were not Party members but intellectuals who thought that Marxism was a nice theory. Haldane could have stuck at this point—as, he admitted, most of his advanced academic colleagues had stuck. They had had enough fighting in the First World War. Their aims had not been achieved. And middle-aged professors were, in any case, receptive to what Haldane called Housman's profoundly ignoble slogan: "Let us endure an hour and see injustice done."

The benevolent non-intervention with which the British Government greeted the rise of the Right-wing dictatorships in Europe would probably have driven Haldane into the arms of the Communist Party whatever else happened. This was, after all, the period during which Marxist predictions were coming true almost daily. Yet, in fact, much did happen. From the mid-1930's onwards a number of personal factors edged him in the same direction. To his daily contact with the problems of the refugees there was added in 1934 the effect of the ban which the B.B.C. imposed on his broadcast on the causes of war. Dean Inge was one speaker in the series. Sir Norman Angell was another, while a third was Lord Beaverbrook. The B.B.C., trying to keep the balance fair, one must hope, invited Haldane to take part; when they saw his text, their courage failed them and they had second thoughts about holding the balance.

Judged by contemporary standards, the talk was innocuous enough, merely putting forward the respectable if not always accepted theory that capitalism is one of the main causes of war. Haldane compared the University of Oxford, which had conferred an Honorary degree on Zaharoff, the arms king, with the Vice-Chancellor of Leeds University, who had recently censured a lecturer for making a speech in favour of peace. And he concluded by saying that if the world really wanted peace, "we must examine all the causes of war, economic and technical, as well as psychological and political. We must be prepared to associate with all sorts of people, from Bishops to Bolsheviks, who share our view". When the B.B.C. refused to broadcast the text in its existing form, Haldane offered to tone down some of the Socialism and cut the controversial material at the end. "They still refused," he wrote later. "I did not feel justified in cutting my pleas for food storage and A.R.P., so the broadcast was not given." However, *The Daily Herald* had a stronger stomach and published the text on November 3rd 1934.

Almost exactly one month later the Walwal incident took place on the Abyssinian frontier and the following year Italy invaded Abyssinia. In March 1936 the Germans re-occupied the Rhineland and three months later a group of officers rose in revolt against the Spanish Republican Government. Haldane was ripe for conversion.

· · ·

Within a few months of the outbreak of the Spanish Civil War Haldane had visited the secretary of the British Communist Party in his King Street headquarters, had visited the Spanish Ambassador, discussed anti-gas precautions with him, and was already preparing for the first of three visits to Spain. During these visits Haldane advised the Spanish Government on the precautions to be taken against gas attack. He advised them on the best way of protecting civilian inhabitants against the steadily increasing rebel air raids. He visited the front as a free-lance observer and wrote extensively about his experiences when he returned to England.

Haldane's pro-Government loyalties were never in doubt, and the strength of his personal feelings is shown in his reply to a letter suggesting that he should meet Douglas Jerrold, an ardent supporter of the rebel leader, General Franco. "I understand," he wrote, "that Mr. Jerrold made arrangements for conveying Franco to Spain by air last year. I have seen the results of this action. I have seen little children torn to pieces before their mothers' eyes. I have seen women crushed under their own houses by the explosion of foreign bombs imported by the 'patriot' Franco. I have seen this occurring many miles from the scene of fighting or even from factories where munitions were being made." And to a suggestion that he might spend a very pleasant evening with Jerrold he commented: "I regard this suggestion that I should take pleasure in meeting such a person as a gross insult, and I demand an apology by return of post. I note that, according to the Press, Mr. Jerrold has also insulted the Catholic Church by describing Franco as a saint. I have said some hard things of the Church, but I trust that I have never sunk as low as that."

Although Haldane wrote and lectured extensively on the Spanish Civil War, his personal impact on it was small—it is remarkable how rarely he is mentioned even in the accounts of the fighting later produced by the British members of the International Brigade. Yet if his effect on the war was slight, the effect of the war on him was considerable and lasting. He spent a total of only a few months in Spain, but they confirmed his belief that only the Communists would stand up to the dictators.

It would be unfair to say that Haldane enjoyed the little of the front-line fighting that he saw, or the experience of being bombed in Madrid and other Spanish cities and towns. He was always quick to feel the suffering of others, and too practised an observer to miss the horrors. Yet if the danger which he experienced in Spain was only relative, it was enough to give him back the excitement of his youth. This man who had actually enjoyed Flanders' fields could not remain unmoved by his experiences. Like Hemingway, who also wanted to recapture his youth, or Chalmers Mitchell who went to the Spanish War at the age of seventy just "to be in it", Haldane was drawn by a need almost as emotional as intellectual. One part of him remained the objective scientist; on to the other there brushed off some of the romantic glory of the International Brigade, and Haldane was in the right mood to be transformed by it. "I first met him," says one of its members, "at a Christmas Party we held in the headquarters of the British Battalion in the village of Mas del las Matas just before we set off for the Battle of Teruel. He struck me as a big shaggy bear enjoying a picnic."

There were two ways in which the Spanish War changed Haldane so that he came out of it a different man. In Britain he had seen people protesting against the rise of Fascism; in Spain he saw people fighting it. It is significant that one of the few times he ever lost his temper with a much-respected colleague, the Dr. Julia Bell with whom he carried out his work on haemophilia, was when she warned him, as he left for Spain, not to get himself killed. "He blew up completely," she says, "saying that if only a few people like him did get killed it would make people in Britain understand what Fascism really was." And in Spain he saw that it was mainly the Communists who were welding together the varied pro-Government parties into a coherent front against the rebels; the situation confirmed his belief that in an imperfect world, support for the Communists represented the least unsatisfactory option. As a footnote to this belief, he saw how different events looked when they were first seen in Spain and then viewed, in Britain, after being filtered through Parliament and Press. His surprise was perhaps a little ingenuous, but it confirmed his worst suspicions about politicians. It also led him to claim that the only thing you could believe in a newspaper was the date. This, presumably, excluded his own contributions.

The Spanish War had one other important effect on Haldane. It turned him, over a matter of twenty months or so, into one of the few British scientists who could speak with authority on air raids as they were experienced during the 1930's rather than during the First World War. This put him on the higher ground when the authorities in Britain were pushed, still protesting, into taking the first A.R.P. measures.

On his first visit to Spain Haldane went to Madrid, having acquired an outfit of black leather jacket, breeches, and motor-cyclist's cap with visor. In this he arrived at the Spanish Ministry of Defence where he was soon advising its members on what gases the Franco Air Force was most likely to use, and what precautions should be taken. Mustard gas seemed the most likely, and Haldane himself was injured during tests of the ineffective gas-masks available. He also discovered what he could about the research still going on in the capital. "Professor I. de Zulueta, in the intervals of hiding the more precious contents of the biological museum in cellars, was continuing his work on the polymorphic beetle *Phytodecta variabilis*," he later reported. "Professor Salan, of Salamanca, was very appropriately breeding the 'explosive cucumber', *Ecballium elaterium* . . . Our discussion of these topics was interrupted by an air raid."

He hitch-hiked to the front, finding the process difficult and his appearance often suspect, and he also made a twelve-hour journey to Alicante with refugees from Madrid. "The train was six hours late," he wrote. "As I was a privileged person, and also suffering from the after-effects of influenza and from violent rheumatism, I was not only allowed to wait in a waiting-room, but even given a first-class ticket. However, if the classless society has not been fully realised elsewhere in Spain, it has certainly been achieved in the railway trains. I got into a coach, third-class as it happened, and forced my way into the corridor." Here, where he slept for most of the night, the children and the dogs relieved themselves on the floor. The windows were closed but, as he pointed out, all smells were obliterated by the long cigars called *dinameros* since they were used for lighting bombs. "It may be that their smoke possesses germicidal power," he wrote. "To a man like myself, already suffering from laryngitis, they were more nearly homicidal." He spent some time in the trenches although he was not involved in action. "As I was bombing officer to the 1st (Guards) Brigade of the B.E.F. in 1915," he subsequently wrote, "I am rather a snob about trench warfare. There was plenty to criticise." He knew more than most of his companions about the business of staying alive in the front line—"whenever my companions started an animated conversation in full view of the enemy I lay down", he commented.

This first visit was followed by a second in the spring of 1937, and by a third during the winter. On the second visit Haldane wore flannels, which together with his accent caused him to be arrested as a potential bourgeois spy. He was soon released but tended to make much of the incident, wrote of himself being brought before a military tribunal, and said that the Spanish had "rounded up a number of foreigners and, I think, one was shot". Sensibly enough, he switched from "bourgeois" flannels to proletarian corduroys, and before his third visit a new pair was presented to him by colleagues at University College. For the ceremony, one of his students had drawn his portrait on a blackboard in the gift corduroys—fat before going to Spain and emaciated on his expected return. Haldane, queerly embarrassed, hastily rubbed out the drawings.

On all three visits to Spain Haldane travelled rough and lived rough, sleeping in stables with refugees and mules, travelling back to Madrid on one cold night on the outside of a lorry, jammed precariously between cases of ammunition. He lived for some days as an ordinary soldier, acting on one occasion as interpreter between an Italian who spoke French and a Hungarian who spoke German. In Barcelona he contributed to the Spanish blood-bank. And he volunteered to act as the *Daily Worker* correspondent at the front to assure "that Eden does not keep the truth from the people in Britain".

It was, however, his observations of what happened in air

raids, of what protection could be given, and of what could not, which were to be of particular importance to the future. In Madrid, in Barcelona, and in many smaller towns, he went about the business of observing, recording, and applying his statistical expertise to the effects of modern bombs dropped under contemporary conditions. Very little was known about this, and much of the work tentatively being done in Britain was purely theoretical or, at best, based on experiences in the First World War.

While Haldane concentrated on the factual problems of protection required for tonnages expected, he was acutely aware of the psychological effects of modern bombing. He admitted that once having been bombed on a Spanish highway he could not drive along a road, either in Spain, or for some weeks later in England, without instinctively looking for cover on either side. He agreed that bombing produced an overwhelming if irrational desire to get underground—even though it might be safer to remain above ground. And he personally went through one experience which greatly moved this man who had noted, without undue concern, the shambles of the Western Front.

He was sitting on a park seat in Madrid when an air raid began. Maybe he felt as he had felt during a broadcast during an earlier raid—"I feel I should like to make a dive for one of the many cellars which are labelled as refuges. But I can't. I am for the moment a citizen of Madrid, and I have to be as brave as the other citizens, women and children as well as men." Whatever the reason, J.B.S. remained sitting. So did an elderly woman on the same seat. Then a bomb dropped nearby—and the woman was killed instantaneously, apparently by a bomb-splinter. The experience severely shook Haldane—more severely, it appears, than anything which he had experienced in Flanders. "It was not that he was frightened of getting killed," explained a friend to whom he later recounted the incident—"it was that he had so many things to do."

One result of the strong convictions confirmed in Haldane by the Spanish Civil War, was a difference of opinion with his mother. The details are unknown, but the feelings aroused can be gauged by a letter from Mrs. Haldane, kept by J.B.S. among his papers, which ran:

Dear Jack,

My most casual acquaintance could hardly fail to know what I feel about the sinking of British ships, so I do not think there is any use in my answering your remarks on the matter. I have read the draft of a letter I wrote to you in December, 1936, and nothing I wrote then applies to this question.

I agree with you that if I had "accused" you of cowardice during the 1914-18 war, it would argue a "pathological state of mind" (I quote from yr. letter dated February 2nd, received yesterday February 7th). I deny that I ever said so, & it is surely late in the day to bring an accusation of that sort against your mother.

I was very proud of you in 1914-18.

Returning from his final Spanish journey, Haldane gave a typical display of the mingled rudeness and charm which was apt to confuse casual acquaintances. On the train from Paris to the Channel he was joined in the restaurant car by a young Australian artist returning from the Mediterranean, her first journey in Europe. "How surprising that there should be no snow in Northern France while there had been a lot further south," she casually remarked to the man at the same table. He gave an irritable snort, and said: "That's the kind of silly remark that people are always making." Unabashed, she explained where she came from and that she thus had little experience of snow. "Oh," he said, "I thought you were just trying to be clever." And he then went on to explain the mysteries of snow.

Arrived in London, Haldane went straight to University College, only to find his laboratory locked against him. The key was a cumbersome affair which he often failed to carry, and he instructed the steward that the door should never be locked. During his absence the steward had been faced with an awkward choice; but he wanted to protect the laboratory and the various personal items which Haldane usually kept in it. He therefore locked the door and gambled on getting advance warning of Haldane's return. He had failed to receive it.

J.B.S. solved the problem simply—by putting his shoulder to the door and bursting it open, splitting the jamb on both sides from top to bottom and tearing out the hinges. He spent the night in his huge armchair, as intended. The following day his colleagues watched the crestfallen steward repairing the door.

.   .   .

Haldane's aid to the Government was not limited to his advisory visits to Spain. In Britain he threw himself wholeheartedly into the "Aid Spain" movement, giving up to one hundred lectures a year, appealing for funds, writing numerous letters to the papers and, from the end of 1937, adding to these activities by becoming the science correspondent of the *Daily Worker*. The *Worker* articles, which represent a high point in his exposition of science to those who knew little about it, began on December 9th with "What Makes the Birthrate fall?" and ended nearly thirteen years later with "They Want to Sterilise the Poor" on August 9th 1950. In between came nearly three hundred and fifty articles, invariably laced with propaganda yet explaining the scientific facts of life with a sureness of touch hardly equalled since the days of T. H. Huxley.

The "Aid Spain" meetings brought J.B.S. into close contact with large numbers of the working class and from the contacts sprang a mutual and lasting respect, largely due to Haldane's commonsense and his genuine feeling for ordinary people. In one Fife village, for instance, he remarked on the absence of the wife in the small cottage where tea had been arranged after a meeting. The woman had been nervous of meeting the great man and had scuttled back to her kitchen once everything had been prepared. Haldane insisted that she came in, immediately set her at ease by enquiring about local conditions, and is remembered nearly thirty years later in the woman's one comment: "He had no airs about him." There was also the occasion when he volunteered to speak at a village institute and found himself faced with an audience of only twelve. There were twenty other members in the games room and it was suggested that they should be called in. "Let them alone," was Haldane's advice. "They will enjoy their game of cards better than listening to me—and in any case twelve volunteers are better then one hundred conscripts."

He always insisted that no special preparations should be made to accommodate him, and that he preferred staying at a worker's house to an hotel. However, he sometimes failed to make himself fully understood. One housewife in whose home he was staying, called on her neighbours with apprehension after he had gravely told her that he was lousy. "I was later sitting next to him," a colleague says, "and I noticed that he was carefully scratching his ankle round some circular object beneath his sock. Seeing he was observed, he leaned over and quietly said, 'Lice.' The insects were in a pillbox, taped to his leg so that they could feed on him."

Work for the "Aid Spain" movement naturally brought J.B.S. into conflict with Sir Oswald Mosley's British Union of Fascists. He met the opposition head-on, as was shown when about two hundred fascists tried to break up an "Ambulance for Spain" meeting at Shoreditch Town Hall. J.B.S. and the local M.P., Ernest Thurtle, were both howled down by the demonstrators, but these had a hard time with Haldane. "It is only natural," he shouted back during their first interruptions, "that the friends of Hitler, who are traitors, should howl down a man who has argued for many months that the unemployed should be given work on A.R.P." When they persisted, he described them as "filthy traitors who are supporting the murder of British seamen", and added the injunction: "Throw them out." After a collection had been made the meeting broke up in disorder, and Haldane was advised by his friends to leave the Hall by a back entrance. He walked out of the main entrance where he was set upon by the Mosleyites. "I can still use my fists, and was not much hurt, though lame for a week or so from kicks," he later wrote.

Haldane's reference to A.R.P. came naturally enough, since his experiences in Spain had led directly on to the campaign for adequate air raid precautions which he was by this time waging. For a man of Haldane's background this was an almost inevitable development. The British Government still appeared incapable of taking seriously the danger of air raids—even though the threat of the German bombers was to paralyse them little more than a year later, at the time of Munich. The Spanish Republicans had the most up to date experience of raids in the western world—and it was undoubtedly true that raids in any coming war would strike most severely at the working classes, cramped together as they were in the most vulnerable areas. It needed little experience to forecast the result: that the Communists would exploit the situation, call for adequate protection, and suggest that conspiracy lay at the root of the Government's stumbling incompetence. Haldane had considerable knowledge of gas, for long considered a major danger; he had served on a Government Committee dealing with air defence; and his ability to see warfare in the mathematical terms which were later to be utilised by Operational Research had been reinforced by his Spanish experience. He was therefore, without any political promptings, a man tailor-made for the campaign which the Communists now led.

This A.R.P. campaign of the immediately pre-war period was supported by many who had no Communist links and by other well-meaning souls who would have been shocked had they known the extent of such links as did exist. These are made clear by the activities of the Haldanes.

On April 7th 1938, Charlotte Haldane wrote to the Communist Party Secretariat suggesting that she should help to set up an organisation to be called the "Women's Committee for Protection from Aerial Bombardment", and that she and Haldane should write a book to be used in connection with the Committee's work. This book should preferably be published by a non-political publisher "whose name would not immediately stamp it as Left-wing propaganda". J.B.S. had already agreed to utilise what he called a named technical adviser, provided he was considered by the Party to be politically suitable for the job, and he accompanied his wife's letter to Communist Party headquarters with one of his own. "In the first place," he said, "I am quite willing to undertake the work suggested in my wife's accompanying letter. This will imply a slight but not very serious postponement of scientific and other work. It will, however, leave me no time during the next six weeks for the extra calls which according to Comrade Pollitt's letter of April 22nd, may be necessary in the near future. However, I can certainly undertake the A.R.P. book if it is thought desirable." At the same time he asked the Communists whether he should accept an invitation for a four-week private lecture tour in the United States. "It is tiring work and I can only put over a fraction of the propaganda which an American could do," he concluded. "Nevertheless, if it is thought desirable I will apply for leave of absence from London University."

The lecture tour was eventually turned down. The book, however, went forward, and was eventually published by Gollancz later the same year, its pro-Communist parentage skilfully played down. It was accompanied, the official historian of the Civil Defence Services later commented, "by meetings which began a deep-shelter campaign by Communist and other Leftwing forces which was to prove a serious source of embarrassment to the Government". Apart from its political overtones, A.R.P. was an important book, one of the first to provide a quantitative framework for a military problem, but one whose lessons were to be mainly ignored. During the following year, J.B.S. stumped the countryside expounding these lessons, organised very largely by the Communists, and maintaining on platforms in village halls, public squares and market places, that the Government was failing in its duty to provide adequate protection against the aerial wrath to come.

Haldane's strongest points in what was—however correct its facts—clearly a politically-motivated campaign, lay in his scientific ability to appraise what modern weapons could do in theory and his experience of what they did do in practice. On one occasion, after addressing a meeting of the Royal Institute of Chemistry, he was strongly criticised by Government officials.

"Gentlemen," he was able to reply, "you may well be right. I haven't been in an air raid for the past three months."

Gas, according to J.B.S., was no longer the main menace. "Calculations about gas are often based on ridiculous misconceptions," he said, when addressing the Royal United Service Institution on "Science and Future Warfare" during this period. "It has been pointed out with perfect truth that ten tons of gas would render the atmosphere poisonous over an area of several square miles if it were rightly distributed; but it is also true that one ton of bullets would destroy the whole British Army if it were rightly aimed." Gas was still, however, public bogey No. 1, and Haldane felt that all possible precautions should be taken, even if only to avoid unnecessary panic. Thus he claimed that babies could be shut up in airtight boxes during a gas attack, and to demonstrate that this was so, constructed a three foot square, four foot deep, steel box into which babies were put by their mothers. When one volunteer mother became anxious, Haldane got into the box and stayed inside for an hour.

"I got rather hot, and towards the end of the hour I think I was breathing a little more deeply owing to the carbon dioxide which I had produced," he said. "However, I could have stayed for two hours without harm."

The dangers from high explosive were what worried Haldane, and for more than two years he hammered away at the authorities with demands for deep shelters, offering, in the summer of 1939, to sit in one of the above-ground Anderson shelters while explosives were detonated nearer and nearer to it. This method of testing the value of his eponymous shelter was quietly rejected by Sir John Anderson, soon to become Minister of Home Security. If the scale of attack had been of the order that Haldane envisaged—"I do take the view that an air raid on London, in which, let us say, the Germans employed a large part of their air force, might kill fifty thousand people or so"—deep shelters would no doubt have justified the expenditure of labour needed to provide them even in a country stretching itself for war. In a country with 1,800,000 unemployed—Britain's figure for the summer of 1938—their provision might have been justified as a social safety-net even though the threat from the German air force was being grossly over-estimated—by many men better informed than Haldane.

In 1938 he put forward an ingenious scheme for tunnel shelters which he claimed could be constructed for as little as £12 per head; when the Finsbury authorities produced a somewhat similar scheme early the next year, he agreed that the second scheme was not only superior in many respects but also cheaper. In the climate of early 1939, however, there was little chance of such schemes getting more than a cursory examination. The situation remained much as Haldane described it in "London is Unprotected", an article in the *News Chronicle*. "If London is raided in the course of the year," he concluded, "it is possible that some of the people responsible for the existing chaos—and very likely some who are quite innocent—will be hanged on lamp-posts. Unfortunately, this will not save the lives of the ordinary people. We have got to realise that we are being betrayed, and to act on this realisation." However, the British are a good-tempered race; on the night of September 7th, the start of the great London raids, they neglected the lamp-posts, tore down the metal gates barring access to Underground stations, and inaugurated their blitz-long use of the stations as deep shelters.

Haldane's long stride into the political waters of A.R.P. eventually brought a result which he no doubt expected and probably feared: he was asked once again to stand for Parliament. A refusal to stand as a Liberal during the First World War had been natural enough for a man of his inclinations. But by 1939 he was far better briefed on scientific problems than most M.P.s, and at first glance would for this alone have seemed a good candidate. Yet he was already bemused by the apparent faultlessness of the Communist cause, and was already its open and powerful advocate—not only through his *Daily Worker* articles but through *The Marxist Philosophy and the Sciences* which had been published in 1938. He was impatient of opposition, a master of the tactless reply, and as a Left-wing member he might have proved an invaluable asset to the Conservatives. The wording of his refusals suggest that he himself was well aware of the fact.

Writing in January 1939, to the Vice-Chairman of one local Labour Party, who had assumed that he was a party member, Haldane said that he wished to advance the effective electoral unity of all anti-Chamberlain forces, but that he would not be anxious to be actually returned—"should you be prepared actually to serve as a member, I would not dream of asking you to waste yourself on [such] a constituency," the Vice-Chairman had written. Haldane said that this was, he thought, the third offer he had had in as many months. "Unfortunately, in your case, there is no question of the reply," he went on. "I am not, and never have been a member of the Labour or of any other political party and it would not look too good if I joined up *ad hoc* . . . I do not think I should make a good M.P. and, indeed, I hope to get back to scientific work completely when there is less need for public activity. Of course, if I thought I could be of real value, I should take a different view, but I actually believe that my scientific work is of some value and that I should make a mess of a political career."

Only a few days later he was asked to stand for Cambridge by the University Labour Party. In his reply he revealingly spelt out his own position as he saw it some seven months before the outbreak of war. "Though not a member of the Communist Party," he wrote. "I am very closely associated with it; for example, I write weekly in the *Daily Worker*, and am very definitely a Marxist. My personal character is such as not to endear me to a number of people who state, probably correctly, that I am rude. Fourteen years ago I was concerned in a divorce case, and although the University Appeal Court decided that I was not grossly or habitually immoral, this will probably lose me votes. I am not very good at getting to know people.

"From my own point of view, the main objection is that were I elected, I should possibly have to resign my chair here and certainly have to give up a good deal of scientific work, whereas at the moment I am turning out more than I ever did in my life. And I doubt whether I should be a good M.P., as I work best as an individual rather than as a member of Committees and the like. Indeed, I think it is quite likely that, were I elected, I should lose the seat at the next election because people took the view that I was not attending sufficiently to the interests of the University or those of individual constituents."

One other point, possibly two, affected Haldane's decision. As a Labour Party member he would no longer be able to speak as he truly felt about Communism. And, in any case, surely he would be required for special work when war did come?

7

A Scientist Goes to War

HALDANE'S activities in the Second World War were unique
—and in more fields than one. Following the signature of the
German-Russian Treaty of Non-Aggression on August 28th, he
had duly taken the Communist line. But before the end of
September 1939, he was working for the Ministry of Information's Directorate of Home Publicity and urging, in an official
memorandum, that "anti-war propaganda must be rigorously
controlled". Throughout the months of the "phoney war" he
was a constant and bitter critic of the Government in the
columns of the *Daily Worker*; but by November 1939, he was
being consulted by Air Intelligence 4, one of the Air Ministry's
most secret departments. As his criticisms continued throughout
the spring and summer of 1940 he was working on very secret
and dangerous assignments for the Royal Navy, and as the first
moves were being made for the official banning of the *Daily
Worker* Haldane—by this time Chairman of the Editorial
Board—was advising the Army on its crucial anti-invasion preparations. And by the autumn of 1940, as the closure of the
Daily Worker grew nearer, he was again involved in some of
the Navy's most closely-guarded work—the preparations to
operate midget submarines.

This dichotomy led at least one colleague—and one who did
not know the full extent of Haldane's official commitments—
to contend jokingly "that in reality he was a member of M.I.5
and had to behave as he did to gain entrée". The possibility
that Haldane was so inwardly shocked by the Russian Treaty
with Hitler that he carried out undisclosed duties for the British
Government—and continued to do so until the Russians were
transformed by German invasion into our allies—is almost certainly ruled out by two things. One is Haldane's personality;
the other is his belief, later frequently reiterated, that the Pact
was simply the result of an Allied failure to unite in time—
made inevitable by the fact that the Allies were capitalist States.
Yet in the nature of things the possibility cannot be totally

excluded. However, the truth appears to be that Haldane's character was of a complexity which the more intelligent of the Service chiefs understood. He was ideologically, though not until 1942 formally, a member of the Communist Party, and he would not desert them in their hour of embarrassment. But he was also a man of honour and of his word. He regarded the occasional absurdities of censorship, and the Fifth Column panic of the summer of 1940 with the contempt which they deserved; but he knew that security demanded that he keep his mouth shut, his pen from paper, and the authorities knew that he knew.

Haldane's most important and most dangerous wartime work was carried out on physiological problems for the Royal Navy. It grew directly from immediately pre-war work connected with the disaster to H.M.S. *Thetis*, but it did not start until the first months of 1940, and long before this he had been caught up in the official machinery. Just when he began work for what was then the Ministry of Information is still not clear, but by September 14th John Hilton, the Director of Home Publicity, was asking University College that Haldane, "doing occasional work for this Ministry", should be given access to his own Department from which attempts had been made to exclude him. Subsequently he wrote a number of articles on semi-scientific subjects which were distributed by the Ministry in the hope of keeping up civilian morale; however, this part-timer for the Government's Home Publicity Department was simultaneously writing to a friend that the current situation in Britain was more chaotic than it had been at the same period in 1914. "This," he commented, "may be a good thing if it leads to more people being genuinely fed up with the war."

He had already offered his scientific experience to all three Services. To the Secretary of State for War, the Hore-Belisha who had been Secretary of the Oxford Union when Haldane had been Librarian, he made one interesting suggestion which arose from his physiological work. "Among the major tasks of the allied armies may be the crossing of the Rhine or other large rivers," he wrote. "I believe that in such a task divers using self-contained dresses with their own oxygen supply, may play a valuable part. Of course a diver cannot walk across a rapidly flowing river. But I believe that, if he were attached to a wire rope, he could cross it obliquely, reaching the other bank perhaps half a mile below his point of departure." Such men might set out on sabotage operations, help the building of pontoon bridges, or even assemble under water for surprise attack. "In this latter case at any rate," Haldane went on, "the apparatus needed would be something like the Davis escape apparatus plus weights on the feet, so that it could be discarded in a few seconds on emergence from the water. Such a scheme is, I believe, no more chimerical than the landing of troops by parachute, and is therefore worthy of investigation. This would include not only topographical and tactical research, but design of a special apparatus, including, if possible, protection against shock from 'depth charges' or shells bursting in the water."

This proposal has a grim reality compared with the scheme which Haldane put forward on hearing that magnetic mines, exploded by the change in the local magnetic field produced by the approach of a steel ship, were being laid down by the Germans. They would also be exploded, he suggested, by the proximity of much smaller magnets; in fact, a one ounce magnet would do the job when it was about one yard away from the mine.

"How are we to get our magnets within a yard of the sensitive magnet attached to the mine?" he went on. "In fishery investigations metallic labels are attached to fish as a routine. The labelled fish live for some years and do not lose their mobility appreciably. Thus a fish carrying a permanent magnet weighing about an ounce should activate a magnetic mine if it passes within a yard of it." Haldane went on to propose that whenever a magnetic minefield was detected thousands of suitable fish with magnets attached should be released nearby, and that numbers should also be released where magnetic mining was expected. "By the end of a year, some hundreds of thousands, perhaps millions, of mine-activating fish would be at the service of this country (and of neutrals)," he went on. The suggestion was never followed up, but its impracticability was not necessarily the main reason; the Admiralty was already at work on its own magnetic mines, and while degaussing, later used by the Allies, protected only their own ships against the new menace, magnetic fish would have been indiscriminate.

It was natural enough that J.B.S. should be thinking of new weapons and their antidotes. Even before the outbreak of war he had been discussing the prospect of atomic bombs in the columns of the *Daily Worker*. On this subject he had initially been as sceptical as most other scientists. "We know very little about the structure of the atom and almost nothing about how to modify it," he had written in *Callinicus* in 1924, "and the prospect of constructing such an apparatus seems to me to be so remote that, when some successor of mine is lecturing to a party spending a holiday on the moon, it will still be an unsolved (though not, I think, an ultimately insoluble) problem." J.B.S. erred in good company, and after the discovery of nuclear fission at the end of 1938 he was quick to seize on its possibilities. He described the latest experiments in the *Daily Worker* in March 1939, and a few weeks later devoted another of his weekly articles to the subject. "Nobody knows how large a lump of uranium is needed before it begins to set itself alight, so to say," he noted. "But experiments are already under way in two British and one German laboratory to my knowledge, and doubtless in others in America, the Soviet Union and elsewhere." Stating that uranium bombs could not, fortunately, at once be adapted for war, he added that his whole article was speculative and he was prepared to bet against immediate success in the experiments then going on. "Nevertheless," he commented, "some of the world's ablest physicists are hard at work on the problem. And the time has gone past when the ordinary man or woman can neglect what they are doing." Privately, he speculated that a lump of uranium the size of a walnut might be able to destroy an area stretching from Piccadilly to Hampstead.

It was known that Haldane's experience spread across many fields of science, and in the autumn of 1939 he was approached by David Garnett, then working in the Air Ministry's top-secret Air Intelligence 4. Garnett quoted Mr. Churchill's recent statement that Britain had an advantage over the Germans "in the higher ranges of Science", and asked whether there had, in fact, been a decline in the volume and the quality of German scientific work since the Nazi regime had been set up. Publication, of books and of papers, might form a useful yardstick, he suggested. Could Haldane help? J.B.S., who was by this time fighting his own guerrilla war with a University College still trying to move his Department from London, replied in vintage style. "Our local Führer, [Sir Allen] Mawer, has decreed that the libraries of this College should be shut," he replied, "and my colleague Professor Fisher was assaulted by the College servants while attempting to get into his own Department. The Library of the Royal Society is also shut, and the Science Library in South Kensington, which is open, is not very good on biological journals. In fact the situation in London as regards scientific periodicals was summed up by a colleague of mine who said that the only scientific information available to him was contained in files marked 'Secret'." He continued with the fully justified complaint that with the exception of the Air Ministry, the Services were using scientists even less than they had done in the previous war, and he bemoaned the fact that the Cabinet lacked any Minister who had contacts with the scientific world comparable to those of Lord Balfour. "I may add that this is not a personal complaint," he continued, "I have sufficient pertinacity and reputation to be able to make some impression on certain generals and admirals. But most of my colleagues are not able to do so."

It was on the admirals that he was in fact making most impression, and within a few weeks he was embarked on what was to be his major war work. This sprang directly from the disaster to H.M.S. *Thetis*, the submarine which three months before the outbreak of war had sunk off Liverpool, while on trial, with the loss of ninety-nine lives. More than forty of the men who died were civilians; nineteen were members of the Amalgamated Engineering Union and others were members of the Electrical Trades Union. These two organisations quickly enlisted Haldane. Both wanted to represent their members' interests as fully as possible at the Public Enquiry into the disaster which was called; both also hoped that Haldane might be able to provide at least some consolation to bereaved relatives by showing that the men lost had probably died painlessly. John Scott Haldane, it was recalled, had as an experiment shut himself up in an airtight chamber after investigating the causes of high death-rate in the slums of Dundee, and J.B.S. was later to claim that his *Thetis* experiments "were merely extensions of this one". He himself had done similar work with Wigglesworth and Woodrow sixteen years previously.

Technically, Haldane's claim that he was merely extending his father's experiment was true; in practice he went much farther, although he later tended to pass off the work as being in the common run of science. He claimed that he ran no appreciable risk and wanted to correct the "somewhat sensational accounts" which appeared in the papers. He was in fact justified in wincing at such phrases as "death-defying ordeal".

However, at the time J.B.S. favoured the limelight, although not for personal reasons. Working with him on the *Thetis* experiments were four non-scientific colleagues; these men, he rightly felt, deserved all the publicity and praise they could get. They deserved it, moreover, for more than the obvious reasons. All four—W. Alexander, Patrick Duff, George Ives and Donald Renton—were members of the International Brigade, while Renton was on bail at the time of the experiments. As a leader of the unemployed he had been one of a party which had entered the premises of a railway company in an effort to show that they were "genuinely seeking work", and he was on trial for this offence.

"I chose these men as colleagues because I had no doubt of their courage and devotion," Haldane said later. He reckoned that men with recent battle experience would be unlikely to panic—even though they were, he noted, refused admission to the Territorial Army. They showed genuine scientific interest, they took notes on their own initiative and their attitude was later summed up by Duff. "I felt bad, but trusted the professor," he said. "I went there hoping the experiment might prevent disasters similar to the *Thetis*. I don't think I would have done it for money." Haldane picked the right men for the right non-political reasons. But he was glad to underline that they would risk their lives in such circumstances, and he was vehement when some papers named them but omitted any reference to the International Brigade. Significantly, when Haldane was paid by the A.E.U. for his work two and a half years later, £65 of the 100-guinea fee went to the International Brigade Association, and £40 to the A.R.P. Co-Ordinating Committee he had helped to found in 1939.

The position in which Haldane believed himself to be *vis-à-vis* the authorities is shown by a letter he wrote at the time to a French friend, saying that he was not, as reported, employed by the Admiralty. "On the contrary," he said, "I was employed by a Trade Union (syndicat) and the Admiralty do not approve of me on political grounds. They would, in fact, be very glad if they could imprison me, as your Government is trying to imprison M. Sampaix."

These experiments in which J.B.S. and the four International Brigadiers took part were carried out in the London works of Siebe Gorman, whose connections with J.B.S. went back more than thirty years, and who put one of their steel chambers at his disposal. The aim was to simulate conditions in the escape chamber of the *Thetis*, and all five men were sealed into the small chamber. The concentration of carbon dioxide was high to start with, and it rose rapidly. After half an hour, air was let into the chamber, but again the carbon dioxide began to increase very quickly. At the end of an hour everyone was panting severely while Duff, who was awaiting an operation for wounds received in Spain, was in considerable distress. The men then came from the chamber and attempted to put on, and simulate the use of, Davis escape apparatus. All had headaches, some vomited, and some were temporarily incapacitated.

This experiment showed Haldane how different men would react to the conditions of increasing carbon dioxide. But it was only carried out after he himself had been sealed up in the chamber for no less than fourteen and a half hours—to discover whether a gradual rise in carbon dioxide pressure had the same effect on him as the abrupt rises he had experienced in experiments carried out years earlier. He entered the chamber at ten at night, going into an air mixture which probably corresponded to conditions in the *Thetis* about nine hours after she had dived. "I slept intermittently most of the time until 8.30," he told the Court of Enquiry in which there sat Captain Oram, one of the four survivors from the *Thetis*. "By 11 a.m. I was panting very severely. I had the start of a headache and some photophobia—pain when the light shone on my eyes. The symptoms got worse pretty quickly, and about 12.30, I think, Captain Oram arrived and had a look at me through the window. I understood him to say I was rather worse than the men in the *Thetis* were when he escaped." Ten minutes later Haldane came out of the chamber. Vomiting and a violent headache passed off and, he wrote in his report in *The Lancet*, he later "felt unusually well".

Whatever else the *Thetis* enquiry showed, it was abundantly clear that certain physiological factors concerned in escape from submarines had not been fully considered. The Admiralty was quick to realise this and by July 24th 1939, had decided to set up under Admiral Dunbar-Nasmith, Commander-in-Chief, Plymouth, a committee to consider existing policy "and to decide what improvements may be possible". Could the committee, the Admiral asked, have the details of Haldane's *Thetis* experiments?

Two days later J.B.S. called at the Admiralty with the necessary information; discussed the situation; and so impressed the authorities that on August 5th he was formally asked to help in drawing up a programme of the investigations considered necessary. Lord Nuffield, the Admiralty added, had offered Oxford University financial support for such work, and the authorities were planning to make use of the facilities there. A few days later Haldane replied with a list of eleven specific questions which he felt should be investigated. And here, for a matter of four months, the matter appears to have rested. The outbreak of war, the translation of Mr. Churchill to the Admiralty, and the long list of urgent investigations which now had to be put under way no doubt provided reason enough.

On January 9th 1940, Haldane was told that the authorities

were anxious to gain information on certain specific problems as soon as possible. "I am directed," wrote the Secretary of what was now called the Medical Director-General's Physiological Committee, "to enquire whether you could arrange for research on any of these matters to be carried out under your direction." Siebe Gorman's were at the same time asked whether they would provide facilities, and within a few weeks all was ready for what was to develop into one of the most unusual, as well as least-known, epics of the war.

The main aim of the series of experiments which Haldane now began was to find out how men might with the least difficulty or danger escape from sunken submarines; however, what was learned would also be of use to divers, while so little was known of the conditions to be simulated that new and fundamental discoveries might well be made. It was necessary to find out how a variety of human beings reacted—in terms of both mental and physical ability—when they were subjected to the pressures met at the depths at which submarine crew might have to escape; it was necessary to discover how they reacted to breathing gases whose constituents were differently-proportioned from those of ordinary air; it was necessary to discover how they would react in conditions of great cold. And it was, as a further complication, necessary to find out how they would react under different combinations of these varying conditions. Fundamentally therefore, and in spite of the strictly practical aims of the exercise, the investigations were into the ways in which the human animal reacted to various abnormal conditions. They carried the investigators out over the known boundaries and into unknown dangers. As Haldane later wrote: "The work is of a very severe character. For example, I was on one occasion immersed in melting ice for thirty-five minutes, breathing air containing $6\frac{1}{2}$ per cent of carbon dioxide, and during the latter part of the period also under ten atmospheres' pressure. I became unconscious. One of our subjects has burst a lung, but is recovering; six have been unconscious on one or more occasions; one has had convulsions."

Recruiting such "subjects" was easier than might have been imagined, and it was so largely due to the confidence which Haldane inspired. The first—and the man who was to become more deeply involved than anyone other than Haldane himself —was Martin Case, the former graduate of the Cambridge period, who had returned from Kenya shortly before the outbreak of war. During the first days of 1940 Case wrote to J.B.S. saying he had given Haldane's name as reference on his application for a Commission. Haldane thereupon wrote to the authorities via the Admiralty saying that he hoped Case would not be accepted as he had more important work for him; and to Case he wrote saying he might be able to get him "a job in connection with research on how to get out of submarines". The word "job" was perhaps hardly accurate, since the authorities were cautious of actually employing civilians for what was obviously, dangerous work, found it difficult to insure them, and appear to have hoped that Haldane himself would deal with such troublesome matters.

This Haldane did, bringing into the unit a Martin Case remembered by his colleagues as "an able, amusing, eccentric man, an intrepid experimental diver, a strange philosophic person who ate and drank nothing throughout the day and had one large meal at night, followed by an ocean of beer, usually somewhere in Soho". Haldane set about recruiting others from among the staff of University College, many of whom were, as we shall see, by this time only partially employed on College work. He would, as one of them later put it, sidle up and say that there was some rather interesting work on which they might be able to help. He couldn't tell them very much about it, but it involved escape from submarines. It might be quite dangerous although he personally would see that all the precautions which could be taken were taken.

This back-handed offer, coming from Haldane, was eagerly taken up. One of the first to accept was Helen Spurway. "She was warned not to dive," Haldane wrote later, "and perhaps correctly. However, I think she was right not to listen to the doctor in question. Other people at that time were risking more than their ease." Another volunteer was Elizabeth Jermyn, his secretary. James Rendel was a third, while a fourth was Hans Kalmus. However, Haldane threw his net wider. Dr. Negrin, the former Prime Minister of Spain, was drawn in as a volunteer; and when the Admiralty objected that trained biologists and similar people were untypical Haldane remembered the *Thetis* work, applied to the Communist Party, and brought in four men who had fought in the British battalion of the International Brigade—a merchant seaman, a machinist, a tailor and a man who was by this time serving in the British Army.

There were delays before the start of the tests—partly due to the Admiralty who until the last minute were unable to gain Treasury permission for the minute sums of cash involved, partly to Haldane who months earlier had promised to deliver a series of lectures at the University of Groningen.

Finally, in March, all was ready and the volunteers arrived, two or three at a time as ordered by Haldane, at Siebe Gorman's works in Westminster Bridge Road.

Much of the work could be done "in the dry", in compressed air which simulated the conditions faced by men escaping from submarines and by divers. For this, Siebe Gorman's No. 3 chamber was used, a metal cylinder rather like a boiler lying on its side, eight feet long, about four feet in diameter, and with at one end a door which closed on to a rubber sealing ring. The chamber had no lights and no telephone link with those outside, messages being given either by taps on the metal walls or by written messages held up to the small glass windows let into the side. Three people could sit side by side in the confined space of the tank, but none could of course stand up. When it was necessary that the tests should actually be carried out under water, a tank about ten foot high, four foot across and filled with water to a depth of about seven feet was used. The man or woman being tested would drop into the tank wearing diving or Davis escape apparatus and the pressure in the air above the water would then be raised, thus simulating the under-water conditions at whatever depth was required.

The practice was for the subject under test to go into the tank, with an observer sitting by his or her side. The pressure would then be raised, with or without variations of the gas mixture being breathed. The observer would sit breathing through a canister containing a mixture of lime and soda to absorb carbon dioxide in the tank, while the victim would breathe the carbon dioxide until unconscious. "But the compressed air by itself," said Haldane, who often acted as a control, "made me feel so queer that I sometimes forgot to breathe through the canister after speaking to the victim, and I passed out too. In this case, someone watching at the window would lower the pressure. The observer outside would in any case be taking detailed notes of how the victim was reacting inside the tank, while the victim would also make his or her own notes until consciousness was lost. One regular test of mental ability was the ease with which the subject used special instruments to lift little steel balls into holes—a test initially used to eliminate the less able candidates for a qualification in dentistry."

Each test was an individual experience. One, which Helen Spurway later reconstructed from her notes, was typical. In this, varying amounts of carbon dioxide were added to air at a pressure ten times the normal—corresponding to the pressure 300 feet below the sea—and the times taken by different people to become unconscious were noted. Dr. Spurway sat in the chamber recording her experiences. By her side sat Martin Case, wearing a respirator and taking gas samples. Outside, watching through the observation window, stood Haldane.

"Have you got everything?" Haldane asked.

"Pencils, Pads, Sweater, Watches, sampling tubes," answered Spurway. "That's the lot."

"What time do you make it?" asked Case.

"Just coming up to 11.40," said Haldane. "It'll be 11.40 in 5 seconds . . . Now."

"Right I'm synchronised," said Case. And then, turning to Spurway: "Are you ready?"

Spurway shouted for the door to be closed. Then, after it had clanged to and they had heard the handles being hammered into position, Case opened the first cylinder of carbon dioxide.

"11.41," Spurway noted on her pad. "Carbon dioxide let in. Sharp smell which persists. Hadn't noticed it before."

"11.41," said Case. "I've got the sample. Tap for the compressed air."

Spurway gave three heavy taps on the tank wall and with a violent hissing the pressure began to rise. "11.44," she wrote. "Roaring in ear, as in fainting, begins. Have become conscious of my change of cons . . ." Then she stumbled over the spelling.

The hissing stopped and a clang on the metal from outside was answered by a responding bang from Case.

Outside, Haldane noted: "Maximum pressure reached. 300 feet. Both breathing heavily."

On her pad Spurway noted: "My fingers felt like bananas," while Case began to open the next cylinder of carbon dioxide, and to fan the air.

"Fanning me makes me feel hyper—I can't spell the wretched word. Hyter-op-hera-tera-herea," Spurway noted on her pad. "A length of word—then it's all over."

Outside, Haldane noted that they had started on the third cylinder of carbon dioxide. "She's looking fairly bad," he noted. "But she's still trying to write. I should think the CO_2 must be up to 8 per cent. Case is taking a sample. 11.55. Case has taken off his respirator. I wonder how long he'll last? He's lifting her left eyelid and looking at her pupil."

"11.29," Spurway noted inaccurately on her pad. "Chase has looked at my eye . . . under my lid. to eye. If they looked if I am still C O N . . ."

"11.59," Haldane noted. "Case has emptied the third cylinder. It must be nearly 10 per cent. No wonder he's looking queer. I can't believe he'll remember to take that last gas sample. Good man. He has. 12 noon. H.S. is twitching. Both look dopey. Yes, they're both K.O.'s now. That gives us two more points on the curve. Stand by to decompress. Right? O.K. Go ahead."

Case wakes up and realises that they're decompressing. "We have reduced pressure," notes Spurway. "But I haven't lost consciousness." Outside, Haldane notes that they're up to the equivalent of 100 feet. Inside, Case says: "It's cold. Put your sweater on." While on her pad Spurway makes a series of notes. "12.5 I am . . . afraid . . . to think about being sick. 12.7. Headache . . . is . . . developing. 12.10. Feel much better. 12.24. Hear the talking outside for the first time. 12.44. Gradually waking up."

Under such tests, great differences in reaction showed up. Some subjects "felt awful"; some felt elated, while one said repeatedly: "I'm going to die, I'm going to die", and was unable to do the necessary sums. One laughed uproariously when told he was cheating in the ball-test by using both hands. Another believed that the observer took a spanner out of his hands as he was recovering consciousness during decompression, and told him not to be violent. "As the observer does not recollect this," Haldane later noted, "it was presumably a dream." At the pressure of 250 feet down, although breathing normal air, all subjects felt abnormal although they described themselves variously as feeling drunk or faint.

"You feel pretty queer at ten atmospheres," noted Haldane. "The air is so thick that you feel quite a resistance when you move your hand, and your voice sounds very odd, as if you were trying to imitate a Yankee twang, and overdoing it very badly. But after a minute or two you also feel changes in your mind, somewhat but not exactly, as if you were drunk. Americans and Irishmen generally get very excited and may be quarrelsome. So do some Englishmen. Dr. Negrin was one of the few who preserved a complete outward calm, though his written notes show that he was feeling rather odd."

Haldane himself was not immune to illusions. He was apt to pursue them vigorously, as shown by the case of Sir Leonard Hill, a distinguished physician and physiologist then in his mid-seventies, who had worked on diving problems for years both with J.B.S.'s father and with Sir Robert Davis, the head of Siebe Gorman. These three older men, all of a generation, were good friends who respected each other's abilities. J.B.S., however, felt antipathy and something like contempt for Hill—for reasons which are unknown but may possibly have had a political basis; being J.B.S., he took little effort to conceal his feelings.

Thus the stage was set for the day when J.B.S., through stupefaction or other causes, gave himself too much oxygen at too high a pressure and succumbed in the chamber to oxygen poisoning. Hill, who was advising Siebe Gorman on purely medical matters and who was watching from outside the chamber, mistakenly attributed Haldane's convulsive movements to asphyxia; he therefore began frantically signalling to Case, who was inside the chamber with Haldane; next he held up written instructions at the window telling Case to increase Haldane's oxygen supply. This Case correctly declined to do—bringing on rage and despair in Hill who thought that Case, too, must be incapacitated.

During decompression Haldane regained consciousness; on complaining of how bad he felt, he was told by Case exactly what had happened. His reaction was fiercely to exclaim: "Hill was deliberately trying to murder me"—a grotesque claim which he continued to repeat for years.

Oxygen poisoning was, due to one reason or another, not infrequent, and on one occasion Lieutenant—now Professor—Kenneth Donald, one of the young naval officers working with the unit, protested to Haldane that he was suffering from it too often. Surely, it was suggested, this might cause some impairment of intellectual qualities in later life—"although I admitted he had a great deal to spare I felt that he should reduce these experiments on himself," says Donald today. "He was angry in his strange but friendly way and proceeded to shout at me. Inevitably, I shouted back and informed him that he was not only a great scientist but also a 'bloody fakir'. We settled the matter amicably and he did agree to seek my approval of the type and number of experiments he did, if only to ensure that he did not do himself unnecessary damage. A little later Haldane decided that he could get convulsant oxygen poisoning by breathing pure oxygen at atmospheric pressure. He demonstrated this to me up to the stage of twitching but not to the major attack. I informed him with some trepidation that I considered this to be a hysterical elaboration. It was not easy to tell him this and also assure him of my high regard of him as a scientist and a friend. I think, however, the point was made and we heard no more about it."

Haldane obviously enjoyed the work. He enjoyed it almost blatantly—so much so that he laid himself open to one criticism.

"Some people thought that he was very shrewd and indulging his penchant for melodrama," says Donald. "He did take many quite serious risks in my presence on many occasions and this criticism, although it may have had a grain of truth, was entirely unfair. On one occasion, he breathed oxygen at 100 feet (4 atmospheres absolute) in a bath surrounded by blocks of ice. Rather foolishly, he suggested that I breathed oxygen as his attendant as well, to allow immediate decompression if necessary. The result of this was that the wet and frozen professor and the young naval doctor both had oxygen poisoning at the same time; and it is only by good fortune that I did not convulse and Haldane did not drown. Again, Haldane convulsed several times in my arms in the wet pressure pot where he was in a diving suit underwater and I was on a platform above him."

The work continued through April and May, Haldane taking part as a guinea-pig—quite apart from controlling the tests—in the largest number of experiments. Case was the next most frequently used, followed by Spurway. One result of the whole series was that the routine for submarine-escape was considerably modified. In addition, the foundations were laid for the further work, carried out by Haldane and Spurway a few years later, which helped make possible both the under-water attack on the *Tirpitz* and the clearing by the famous "P" parties of the under-water mines and time-bombs which blocked the captured Normandy ports.

There were also various *ad hoc* problems which were usually dealt with by Haldane himself and in one of which he suffered an injury to his spinal cord that was to give him intermittent pain for the rest of his life. "This is due to a bubble of helium formed in this organ while being decompressed while testing in 1940, on behalf of the British Admiralty, a claim by an American firm that a helium-oxygen mixture is safer for divers than air, as being less likely to cause 'bends' and other symptoms during a rapid ascent," he later wrote. "I was decompressed according to a time-table on which I had frequently been decompressed without harm after breathing air. I developed fairly intense pain, and have had some discomfort ever since when sitting on a hard surface. I do not complain. I have learned to be sceptical of American salesmanship, even if I learned it the hard way."

Early in the experiments Haldane discovered that while oxygen is a tasteless gas at atmospheric pressure it begins to acquire, at about five or six atmospheres, the taste of rather stale ginger beer—"a trivial discovery which, for some reason, pleases me greatly", as he described it in his Personal Note for the Royal Society. One result, which he characteristically relished, was that he could now warn young men against believing what they read in the text-books. Oxygen was not, as claimed, quite tasteless; he knew; he had tasted it. Another point, of which he made much, was that this minor discovery illustrated a point in Marxist dialectics; here, after all, the very quantity of a thing altered its quality.

The common coin of experience in all these experiments was loss of consciousness, the onset of fits, or mere nose-bleeding—"we could usually track down the Professor, paper-chase fashion, by following a trail of small bloody pieces of cotton-wool", say some colleagues. To these were also added the effects of cold. Cold alone, cold and carbon dioxide, and cold and high pressure, had all to be investigated, and Haldane and Case alone took part in the necessary experiments. They were each "immersed in a bath of melting ice in the pressure chamber, wearing a shirt and trousers. Immersion was not complete but ice was piled so far as practicable, on portions of the body above water level." Haldane alone subjected himself to the effects of cold, pressure and carbon dioxide, being immersed in a bath of ice for twenty-one minutes, breathing up to 6·5 per cent carbon dioxide and then, when he began to shiver, waiting while the pressure was increased to ten atmospheres. "He was soon unable to speak coherently (the partial pressure of CO_2 being 6·9 per cent) and lost consciousness after three and a half minutes," his report commented.

One other unexpected discovery was made after Donald had pointed out that much classical respiratory physiology was founded on physiological idiosyncrasies of J.B.S. and his father.

"I suggested," says Donald, "that the 'off-effect' of carbon dioxide, which consists of vomiting after the cessation of breathing high carbon dioxide, and which J.B.S. thought to have been important in the *Thetis* disaster, might be a personal idiosyncrasy. As a result of this argument, Professor Haldane, Commander Mould, G.C., G.M., a famous and heroic Australian mine disposal officer, and myself, were sealed in a chamber for nearly eight hours. Haldane analysed, on the Haldane gas apparatus, the fall of oxygen and the rising carbon dioxide, and sprayed mercury and chemicals in various directions as the gaseous environment became more and more desperate. At one stage he called his famous father's famous apparatus a 'purple bitch' and threatened to destroy it.

"If I remember rightly, we were breathing something like

11-12 per cent oxygen and about 9 per cent carbon dioxide. Haldane then put on oxygen breathing apparatus and did, in fact, vomit monstrously. I repeated this and it had no effect apart from relieving my somewhat asphyxial sensations. However, Mould also had some nausea. In fact, we were both right; the 'off-effect' does occur in some people, but there is extreme variation. After this, we then put on a mask to absorb the carbon dioxide. This was a highly dangerous experiment and both Haldane and I felt we were going to die. Haldane, in fact, said he wanted to die. After these experiments, he dared me to drink three large bottles of beer as he was interested in the effect of alcohol in the hypoxic (low oxygen) state. This I did but felt little difference. I am still wondering why Haldane did not drink the beer."

In the middle of the first spell of the difficult and dangerous work, for which special qualifications of training and courage were necessary, Haldane's carefully-planned series of experiments were threatened—not by the enemy but by Whitehall. Martin Case, he was informed, was to be called up for military service. He had barely dealt with this when there was thrown into the work the spanner of Regulation 18B, which as the threat of German invasion increased during the summer of 1940, permitted the wholesale rounding-up and internment of anyone suspected of German sympathies. In the conditions of the time the rough justice of the measure can be excused if not justified, and those who suffered most usually complained least; nevertheless, the administration of the Regulation involved some grotesque miscarriages of justice.

There was, in this case, the extraordinary example of Hans Kahle. A professional soldier, Kahle had served in the German Army during the First World War, and had later become a dedicated Communist. Historians of the Spanish Civil War noted that when detachments of the International Brigade marched through Madrid in November 1936, the Franco-Belgian "Paris Commune" battalion was led by a former French officer, M. Dumont, while the German Edgar André battalion was commanded by Kahle—two men who had fought in opposite trenches during the 1914-18 war. Kahle had come to England when the International Brigades were finally withdrawn from Spain, and, after the signature of the Russians' pact of friendship with Germany, had naturally attracted suspicion. However, Herr Kahle was a man of honour. He did not wish to fight against his own country, but he was willing to risk his life for the country which had given him shelter. When approached by

Haldane in the spring, he had been told only that the work in hand was intended to save the lives of British sailors, and that it was dangerous. He had immediately volunteered, and his services were, Haldane later wrote, particularly valuable for certain reasons. "He is a fattish man of middle age, who finds great difficulty in opening his Eustachian tubes. He is therefore an ideal subject for testing the effect of benzedrine of any subject so far," he wrote. "Of all the subjects he is the most likely to be killed or injured. In the national interest it seems better that he should run this risk rather than a British subject."

However, in the middle of June Herr Kahle disappeared. Neither Haldane nor the Siebe Gorman workers knew where he was. Neither did his relatives. Nor, for that matter, did the police who on one occasion appear to have rung up Siebe Gorman's to collect Kahle under the 18B Regulations.

I "know him to be a thoroughly genuine anti-Nazi and a good friend of this country", wrote Ellen Wilkinson, then Parliamentary Secretary, Ministry of Pensions, an old friend of Haldane who had written to her for help. "Believe me," she added, "it isn't much that the parliamentary secretary and her department can do with H.O. [Home Office]." However, it was now discovered that Kahle had, in fact, already been arrested. The authorities were sorry. The Admiralty informed the Home Office and the Home Office informed the Directorate of Prisoners of War. On July 5, Haldane was told that Kahle had now been released although he still failed to put in an appearance. A fortnight later a Metropolitan Police Inspector formally informed Siebe Gorman that Kahle had, in fact, already been transported to Canada for internment.

Haldane immediately interceded for his return. "Of course," he wrote to Commander Fletcher, M.P., "if you can get me a fat Tory M.P., aged about fifty, that might be equally good. But frankly the work is unpleasant and rather dangerous." Kahle was eventually returned to Britain—but months later, and too late to take part in the rest of the submarine-escape experiments.

These experiments were finished during July. On the 22nd, Case and Haldane signed for the Admiralty a "Report on effects of high pressure, carbon dioxide and cold", and subsequently there arrived from the Lords Commissioners of the Admiralty thanks for all those who had taken part, and for Haldane "an expression of their cordial thanks for the services which you have been good enough to render, not only in organising the research work but also in taking a personal part, at risk and great discomfort to yourself, in a large number of experiments".

Case and Haldane were also encouraged to describe their work at some length in the *Journal of Hygiene*, a curious fact since publication gave the enemy an indication of what at least one prominent scientist had been doing. Haldane used the opportunity to send Bernard Shaw an account of his experiments. Shaw replied by posting Haldane a number of his own recent publications and shortly afterwards followed up with a letter protesting against Haldane's "suicidal experiments" on himself.

By the time that he received Shaw's letter, Haldane was already engaged with Case on an investigation quite as unpleasant and dangerous as the earlier one. Admiral Sir Max Horton, Flag Officer Submarines, had naturally taken a keen interest in the work of the Dunbar-Nasmith Committee, and in the summer of 1940 had asked for Haldane's help on one of the most secret projects of the naval war. It had been decided to re-introduce miniature submarines, built during the First World War but not extensively used. The problems involved had to be studied in the light of modern conditions and knowledge. Would it be possible for men to leave the vessels while they were submerged, to cut a steel net protecting an enemy harbour or to fix a bomb to a ship, and then to re-enter such vessels safely? These questions had to be answered before work could continue and plans be made.

In mid-August Haldane therefore spent three days at Portsmouth, discussing the tests that would be necessary and advising on the construction of the test-apparatus. The following month he returned, this time with Case. What the two men found waiting for them was the mock-up of a miniature submarine's cabin. Its volume was about 100 cubic feet—less than five foot by five foot by five—and it was, even judged by the uncomfortable vessels in which men were later to attack enemy targets, a crude affair. Into it, Haldane and Case were to cram themselves and then to report upon their reactions.

The first brief test was carried out on Saturday September 21st. The mock-up, made of steel plates as the genuine article would be, stood in a naval workshop, and for two hours the men sat inside it, first with the "hatch" open, then with it closed, carefully recording the temperature and the varying concentrations of carbon dioxide which their breathing produced in the confined space. This was only the beginning.

On the following day they went into the tank in the afternoon. The hatch was battened down, the mock-up was swung by a crane and was then lowered into the waters of Portsmouth Harbour. The busy life of the harbour continued, and the wash of the ships entering or leaving soon had the tank swaying violently. Eventually it broke loose from the weights which should have kept it in position on the harbour floor, and the two men inside were badly thrown about. Use of the gas analysis apparatus was difficult, but it was later found that the increase of carbon dioxide had been rather high. First Haldane and then Case noticed an increase in their breathing. Haldane had a suspicion of eye irritation and Case of headache. Before three hours had passed they found that during such exercise as they were able to take, their increase in breathing was very marked. Before four hours had passed they were both panting hard and feeling pains in the head and eyes. This was all interesting, but after two minutes short of four hours they were drawn up out of the water and the escape hatch was opened. Had they remained for another hour, Haldane estimated, they "would have had severe headaches and probably vomited". They could probably have survived for another three hours.

The following Wednesday week both men arrived at Portsmouth once again. This time something far more ambitious was planned. They were to stay inside the tank for two days, and would be kept both alive and comfortable with the help of oxygen from two cylinders, and boxes of soda lime which would absorb the carbon dioxide. Two sets of equipment for analysing the gas were necessary and these, combined with the rest of the apparatus, further cramped their already cramped positions. In the autumn afternoon they were, as Haldane later described it, "screwed up like so much shrimp paste in a jar", lifted by crane, and lowered to the bottom of Portsmouth Harbour.

The cabin was too shallow to stand up in, and while there was space for one man at a time to lie down by thrusting out his feet into the escape chamber, his companion had to sit. They had electric light and were linked by telephone to their colleagues in the world above water, but both light and telephone worked only intermittently.

The tank had been on the harbour bottom only a short while when water began to seep in past one of the screws which secured the hatch. This was quickly stopped. Above water, attempts were made to slow passing ships, and thereby to limit the wash. These were not always successful, and shortly before dusk one vessel passed the site at such speed that the tank was lifted up. One of its weights came adrift, and it then settled at an angle which would have made both gas analysis and sleep very difficult. Neither Haldane nor Case were as yet experiencing trouble from too much carbon dioxide or from too little oxygen; but the water from their breath condensed on the walls and in the confined space it was impossible to escape the constant drips. Both their scanty clothing and their scanty bedding was soon soaked so that, as Haldane said, "we were wet as well as cold".

Later that evening it was decided that since the angle of the tank made gas analysis so difficult, the rest of the forty-eight hours should be spent above water, on shore, and the crane slowly began to raise its load. By this time, however, the sirens had sounded; an air raid on the harbour was in progress. Then, whether due to the raid or to other reasons Haldane never found out, the crane jammed, leaving the tank with its two men swinging in the air as the raid continued. Eventually it came to rest on dry land.

Throughout the rest of that night, for the whole of the following day and the whole of the following night, the two men remained sealed up, continuing to record the varying gas samples. "We kept a log of the foulness of the air," Haldane wrote later, "and showed that, if the gas analysis apparatus failed, a man could judge when the oxygen was needed by the fact that a match would not burn, and tell when carbon dioxide must be absorbed by his own slight panting."

When the hatch was at last opened soon after midday on October 4th, both men were stiff as a result of their cramped positions; but they had no headaches or other symptoms which could be attributed to bad air. This was vital knowledge. What they had shown was, as Haldane wrote in his official report, that "with one oxygen cylinder and three containers, two men could live comfortably for three days. They could also live less comfortably, but without serious loss of efficiency, for twelve hours without any reconditioning of the air". Perhaps only Haldane, with his family motto of "Suffer", could have used the word "comfortably".

Physiological work for the Admiralty continued in various guises throughout the whole war, much of it in Siebe Gorman's Experimental Diving Department which towards the end of 1940 moved to Tolworth, on the outskirts of London, after the firm's headquarters in Central London had been bombed. The experiments went on under a variety of sponsors, and Haldane's papers reveal how much he did for the sub-committee on under-water physiology, part of the Royal Naval Personnel Research Committee of the Medical Research Council.

In 1943, he supervised a series of experiments with Helen Spurway, Hans Kalmus and Dr. Philip, planned to discover whether men were more liable to oxygen poisoning after they had been subjected to the excess carbon dioxide which would accumulate in a sunken submarine before escape attempts were started. On one occasion this work had to be stopped when Helen went into convulsions. The experiment on Kalmus ended when serious facial twitching developed, while Dr. Philip suffered from severe headaches and vomiting. Later, when the attack on the *Tirpitz* in Arctic waters was being planned, Haldane had the task of submitting himself to a pressure of ten atmospheres and of then being plunged into water at o°C. "an undress rehearsal for getting out of submarines in the Arctic, adding a little CO_2 to make it more life-like" as he later described it. "The combination gave me the K.O. But the cold hadn't."

Physiological work for the Royal Navy—and for the R.A.F. in 1941—was merely the most dangerous of Haldane's contributions to the war. Both he and Helen Spurway were also used for a great variety of statistical investigations—by the R.A.F., the Ministry of Aircraft Production, and the Army. These concerned such matters as the theory of random patrolling—of interest to Coastal Command's search for U-boats on the Western Approaches—the problems of markers dropped by Bomber Command during its raids on Germany and, later, the tactics which offered the highest chances of shooting down the V1's or buzz-bombs. Connections- with Haldane's earlier work were sometimes greater than might be expected. Thus the problem involved in "The interpretation of certain casualty statistics", a paper J.B.S. produced for the Army, was similar to one occurring in human genetics; and in another, on the distribution of bombs during a raid, he drew a striking parallel between the problem and a passage in Galton's *Natural Inheritance*—the link between the statistical chances of a bomb falling on a certain point and the statistical chances of inheritance being greater than at first appeared.

There is no doubt that Haldane's wartime work for the Services went further than the published records indicate. When in 1940 it was suggested that oil could be used to set fire to the sea as an anti-invasion measure, "it was to Professor Haldane that I turned for advice", says General Ritchie, then on the General Staff, "and I must say that he was most helpful." In October

1944, J.B.S. made a brief visit to the forward troops in Holland, for an unspecified purpose; interestingly enough, at least one of the divisional generals he visited asked Haldane to send out a weekly publication which, it appears, he himself was unable to get.

As the spring of 1944 approached, and with it the certainty of Allied invasion of the Continent, J.B.S. appears to have felt that he personally would be involved in the rising climax of the war. "In the event of my death during the next few months," he wrote to the Provost of University College on March 2nd, "I wish to commend the Department of Genetics to your notice." He went on to suggest how the Department should be continued, and specifically asked that the insurance which would fall due on his death should be used to carry on the work.

Shortly afterwards, Haldane remade his own will, leaving all he had to Helen Spurway "as a token of my deep and sincere appreciation of her unselfish devotion and courage in carrying out various experiments designed to save life during underwater operations in the present war at the risk of her own life." If Helen died before him, his estate was to be divided between four of the other colleagues who had worked with him on underwater work—Elizabeth Jermyn, Dr. Kalmus, Dr. Philip and James Rendel.

8

A Scientist Fights the War

HALDANE'S physiological work for the Admiralty, and his *ad hoc* jobs for a variety of Ministries, occupied only a part of his time during the war. He was still, as he was sharp to point out, the Weldon Professor at University College. As such he continued with as many duties as he could, despite the evacuation of much of the College, despite the first hammerings of the blitz and despite what can only be called—even when due allowance is made for his facility for making the most of a grievance —the studied opposition of the College authorities.

In June 1939, more than two months before war broke out, they had tactlessly suggested to Haldane that if University College was evacuated to Bangor in North Wales, as was then planned, he would be unable to carry on with his work since no suitable accommodation would be available. "As the College cannot itself, in the event of war, make use of your services," the Provost added, "I am sure you will realise that it would be its earnest desire that you should, in the event of war, forthwith undertake any form of service (National or personal) which may be open to you." The request was perhaps no more than reasonable. To Haldane it appeared like attempted dismissal, and it was to colour most of his reactions during the period of guerilla warfare between himself and University College that began a few months later. He replied that to close down his department would waste many years' work. He enquired amiably enough as to what was to happen to his workers. But he realised that he had been warned.

During the next few weeks Haldane became involved in the *Thetis* enquiry and he received the first enquiring letters from the Admiralty about investigations which might follow the enquiry. Then, towards the end of August, as the last hopes of peace began to dissolve, he was told to evacuate his Department from University College within three days.

The reaction might have been expected. Haldane refused to budge. The official College machinery, which had operated effectively on the rest of the evacuation plans, thereupon clanked into action against J.B.S., and he and his colleagues became, as he put it in a report to the Rockefeller Foundation "subject to a certain amount of siege by the College authorities". A wooden bar was placed across the door to his room, a move that deterred Haldane as little as might have been expected. He quickly got rid of the bar. It was suggested that his heating, lighting and/or water might be cut off if he refused to leave his rooms, but these threats had no effect and they were not implemented. Some of his apparatus was taken away and moved up to Bangor; within a month Haldane had, as he reported, "succeeded in recovering it". Other equipment was moved to the cellars and at least some of this was taken back to his rooms.

All this was successful as far as it went. But Haldane had to face the fact that all normal College facilities had ended with evacuation, and he was forced to take a number of unpleasant steps. Most of his mouse and rat colony had to be killed, although he made a careful selection from it and sent the lucky few to the United States where it was hoped that the chosen strains might be continued. Hans Grüneberg, thus rendered unemployed, was sent to the library where he settled down to write a valuable book on his mouse-work. Dr. Philip was despatched to John Innes with instructions to carry on work there with her stocks of *Dermestes vulpinus*.

The hard core of the department that remained in Gower Street consisted of Haldane; Helen Spurway who was soon giving practical classes in genetics at Birkbeck College, which had not been evacuated; and Haldane's secretary, Elizabeth Jermyn. Surrounded by the funereal emptiness of much of the buildings, Haldane carried on with his job. "We hope to get at least another three months' work done, raids or no raids," he wrote to the Rockefeller Foundation on September 22nd. "I reckon our chance of anything worse than broken windows as a fraction of 1 per cent. In fact I will bet you that more people die in London during this war from preventable diseases than from bombs."

Here, of course, was a situation Haldane relished. In the first place he was defying authority. In the second, he was doing what he believed to be scientifically correct. The third factor, which he no doubt considered almost as important as the other two, was his view that the College insistence on evacuation revealed a faint-heartedness out of keeping with the situation. How, after all, had the Spanish behaved? "I do not want to go," he wrote, "since de Zulueta carried on in Madrid during the siege for at least eighteen months, and London is not yet a second Madrid; but I hope that, if necessary, we shall copy Madrid and Warsaw rather than Vienna and Prague, since it is much better to be blown to bits while doing your job than beaten up, and then shot in a cellar."

Haldane had barely begun to settle down to his work under wartime difficulties when two events took place which strengthened his determination not to be moved. The first was receipt of a letter from E. L. Tanner, the College Secretary, who had the temerity to ask whether Haldane had "been able to secure any paid work, National or otherwise", so that the necessary deductions could be made from his College salary. One can imagine Haldane literally clenching his fists as he read the letter. "I protest strongly against the suggestion made in your letter that I should abandon my post as Weldon Professor for any other than national purposes," he replied. "At the present moment I am giving occasional advice to two Government Departments, and (apart from one visit to Farnborough), am remaining in London at the written request of one of them. In peacetime I should not have asked either of these departments for remuneration, nor do I intend to do so now, since I do not regard occasional work of this character as in any way incompatible with my tenure of the Weldon Chair."

While Haldane was thus busy sticking to his guns, his colleague R. A. Fisher, the Galton Professor of Eugenics who had over the years provided his own statistical explanation of evolution, was involved in action. J.B.S. long regretted that this good luck missed him. Fisher, like Haldane, had been informed that he must move to North Wales with his department. Unlike Haldane, Fisher lacked the support of the Services, and the College exercised its authority, decreeing that while Fisher himself might be allowed to enter his own rooms, none of his staff should be allowed to do so. By the end of September, passions were riding high and on October 2nd Fisher outlined his feelings in a strong letter to *The Times*.

The following day, he and his secretary, Miss Simpson, approached University College. While Fisher engaged the Beadle in conversation, Miss Simpson climbed the railings, intent on visiting the laboratory as instructed by her Professor. At the last moment the Beadle caught sight of her and ran to intercept. The details of exactly what happened are, as might be expected, somewhat conflicting. One popular version has it that Fisher, saying: "What, assault my secretary would you," threw himself at the Beadle. Both were soon rolling on the College lawns, locked in combat.

"Haldane was really jealous of this episode and obviously wished that he could have had Fisher's luck," James Rendel said later. "He gave Helen instructions to keep out of his way if he had the fortune to get into a fight with a Beadle and, if she had time, to whistle up a press photographer."

While Haldane missed the fight he relished the story. It came at a convenient moment, and the following day, in a long letter to the College Trustees complaining of "the position under which I am attempting to carry on as Weldon Professor", he said: "As you are perhaps aware, the college servants yesterday assaulted a lady who was engaged in calculating tables for the British Association in the department of my colleague, Professor R. A. Fisher. She was somewhat severely bruised, as I saw for myself, and Professor Fisher was also injured while assisting her. Women working in my department have been threatened, but not so far assaulted." And of the Rockefeller Foundation he asked: "Do you consider that as a scientific worker with obligations to your Foundation as well as to University College, it is my duty to see that research is continued even if this leads to my assault and/or dismissal. My own view is that, when culture is being attacked over a wide area of our planet, this is the correct attitude. If so, I propose to 'hold the fort'."

This was pitching the story a little high. However, Haldane clung delightedly on to what was basically a valid grievance and elaborated on it when, in March 1940, he gave a series of lectures in Groningen. These lectures were subsequently published as *New Paths in Genetics* and in this printed version Haldane claimed that Fisher had given him useful advice "until, as a result of a brutal assault by employees of University College, London, while attempting to enter his laboratory, he was compelled to leave London". The implication was, of course, just not true, and the passage produced earnest requests from University College for its deletion. As usual in such situations, Haldane counter-attacked, saying that the assault was more discreditable than he had stated and blandly ignoring the real point being made—that Fisher had left London not because of intimidation but because of the steadily worsening situation in London, which was itself to drive Haldane from the capital late in 1940.

Throughout the summer J.B.S. as we have seen, spent a great deal of his time at the Siebe Gorman works in Westminster Bridge Road. He carried on in University College with such work as was possible—and the stream of papers and notes to *Nature, Biometrika* and the *Annals of Eugenics* continued almost undiminished. And throughout the year his political involvement with the Communists continued to increase. All these activities were to be made more difficult with the coming of the blitz in early September. Both in London and in Portsmouth the physiological work was harassed by the raids. The bombing further increased the problems at University College.

At last, in November 1940, following the increase in the bombing which appeared likely to continue throughout the winter, Haldane agreed that what remained of his department should be evacuated to the Rothamsted Experimental Station at Harpenden, some twenty-five miles north of London. Accommodation was a major problem, since the area had been filled by evacuees a year previously, and it was only with difficulty that rooms were found for J.B.S. and his colleagues. They had not settled down for long before he decided to rent a house on the outskirts of the village and this soon became a home for Haldane himself, for his secretary, for Helen Spurway, and for a doctor already working at Rothamsted.

Space in Rothamsted itself was also at a premium and Haldane's entire department worked in a single room with J.B.S. himself in the middle and the rest of the staff flanking him, an inconvenience which he did not seem to notice. His tall and commanding figure soon became a familiar feature of the Rothamsted scene, one at first sight almost irreverently like those of the retired Army officers who seemed thick on the ground in the Harpenden area at the time. He was always impressive and he was now made more so by the thickness of his moustaches. During the First World War he had let them grow so long that they almost flapped—so that, he told his friends, "they frightened the enemy just as much whether I was advancing or running away". By the start of the Second World War, they had been trimmed down into what increasingly became an imitation of the Hitler moustache. This would never do. Once again, he encouraged them to grow into a bushy luxuriance—"If I have to look like a dictator, I prefer to look like the Russian one."

At Harpenden, Haldane joined in the usual Rothamsted social affairs, contributing a photograph of himself as a baby to a display at which the staff tried to identify present people with past prints, booming round the place with an affable unconventional *bonhomie*, and arguing interminably with R. A. Fisher on every subject under the sun. "I particularly remember sitting with him and Fisher during tea when the question of the gold standard cropped up," one of his colleagues writes. "Somebody asked what they thought of it, and the two agreed that it was a question of how far faith could be based on a material object—one of the profoundest remarks I have heard in ordinary conversation." J.B.S. had not been long at Rothamsted before he contributed to the staff magazine a characteristically witty article in which he described the difficulty of finding people in the laboratories. The older rooms had solid doors and the newer ones had circular glass windows in the door. According to Haldane, if you looked through the windowed doors you could see that the worker wasn't there: if you opened the solid door and looked in, he wasn't there either.

"He worked at all sorts of odd moments," says James Rendel who had by this time rejoined the department. "His attaché case held enough in the way of notebooks or envelopes for him to have a spare piece of paper to do algebra on at any moment, and out it came, in a bus, in a tube, no matter where, in odd moments or for long stretches. This attaché case seemed typically to hold paper, an empty tin of Exmore Hunt in which was a safety razor blade and some thick twist, a pair of pyjamas and latterly a deflated air cushion. At meetings he would arrive and stare between the top of his glasses and his eyebrows at the audience; pick a spot somewhere in the middle usually of a full row, spring on to the desk top, all seventeen stone of him, teeter along in the middle, flop down on to his seat and cough, once more staring round between rims and eyebrows. Then open flew his attaché case and out came papers and pyjamas and tin and cushion. This was first blown up with much puffing. Then back went the pyjamas and papers—all bar one envelope. Then he settled down to carve up his thick twist into the lid of his tin with his safety razor blade. He was excellent at meetings. He understood everything. He summarised it well if in the chair and always had a pertinent point to make about a speaker's contribution. Haldane in the audience was a godsend to the speaker. Even the dullest and more incompetent would find when Haldane sat down that he, the speaker, had said at least one interesting worthwhile thing."

J.B.S. was stationed at Rothamsted for four and a half wartime years, but it is scarcely surprising that few major papers came from him during this period. He continued to write extensively, but much of the purely scientific matter which he published during this period—and it was interspersed with a good deal of popularisation, politics and polemics—has the nature of footnotes to the main themes in which he was interested.

A good deal of it was statistical, like the work he carried out on the data assembled by Elton on fox pelts marketed in Canada during the century which ended in 1933. The proportion of silver fox pelts showed, Haldane proved, that the simple recessive gene which produced a silver rather than a normal red fox must have represented a selective disadvantage of about 3 per cent per year, since the more valuable silver foxes were more likely to be shot—an illustration comparable to that of the *Biston betularia* which he had described in his first paper on the mathematical theory almost twenty years previously.

Looking at the complex record of Haldane's wartime activities, it seems surprising that he managed to produce the volume of work that he did produce. His extra-curricular activities were vast, and he had hardly settled himself into his new quarters at Harpenden before he was faced with a crisis that was both personal and political—the Government's suppression of the *Daily Worker*, the Chairman of whose Editorial Board he had become in 1940. For Haldane's support of the Communist Party had not only apparently survived the twists and turns of policy which had followed the pact between Stalin and Hitler; it had even appeared to grow during the months which followed the outbreak of war.

. . .

It was in support of more effective A.R.P. measures that Haldane spoke, often under Communist tutelage, all over Britain during the first year of the war. In most places he was enthusiastically received. But he was sometimes badly briefed, as when he went to Doncaster where he spoke under the auspices of the *Daily Worker*. "I said that I was informed that the subsoil of Doncaster made deep shelters there impossible, and recommended semi-bombproof surface shelters," he wrote to J. B. Priestley. "Two men got up in the audience and wiped the floor with me. One described a tunnel in a sandstone quarry, thirty feet deep and 300 yards from the hall where I was speaking. The other described a tunnel where he had worked, and which he said could be extended. This was only about thirty feet down, but still fairly safe. Neither was used as a shelter, and the local Communists had never heard of them."

At times he was even more seriously let down. Thus in October, 1940, at the heart of the German blitz, he appeared as the President of the Oxford University Labour Club to speak at an important meeting in the city. He was, he said, convinced of the extraordinary corruptness and inefficiency of the present ruling class. And he then went on to castigate the Tory City Council for having passed a motion asking for deep shelters. "They must know the Ministry of Home Security will not permit them to build deep shelters. The Council are, therefore, by this resolution, deliberately trying to shirk their responsibility to the people of Oxford," he claimed. "They are demanding something they know cannot be started and are then going to say, 'We carried this resolution for deep shelters and we have done all we can for you'. This is a good example of Tory Fifth Column work."

This was fine inflammatory stuff in the best *Daily Worker* tradition—until someone pointed out that the resolution had been tabled on behalf of the Labour Party Group on the City Council. J.B.S. said he must have been misinformed. He apologised unreservedly. But he had been campaigning for deep shelters for a long while. "We certainly did not expect to get a slap in the face," wrote one Labour member.

Haldane's impressive figure, the facility with which he could argue his way out of a tight corner, and the obvious sincerity of his beliefs, combined to help him from such difficulties. So did those characteristics which appeared as cultivated eccentricities but were in fact the result of a tightly-packed life. Thus at Bristol he first made a good speech to a large audience before settling down in his chair and taking out large numbers of serpentine-cum-tapeworm galley-proofs. "He then proceeded to immerse himself in these, so much so that he did not notice that they were streaming down over the edge of the stage into the laps of a delighted audience," says one of its members. "At question time he did not come to the surface at all, and finally, when people got annoyed, had to be shaken by the chairman, who repeated the last question, before he began to function." This was the genuine Haldane, and not the showman, as it might at first appear; however, the show did him no harm.

On A.R.P., Haldane had an arguable case, and the replacement of Sir John Anderson as Home Secretary and Minister for Home Security by Herbert Morrison only fanned the contempt which he showed for the authorities responsible for air raid measures. His dislike of Morrison verged on paranoia, and in his personal notes for the Royal Society he commented: "My only public honour has been that Mr. Herbert Morrison has described me, by implication, as a bastard (Hansard, Jan. 1941). From an ex-conscientious objector who has refused bombproof shelters to women and children because he was afraid that men would not leave them, this is an honour indeed." Writing to a friend of Morrison's statement about men not leaving shelters, he noted: "This is certainly in accord with his past." His attitude was only partly due to Morrison's record of conscientious objection—although typical of the J.B.S. who could exclaim disgustedly at a pre-war anti-Fascist demonstration: "The trouble with these pacifists is that they won't fight." Morrison was, in addition, responsible for the campaign which finally closed down the *Daily Worker*.

It is not surprising that Haldane should have felt his involvement in the *Daily Worker* and in politics increased by the outbreak of war. "I believe that a scientist is all the more use in the world if, like Benjamin Franklin, he takes an active part in politics and does not always behave like a perfect gentleman," he wrote of this period. "This is particularly so in a time like the present when big things are happening, and what would have been regarded as legitimate political activity fifty years ago is ranked as sedition." It was natural that he should feel deeply involved. What is extraordinary is that he should meekly have followed the convolutions of the Party line, accepting the need for war until the last moment and then duly falling into step as the results of the treaty between Stalin and Hitler became apparent. No one now doubts that the treaty was on the Russians' part a defensive step aimed at keeping the Germans at arm's length for a little longer; few doubt that the Winter War with Finland was part of the same protecting operation, however odious it might be. Yet the end-result of much Communist propaganda between September 1939 and the invasion of Russia by Germany in 1941 was in practice as potentially damaging to the Allied war effort as if it had been carried out as part of Goebbels's policy. In this propaganda Haldane played his full part.

The way in which his scientific articles were used was well illustrated by that on "The Study of Change", which the *Daily Worker* published on June 29th, 1939. "Kekule, the scientist who studied atomic formation of chemical compounds, drew inspiration from the formation of people in the street", read the introductory note above it. "Now scientists observe how atoms, in unstable conditions, alter the nature of substances. Professor Haldane points out the similarity in human affairs. This picture—of an unemployed workers' demonstration—illustrates how human 'atoms' can act to change the structure of society." A similar twist was given to many of the extraordinary series of articles which Haldane contributed to the *Daily Worker* during the first fifteen months of war. Writing on ventilation in wartime, he warned against the dangers of putting too many men in too few huts and barracks, and added that this could "be prevented if soldiers, sailors and airmen report any cases of overcrowding to their M.P.'s." Dealing with camouflage, he quoted part of a Nature article mentioning deficiencies and added: "If this is true, numerous factory workers will be needlessly killed, when daylight raids begin." When workers were standing at their machines almost round the clock during the desperate days of June 1940, Haldane ignored the short-term need and stressed the long-term drop in production which would have taken place had the conditions been kept up. Why was the present policy being operated, he asked. "Partly no doubt as a result of Fifth Column work," he replied. "But largely through the sheer blind hatred of the workers, like the blind hatred of the Soviet Union which nearly forced Britain into war with it." In other articles he warned that "our ruling class is not greatly interested in the safety of munition workers". In December 1939 he denounced the Allied blockade, while in dealing with the blood transfusion service a few months earlier he pointed out that venereal disease could be transmitted by blood transfusions. "I do not want to start a panic," he added—the very thing that might have been started had the *Daily Worker* had more than a derisory circulation.

Haldane had been among those who had protested, as in the spring of 1940 Britain had slid towards intervention in Finland and what would have been a disastrous war with Russia. He saw correctly that she had been stopped at the very brink of catastrophe by the course of events and not by any act of the Chamberlain Government. What he later totally failed to see—judging by the evidence of his *Daily Worker* articles and assuming that they can be taken at their face value—was that the invasion of Norway, the supersession of Chamberlain by Churchill and the successful German campaign in France, had created a totally new situation. Support for Communist policy during "the phoney war" might have been an intellectual luxury but it was one which the country could stand. From the spring of 1940 onwards, every soldier complaining about ventilation, every man refusing to work overtime to repair the losses of Dunkirk, lessened the chance of survival which was the only alternative to submission. A moron, or a traitor, might have been expected to encourage them; it is one of the curiosities of human nature that Haldane, who was neither, also continued to do so.

The explanation probably springs from a form of geological fault which separated Haldane's actions on to two distinct planes, enabling him to be unreservedly loyal to the Services and as unreservedly loyal to the Party. This discontinuity separated his ideals from his realisation of the way in which they would or could be carried out in practice. Thus he denied to a complaining correspondent that he wanted Hitler to win the war. "On the other hand I take the view that the present policy of the British Government is getting more like Hitler's every day, and that it is unlikely to secure a victory over Hitler except after enormous loss, and then very doubtfully," he wrote. "I believe that the correct policy is one of alliance with the revolutionary forces which exist in the countries under Hitler's domination. But it is futile for the British politicians who helped Hitler to crush the German working class movement to appeal to the German workers, or for the men who supported the Chamberlain betrayal of Czechoslovakia to appeal to the Czechs."

In spite of his articles in the *Daily Worker*, Haldane certainly made no conscious effort to encourage a German victory, and when a reviewer in *Reynolds News* wrote in March 1941 that "Mr. Pollitt and Professor Haldane want us to lay down our arms", he enquired of his lawyer whether this was libellous— adding that what he was advocating was in fact a "People's Peace", "that is to say a peace based on appealing to revolutionary elements in Germany rather than on negotiation with Hitler". The unreality of appealing to a nation as firmly behind Hitler as it was to remain until the end of the war, at first makes it difficult to believe that Haldane was writing seriously. Yet this was in fact the case, and if his views on Germans in Germany had little connection with reality the same was even more true of his views about the British Government. Helen Spurway's were similar to his, and her assessment of affairs at least comparable. During the weekend of June 22nd, 1941, she was staying with her parents, and it was in their home 'that she heard the morning announcement that Hitler had invaded Russia. "I started back to Harpenden as quickly as I could," she says. "I thought that the British Government would support Hitler, and that J.B.S. would be one of the first people to be arrested."

Certainly by this time Haldane's links with the Party had been greatly strengthened; by this time, also, the Communists' harassment of the war effort had become too strong to ignore. In June 1940, as the country prepared for the Battle of Britain and as Haldane complained that the workers were being driven too hard, those responsible for the *Daily Worker* had begun to see the writing on the wall. They realised that they might soon be the target for attack, and as part of a defensive operation they announced, on June 8th "an important, indeed historic, step in the development and defence of the *Daily Worker*". This was the formation of an Editorial Board, nicely balanced to attract as many sections of the community as possible, consisting of Sean O'Casey, R. Page Arnot and Councillor Jack Owen, and chaired by John Burdon Sanderson Haldane.

The move was astute. Little more than a month later the Board received a letter from Herbert Morrison threatening to suppress publication of the paper unless it ceased what he described as its "systematic publication of matter calculated to foment opposition to the prosecution of the war". Haldane promptly asked Morrison to list the items complained of, but received the answer that the Home Secretary could not "attempt, by reference to particular items, to give [him] guidance" on how to avoid suppression. The "general tenor" of the paper would determine whether action was taken, he added.

As summer gave way to autumn the Royal Air Force held the sky suspended, winning even the grudging admiration of the *Daily Worker*. But with the coming of the blitz and the heavy destruction by the German bombers of British homes, the opportunities for criticism ripened once more.

On the evening of January 21st 1941, Police officers, acting under the 18B Regulations, duly suppressed the paper, and in the House of Commons the following day Morrison explained that it had been closed down, together with the news-sheet *The Week*, since the settled policy of the papers was "to try to create in their readers a state of mind in which they will refrain from co-operating in the national war effort and may become ready to hinder that effort". The *Daily Worker* had, it was added, since the end of September 1939, when it had swung behind Moscow's policy, "by every device of distortion and misrepresentation sought to make out that our people have nothing to gain by victory". This was a logical enough policy for the Communists; but it was a difficult one for Britain to stomach as she faced, alone, a victorious Germany upon which the Russians still smiled benevolently.

Three months later Haldane wrote as Chairman of the Editorial Board to the Home Secretary, claiming that the paper's attitude had been both misunderstood and misrepresented. Would Morrison receive the Editorial Board and consider a reasoned case for lifting the ban? Mr. Morrison refused. The *Worker* kept the nucleus of its staff in being, maintained an information service to as many former readers as was possible, and awaited events. There was not long to wait.

On the night of June 21st, the German armies massed between the Baltic and Bohemia swept eastwards into Russia. "The past, with its crimes, its follies, and its tragedies", flashed away and Churchill, far from applauding Hitler and locking up J.B.S., swung Britain into the fight on Russia's side. Haldane, still free, immediately telegraphed Churchill: "In view of your statement re turning-point of war and tasks of all free people, ask you consider immediate withdrawal of order suppressing *Daily Worker*." However, the record of the *Daily Worker* was a part of the past that refused to flash away quite so easily. The ban remained.

A few weeks later the Editorial Board under Haldane's chairmanship issued a re-statement of policy. If the ban was lifted, this said, the paper would give its full support to the Government and do everything possible to strengthen British-Soviet unity in the fight for victory; would direct its influence in the factories, mines and trade unions towards securing the maximum production for victory; and would "handle international affairs from the standpoint of encouraging the liberation fight of the people in the countries enslaved by German Fascism". The implication of the second aim throws an interesting light on Haldane's industrial campaign of the previous summer. There was still no response from the authorities, who possibly had in mind the repercussions should the *Worker* be re-started and Russia then collapse under the weight of German attack as at first seemed likely. However, Russia held on. Admiration for her grim defence brought growing support for a lifting of the ban on the *Daily Worker*, and on January 1st 1942, as the ban entered the last month of its first year, Haldane once again wrote to Morrison asking for this. By now he had additional reason for supporting the Party. For his wife Charlotte had defected, and had J.B.S. harboured earlier doubts these would now have been submerged by the requirements of loyalty.

Charlotte Haldane had gone to Moscow as the first British woman war correspondent. As she wrote in her autobiography *Truth Will Out*, one of her first acts on returning to England had been to explain her new attitude to J.B.S. "My reports caused him, undoubtedly, considerable surprise and mental uneasiness," she later wrote. "But he was intellectually and emotionally incapable of assessing their objective value; tied, as he still was but I no longer, to the propaganda of King Street, to Party discipline, and to the sacred text of Communism, the works of Marx, Engels, Lenin and Stalin."

Haldane appears to have reported his wife's defection to William Rust at once. It had broken whatever links still remained between them and it had, contrariwise, strengthened Haldane's loyalty to the Communist Party. Some months later, in May 1942, J.B.S. formally announced that he had become a Party member. "You may have seen," he wrote to Case, "that I have joined those nasty reds." Two years later he joined the Executive Committee.

From this time onwards Haldane's life apparently became increasingly dominated by the demands of Communism and by those of the *Daily Worker* which was allowed to resume publication. He continued to work for the Services. He continued his University College work at Rothamsted, much decreased though it had by this time become owing to the circumstances of war. But a growing amount of his time was now devoted to conferences concerned with the Party or with the *Daily Worker*, to answering the scores of letters which came to him from readers —asking for advice on personal problems, putting up ideas for new weapons, demanding information on heredity or sex. One writer offered to give his £1,000 War Loan interest free to J.B.S. and the Red Dean. The Duke of Bedford wrote about his animals at Woburn, saying: "If we end up with a Communist revolution I shall expect you to see that even if your followers guillotine *me*, they take proper care of the Pere Davide deer and the European Bison." And one reader who asked whether Haldane had really said that his indigestion was cured by reading the *Daily Worker* was told that this was not true. "I said that since I had read Lenin and others who pointed out what was wrong with our society, I had not had gastritis, a complaint which is undoubtedly largely due to worry and anxiety," Haldane replied. "The deaths from gastric ulcer went up quite regularly with air raids in 1940 and 1941. Whether my gastritis went away because I became a Marxist, I am not prepared to say. But I think it quite probable . . . Doubtless other people have recovered from gastritis after psycho-analysis or religious conversion. I see no reason to withdraw my statement."

And as the enemy air raids declined and the enthusiasm for Russia surged up, Haldane became, inevitably, drawn into the long series of British-Soviet rallies. He also joined, equally inevitably, the vociferous demand for a "Second Front Now", that demand for a European landing in 1942 or 1943 that would certainly have meant a bloody repulse for the Allies—and whose consequences might well have enabled the Russians to reach the Channel coast before the end of 1945.

By this time Haldane was pushing himself too hard. Some of his meetings were successful. At others he behaved as he did at a big Anglo-Soviet rally held in a North London super-cinema. Throughout the meeting he kept up a critical running commentary to his neighbour. When he finally spoke he was badly barracked by a disgruntled audience. He either lost his temper or his nerve—probably the former—and walked off the stage.

These things were noticed. One former friend, writing a ten-page letter to him "as a Party duty", complained: "It is bad for the Party that its No. 1 scientist should so behave as to get himself laughed at by those who have no direct dealings with him, and loathed by those who do. It is bad for the Party that a member of its central committee should get the reputation of being always ready to do down or discourage a young worker, that he should publicly humiliate younger men specifically gathered to do him honour, that he should give on public platforms exhibitions of indiscipline, egotism and contempt for his audience."

One reason for such increasingly cantankerous attitudes was over-work—"four days a week on a tiring and dangerous job" as he wrote to one friend, adding: "I can't undertake editorial work at present. It may well be that I should be of more use to humanity in the long run if I did so, and let certain sailors die. But I can't do both." Even his imperturbable acceptance of Communism in theory may have been scratched by reports that filtered out from Eastern Europe of Communism in practice. His physical health, moreover, was now beginning to suffer from the combined pressure of wartime experiments and continuing strain. He wrote to the Admiralty concerning the insurance which they eventually carried for him against his death or disablement, and noted that he now had mechanical injuries to his back, received during the pressure chamber experiments of 1940, and that these caused him some pain; he noted anaesthesia and paraesthesia due to bubble formation, possibly in his conus; loss of memory for recent events; occasional vertigo; exaggerated reflexes indicating pyramidal degeneration, and pain in his frontal sinuses.

However, he was still anxious to see all that he could, and as the war in Europe ended he jumped eagerly at the chance of visiting Moscow with a delegation of British scientists invited by the Russians. The Executive Committee of the Party decided otherwise; he could, he was informed, do more useful work in England.

9

Lysenko: The Inescapable Choice

LIKE a majority of scientists, Haldane was deeply affected by the new relationship between science and the ordinary people which the war brought about. For the first time, science had not only been a major weapon for victory but had been seen to be such by thousands of Servicemen. The physicists had enabled them to pin-point approaching planes before they were visible, and to track down U-boats deep in the Atlantic. The chemists had enabled them to burn out concrete emplacements. And in August 1945, the apocalyptic nature of "the bomb" which had concluded the war with Japan left no doubt that in the counsels of the world science had become the fifth estate. Haldane, who had always felt it a duty to explain science, enthusiastically allowed himself to be swept up in the post-war movement.

Yet it was not only this deep undercurrent of changing public opinion in which he was to find himself involved. The end of the war meant a lifting of the voluntary censorship which had tended to obscure the darker side of the Russian military miracle and of the conditions which made it possible. No one doubted the heroism of the Red Army, but awkward questions began to be asked—about the Russian decision which had left the Warsaw Poles to their fate in the summer of 1944, about the Katyn Forest whose question-marks were to be delicately obscured in the Nuremburg Trials. It was remembered that we had, after all, gone to war "to save poor little Poland", and closer contact with the Russians in the four-power government of Berlin left little doubt as to the chances of implementing that vow. The scientists meanwhile, indignant though they might be at Churchill's banning of visits to Russia by scientists with knowledge of "the bomb", yet became increasingly disturbed at what appeared to be the extraordinary State direction of science by the Russian Government. This was in some ways merely a continuation of the process which had been noted even before the outbreak of war; but the process, whose progress had been blanketed by wartime conditions, was now seen to have crept on apace and to be moving swiftly to a climax.

Haldane was to be poignantly involved in this crisis of his times. His simple loyalty to Communist friends, combined with his continuing belief that beneath the current situation there lay a firm basis of sound Marxist commonsense, led him to defend the indefensible. He was for long supported by the belief that since he was in the minority he must be right. And, having decided that he had been mistaken, he refused "to join in the fashionable chorus of anti-Stalinism because, to quote Shelley [on Napoleon I]:

> "I know that virtue owns a more eternal foe
> Than Force or Fraud: old Custom, legal Crime,
> And bloody faith the foulest birth of time."

The agonising reappraisal that this was to involve lay in the future as J.B.S. moved back to University College at the war's end. First of all, he took a moment from work to regularise his personal affairs. In the spring of 1945 Charlotte had at last divorced him, bringing grounds of desertion in an undefended case. Only the terms of alimony had to be settled, a matter made difficult by the casual offhandedness with which Haldane customarily treated the mundane business of banking accounts, cheque-books and financial affairs in general.

Now he quietly married Helen Spurway—a marriage whose prospects had seemed distinctly uncertain to many mutual friends. In fact, the marriage not only worked but worked well. Had Haldane's aim been high position in the scientific or academic hierarchies the story might have been different; the outspoken views of his new wife, uninhibitedly proclaimed in the broadest of terms, were not endearing to all, and they tended to conceal her extraordinary qualities of bravery and kindness as well as her scientific ability. Yet Haldane had long ago, by instinct and personal inclination, determined to ignore the road that led to Provostships, to Vice-Chancellorships or to any other high administrative post. The pot-boilers could do that, he claimed; as long as he could carry on with his research, publish his papers, tell the world how it should run its business on Communist lines, then so long would he be doing the job that Nature intended. All this Helen Spurway enabled him to do, understanding his work, protectively safeguarding him when necessary, seeing that he did not become too enmeshed in the trivia which would occasionally wrap themselves round him when he played the absent-minded scientist.

Years later, after Haldane's death, one of his students wrote that it would be impossible to write the life of J.B.S. while Helen Spurway was still alive. The remark was revealing and well-meant; yet it showed only a partial and a largely superficial understanding of either Haldane or of Spurway. J.B.S. was not the man to marry a woman who would try to duck the truth. He knew all his future wife's failings long before he married her; and he knew also that her strength lay in a facility for brutal self-criticism if that were necessary. It is true that from the early years of their marriage he began to secure her future, buying for her the Goodwill and Copyright of the *Journal of Genetics* in 1946, and then steadily increasing its already international reputation. It is true that he helped secure for her a Lectureship at University College. It is true that when he contemplated retirement from University College in 1958, he contemplated seeking posts both for himself and for Helen, a decision which would naturally have limited the possibilities. But all this had to be weighed against the constant companionship of a sympathetic co-worker as he carried on at University College, lectured at foreign universities, or responded to the continuous demands for popular articles. Both Haldane and Spurway took a humble and civilised view of human frailty. Both knew the other's stubborn contrariness, and both knew that the other knew. Few marriages can have worked out better —despite the continuing lack of a son.

In 1945 J.B.S. resumed his work in London as University College's Weldon Professor, with Helen as his assistant, and also with a number of his pre-war staff. Hans Kalmus, Hans Grüneberg and Ursula Philip were only three of these who returned and who helped to build up Haldane's department during the next decade. During this period he himself produced a formidable amount of work, ranging across much of genetics and covering such subjects as the formal genetics of man, the rate of evolution, the mutation rate of the human gene, the effects of nuclear explosions on human mutations and the cost of natural selection.

This work was carried out against a background of continuous political dispute, for Haldane by now provided the scientific spearhead of the Communist Party's propaganda. His attitude inevitably became the main debating-point in the Lysenko controversy which split the scientific world. And even after he had retired from this particular issue, leaving, so far as the public was concerned, only an enigmatic smile, his opinions were still regularly thrown into the pool of argument, with the spray not infrequently drenching both sides.

170

Haldane's position *vis-à-vis* the Communist Party, as distinct from his belief in Marxism, is more complicated than is usually supposed. In 1946 he had visited the United States with the Party's approval and had made an impassioned speech to Party members in Madison Square Gardens. He continued his articles in the *Daily Worker,* and he continued to serve on the Party's Executive Committee. However, before the end of 1948, before the Lysenko argument reached its climax. J.B.S. was already threatening to resign from the party. Always happy to carry on a running war with the Establishment, he was, judging by the draft of his resignation letter, just as happy to do the same thing with the body of the Communist kirk. Haldane's draft ran:

Dear Comrades,

It is with deep regret that I must ask you to accept my resignation from the Communist Party. My reasons are as follows. A number of comrades, some of whom have been recommended to me by leading Party members, have, in my opinion, let me down. I give only two examples.

When in New York two years ago I was recommended by the American Party organisation to employ the services of Comrade . . . then of the 'New Masses'. I had a book to dispose of, and agreed to give him a power of attorney to sign a contract on my behalf, the royalties of the book to be given to the *Daily Worker*, apart from some advance royalties. Neither the *Daily Worker* nor I have seen a cent of the money, nor has Comrade Ainley been able to discover . . .'s present address. On the other hand, [he] has signed, on my behalf, a contract with an American firm of publishers which gives them half the royalties from the English edition of this book, and the right to publish my next two books.

Comrade Rust recommended me to employ Messrs. . . . as solicitors, and I understand that at least one of the partners is a Party member. This firm first placed me in default as regards a legal action, and has now, without my written consent, agreed on my behalf to the signature of a deed which, among other things, will make it impossible for me to hand over to the Party or related organisations any of the capital which I may inherit on my mother's death under my late father's will . . .

I do not of course accuse either . . . or . . . of fraud or negligence. I have no doubt for example that . . .'s deal was a perfectly proper one from the point of view of American business morality. Still less do I suggest that Communists are less honest than other people. They are usually more so.

But the result of these and other transactions is that I no longer feel the confidence in other comrades which is essential if I am to remain a member of the Party. Such mutual confidence is not necessary between members of a more loosely knit organisation such as the Labour Party, but it is so within an organisation which may find itself in a revolutionary situation.

I hope to continue with articles for the *Daily Worker*, and shall do so in the immediate future, but I must find out exactly in what situation . . . have left me before I make any definite promise.

I have no intention of publicising my resignation from the Party which is fighting against the American domination of Britain, though of course were I attacked in the Party press or otherwise I should have to state my reasons for resigning. It would, I think, be very much better if it came out at a later date that I had for some time ceased to be a Party member but continued to support the Party's general policy. In particular I do not want to add to the present difficulties of our American Comrades by publicising . . .'s transactions. It is of course inevitable that the Comrades in this College should learn of my resignation, and they will doubtless take such action as seems fit to them. I would add that I have been contemplating this action for some weeks and it was mainly my present wife who dissuaded me from taking it earlier. I would also add that all letters sent to me are opened by my secretary.

I am extremely sorry to have to take this serious step, but I am sure that if I remained in the Party without the feeling of mutual confidence which a Party member should have, I should be unable to fulfil my obligations. Yours fraternally, J.B.S. Haldane.

Whether or not Haldane sent the letter of which this was the draft is not clear. If so, as seems likely, he was eventually talked out of resignation since, in his own words, he finally left the Party because of Stalin's interference with science, an interference soon to be exemplified in the Lysenko dispute.

.   .   .

There were two separate aspects of this classic controversy. Scientifically, what was at issue was the validity of the theories put forward by Trofim Denisovich Lysenko. Politically, the question was whether the Soviet Government did or did not use its crushing power to stifle all criticism of Lysenko's theories and to dismiss or murder those who refused to knuckle under.

The first of these questions is more complex than is popularly supposed—"What on earth do you mean by *the* Lysenko theory?" J.B.S. wrote to a correspondent. "He enunciated about fifteen. Some of them, for example Michurin's theory as to the effect of grafting on hybridisation, have been fully confirmed. Others have not." After Haldane's death one friend wrote that J.B.S. had "never abandoned the thought that there might be something in some of Lysenko's ideas. Nowadays, after transformation and transduction have been appreciated, the possibility seems more likely than it did at the time".

As for the second question, the enormity of the Soviet's actions might have been seen more clearly had the argument not been smudged during the later 1940's by the extravagances of the "Cold War". Interestingly enough, when Haldane's break with the Communists came, it came not over the rightness or wrongness of Lysenko's views but because of the jackboot manner in which Lysenko's opponents were dealt with. But both questions were of course deeply interlocked; Haldane was from the early 1930's increasingly involved in both; and the tangled story is best explained chronologically.

Lysenko's experiments were carried out at one of the research stations in the Ukraine set up by Vavilov, the geneticist whose guest Haldane had been during his visit to Russia in 1928. First, Lysenko had claimed that by treating wheat grains before they germinated, the plants could be induced to mature more quickly —a process which came to be known as vernalisation and which, if practicable, was obviously of immense importance to Russia, whose farmers would be able to cultivate even farther north. "What Lysenko had done was not new but the expectations he based on it were altogether new," Professor Darlington later wrote. "What followed, however, went far beyond these expectations. Each year for the next decade Lysenko enlarged the scope of his published achievements. First, he claimed that many other crops could be similarly improved. Next, he claimed that one treatment would change the race for all time: the acquired characteristics would be inherited. Then, taking a hint from a Russian fruit grower, Michurin, he claimed that he could change the character of all plants by grafting. In this way he could cross species never previously crossed, and the hybrids were fertile; further, by using mixed pollen he could change rye into wheat; and so on. The pace never relaxed. As Lysenko, in deadly earnest, charged forward into his new world, some said it was Soviet Biology while others declared it was just make-believe."

The quick clasping of Lysenko to the Soviet bosom was easily explicable, since the core of his theories could be simplified down to answer one simple question—could certain living organisms pass on to future generations any of the characteristics which they had acquired during their lifetime? Now short-stalked strains of peas, hairy strains of gooseberries pass on their qualities of shortness of hairiness according to Mendelian principles of segregation. A similar pattern applies to human beings, although the human organism is so complex that this fact is frequently concealed. But could characteristics produced not by inheritance but by environment be passed on in the same way? Or did a new generation go back to square one, as far as these were concerned, and start only with the built-in characteristics with which its parents had been endowed at birth? During the eighteenth century Lamarck had claimed that such transmission of acquired characteristics was possible. The theory had wilted with the rediscovery of Mendelism and had apparently died during the first decades of the twentieth century as the mechanics of Mendelian inheritance were discovered. Some exceptions were known—colchicine, for instance, causes hybrids of certain kinds to breed true although they would not otherwise do so—and a few others were suspected. Yet these were rarities, and Lysenko's ideas suggested something very different. His theories did not merely open fresh agricultural possibilities for a country which stretches from the Arctic to within a few hundred miles of the Tropic of Cancer. Lysenko implied that all life, including *Homo sapiens*, might be susceptible to heritable conditioning. Men might not be born biologically equal, the small fact which invalidated much Soviet theory. But, given sufficient control, surely they might be bred equal? Even if this were not feasible, the possibility of "tailoring" the human race to desired requirements was, barring a better word, a godsend to the Russians and one of immense political and social significance to the régime.

Little wonder that Lysenko was encouraged; that Vavilov, the exponent of classical genetics, came increasingly under a cloud of Government displeasure!

Haldane was sceptical of the reports of this change that began to seep out from Russia during the 1930's. He was not entirely uncritical of the work which Lysenko was publishing—although as far as Haldane was concerned it had the virtue of being unorthodox. Yet his attitude to reports of the official Soviet atti-

174

tude were very different. In the welter of lies and misrepresentation which the ideological conflict in Spain soon stirred up on both sides there was, it is true, some difficulty in making any objective assessment of news from, or about, Russia; even so, it is difficult not to see a rather casual attitude in one of Haldane's first comments on the impending struggle, made in *Nature* which had reported recent attacks by Lysenko on Vavilov. "If the attacks have led to a curtailment of Vavilov's work, the situation of genetics in the Soviet Union is indeed serious," he wrote. "If not, hard words break no bones, and the outlook for genetics in Moscow is at any rate no worse than in London, where I understand that the only department of genetics in the University of London is shortly to come to an end."

There was some reason for Haldane's caution in accepting all the tales of what was happening in Russia. In the summer of 1937 he had received a letter from Vavilov, and other Russian professors, denying that either Vavilov himself or one of the other signatories had been arrested, as reported. And as late as June 7th 1939 Vavilov had himself cordially accepted Haldane's request to write an article for *The Modern Quarterly*.

The position was to be radically changed late in July 1939, less than a month before the Soviet-German pact set the stage for war. Vavilov now wrote to England formally and suddenly saying that the Russians would not be able to take part as planned in the Seventh International Congress of Genetics to be held in Edinburgh the following month—a Congress to which he had already been elected President. But at the same time he wrote another, and totally different letter of explanation to one of his friends in Scotland. Haldane received a confidential copy of this second letter. And from now onwards it must have been increasingly difficult for him to believe that Vavilov was not acting under duress.

This was the position as war broke out—with the shadows no doubt lengthening over Vavilov and his genuine defenders handicapped by the passionate exaggerations produced by the Spanish War in which everything to do with either side was either jet-black or snow-white. This human reluctance to look at the facts impartially tended, during the next few years, further to obscure the growing insecurity of science in Russia. At first it was too easy to over-state the case against the country which together with Hitler's troops had made a meal of Poland —just as, a year or so later, it became fashionable to ignore any murders committed by our Russian allies.

The wartime skirmishing which preceded the Lysenko crisis

itself was opened by a letter to *Nature* from A. V. Hill. "Russian geneticists," Hill wrote, "are torn by faction about the application of dialectical materialism to genetics." He added that while solid achievements had no doubt been made by Russian scientists, "it would be easier . . . to recognise it and give it credit if it were not overlaid by fraud and propaganda". This brought Haldane out of his corner—even before he was asked by the Communists whether he was replying to Hill's letter. Vavilov, he agreed, had been attacked because his theories were unduly mechanistic. So, of course, had his father, John Scott Haldane; but his father had not been sacked and neither had Vavilov "up to September 1st of last year" (1939). In any case, Haldane added, if criticism went on they would end up by being at war with Russia—"a new argument for hushing up the evils in the Soviet Union", as Michael Polanyi put it as the argument opened out during the next few weeks. Hill quietly noted that a resolution adopted by the Astronomy section of the Academy of Sciences had started by saying that: "Modern bourgeois cosmogony is in a state of deep ideological confusion resulting from its refusal to accept the only true dialectic-materialistic concept, namely the infinity of the universe with respect to space as well as time . . ." A *cause célèbre* was refurbished by asking, yet again, whether Peter Kapitza, who had returned to Russia from Rutherford's Cavendish Laboratory in 1934 had or had not been kidnapped, and a good many similar red herrings were drawn across the argument. Finally, J. D. Bernal produced a letter explaining why the detractors disliked Soviet science. "Science in the Soviet Union means something different from what it means in this country," he said. "There it is an integral part of social life and neither an elegant pastime nor a cheap source of profit. The real basis of objection is that in the Soviet Union science is organised as a part of the productive scheme and that this organisation is conscious and in accord with the philosophy of dialectical materialism." This was, of course, just what Hill and others had been objecting to—that the organisation of Russian science was consciously "in accord with the philosophy of dialectical materialism". Science, they argued, should be organised in accord with the philosophy of science.

The debate continued sporadically throughout the war, with Haldane quick to ward off attacks or, where defence was impossible, as quick to draw a suitable red herring across the trail. His attitude to the political issue was far less flexible than his reaction to the scientific problem that Lysenko and his theories raised, and this first issue taxed all his ingenuity. In 1941, for instance, Hill wrote of science in Russia as well as in Germany, "bolstering up theories which the official philosophy of the State prescribes". Haldane found it impossible to deny this; on the other hand, he insisted that "the fields of scientific research in Great Britain are to a considerable extent determined by the wishes of rich men and women", and that there was no chair of genetics in England which gave scope for experimental work, "because no rich person has endowed one". He was very apt at this kind of riposte. When, years later, it became impossible to deny any longer that Vavilov had been sent to his death in Siberia, Haldane attempted to qualify this, claiming in a letter to Bertrand Russell that a closely parallel case was that of Sir Victor Horsley, the eminent brain surgeon who had died in the Middle East in 1916. According to Haldane, the trouble here was that Horsley had "protested against treating cases of skull fracture with brandy. The case against those who sent him there would, in the long run, be weakened by stating that he died in the Tropics".

Had the argument of Haldane and his Communist colleagues been that subordination of science to the State was a temporary if necessary outcome of the anguished times through which mankind was passing, it is conceivable that they might have won more support; it is certain they would have won more respect. As it was, many scientists agreed with the reviewer of Haldane's *Science Advances* who wrote in *Nature* shortly after the war that it was difficult to believe the author to be "really concerned first and foremost with that task of explaining science to the public which he believes is the responsibility of men of science in a democracy. His first concern is not to advance science but to advance Communism, and one suspects that Communism and not science should be the title word". It was time, the reviewer went on, "that protest was made against the view that subjective exposition can advance the cause of science, and Professor Haldane's carelessness in this respect may well alienate the support of those whose help is badly needed". Such pleas had, of course, the opposite effect. The more that authority, in the shape of A. V. Hill, *Nature*, the Royal Society *et al*, claimed that Haldane was suborning the scientific facts to suit his purpose, the more it became personally necessary for him to continue the process. Nothing would have stopped him—except, perhaps, a pat on the back.

On the purely scientific issue, however, he continued to remain more cautious. His attitude is shown by a letter to Lysenko himself which he wrote in January 1945, after the Russian had referred to Haldane's *New Paths in Genetics* and had sent J.B.S. a copy of his own *Heredity and its Variability*. "I should like to add that the book of mine to which you refer so kindly was written in 1941," said Haldane, "and that as a result, if I wrote it again today, I should modify my views in several respects, perhaps bringing them nearer your own." However, this was not all. "Unfortunately," J.B.S. went on, "it is extremely difficult in this country to obtain accounts of the actual experimental results on which your views on genetics are based, and I should be very grateful if you could obtain some reprints giving accounts of the facts in question, as well as the general conclusions based on these facts." In this last sentence Haldane was striking, as he must himself have realised, at the very Achilles' heel of Lysenko's work. Where were the experimental data on which the theories were based? Could they be checked? Could they be repeated? These were the questions which were to be asked continually during the next few years.

In spite of the lack of answers, in spite of the dogmatic assertion of Soviet control of science which became increasingly apparent during the immediate post-war years, it is possible to claim that thus far Haldane was merely giving Lysenko and his supporters the benefit of the doubt, happily doing so since most of their detractors formed part of the British scientific establishment; to claim that those who were most sceptical of Lysenko's alleged achievements were influenced, if perhaps unconsciously, by their detestation of the totalitarian system which appeared by this time to have sent Vavilov to his death. As *Discovery* aptly put it, "Outside the U.S.S.R., judgements on the controversy were often coloured as much by political convictions as by consideration of the scientific facts."

The situation altered dramatically in the summer of 1948. At a meeting of the Praesidium of the U.S.S.R. Academy of Sciences held on August 26th, twelve resolutions were passed which abolished existing laboratories, called for the removal from Scientists Councils of those who supported "Morgano-Weismannite genetics", and for the popularisation of a "critical exposure of the pseudo-scientific Morgano-Weismannite tendency". A pledge was given to "root out unpatriotic, idealist, Weismannite-Morganist ideology", and it was further claimed that "Michurin's materialist direction in biology is the only acceptable form of science, because it is based on dialectical materialism and on the principle of changing Nature for the benefit of the people".

Here, in tragic detail, was the mirror-image of Hitler's blessing of the Nazis' racial theories; mumbo-jumbo was to be transformed into science by a wave of Stalin's magic wand. As Julian Huxley put it at the time, the announcements "demonstrate that science is no longer regarded in the U.S.S.R. as an international activity of free workers whose prime interest it is to discover new truth and new facts, but as an activity subordinated to a particular ideology and designed only to secure practical results in the interests of a particular national and political system".

What did Haldane do? Contrary to popular opinion, he did not jump to Lysenko's defence. He suggested, in the *New Statesman*, that he wanted to read the original documents in translation, and a Communist Party official who told him that "an abridged English translation of the key parts of the discussion" was being made, received a brusque reply. "An abridged translation will be of very slight value," Haldane wrote to him, "and I personally refuse to commit myself till I have the *whole* thing. I regard it as a matter of great political importance, and have already seen Emile Burns about it. I have been promised a German translation, but have no great confidence in the promise. If we can get a full translation I can and will move in the matter. If not I must refuse. Will you please try to get it done somehow?"

To those with any experience of Haldane it must have been clear that he was digging his heels in. They should have been warned.

From now onwards Haldane's actions began to be governed less by what was expedient for the Party and more by what he felt was right in any particular circumstances. It is true that when he asked whether he was to resign from the Soviet Academy of Sciences, like Sir Henry Dale, President of the Royal Society, he replied "Certainly not. It would have been more scientific if Sir Henry had waited until a translation of Lysenko's work was published in London". It is true that when he wrote an article on "Where I disagree with Lysenko" for the *Daily Worker*, he similarly dodged the issue by referring purely to the biological issue and not to the intrinsically more important political issue which concerned the freedom of science. Yet he also wrote in "Biology and Marxism", a lengthy article for the *Modern Quarterly*, that he had found "that the principles formulated by Mendel, and by Morgan and his school, work in a variety of organisms". Furthermore, he went on: "Some Marxists have reacted too strongly against the application of biological notions to mankind, and assumed that all differences between human beings are due to differences of environment . . . But we know in practice, and should, I think, admit more fully in theory, that different people have very different abilities, that some are capable of making greater contributions to society than others, and that this would be true had they had equal opportunities." This might be commonsense but it was also the stuff of heresy.

In these circumstances, which developed in the autumn of 1948, Haldane began to show his characteristic quality of not giving a damn for anybody. In doing so he contrived to get the worst of both worlds. To his Communist colleagues he was in perilous danger of back-sliding, and from now onwards began to be regarded with caution. To the rest of the world he was still the Communist apologist, defending the indefensible and, in the process, betraying those objective standards which most non-Party scientists did their best to uphold. It is certainly true that J.B.S., pushed back against the ropes by the overwhelming majority of his fellow-scientists, refused publicly to admit his error and turn upon his former colleagues.

His loyalty was stretched, and no more so than during the symposium organised by the B.B.C. on the evening of November 28th. The speakers were Dr. S. C. Harland, Director of the Institute of Cotton Genetics in Peru; Cyril Darlington, by now Director of John Innes; R. A. Fisher, by now Arthur Balfour Professor of Genetics at Cambridge; and Haldane himself. An extraordinary, if generally unappreciated, piquancy was added to the situation by the fact that Haldane had a decade or so earlier come successfully to Harland's aid in an important Court case, and that both Darlington and Fisher now occupied posts which Haldane himself would dearly have liked to occupy. However, it was not this which—in the words of John Langdon-Davies who used the broadcast as the main illustration of his "Russia Puts the Clock Back"—induced the B.B.C. to take "special precautions against possible murder by having each of the four conspirators record their contributions under circumstances which insured against their meeting on the stairs". Passions had been brought to boiling point by the straight issue of State control over scientific thought.

The broadcast was in some ways an astonishing affair. Haldane knew that he was virtually defenceless. He already had the gravest doubts about the propriety of the particular cause he was defending. But he distrusted the uses to which his opponents would put any victory they might achieve. And he therefore continued to fight a defensive action in which one can hear echoes of the legal attitude rubbed off on to him from his uncle, and of his stubborn Scottish reluctance to admit defeat. He returned, time and again, to the 500-page report; he dodged about the scientific issue, and he skilfully evaded the main issue of scientific freedom. As Chesterton wrote, it is always a fine sight to see one man fighting against five, and one man fighting against three has something of the same quality. Haldane did his best—and the fact that he was immediately stigmatised as the outright defender of Lysenko worried him not at all.

The protests of the comrades worried him almost as little. For while the rest of the world seized upon the main burden of Haldane's broadcast, the Party members seized upon its qualifications. The *Daily Worker* report of the broadcast was easily read as suggesting that Haldane had, in fact, come out in unqualified support of Lysenko. Shortly afterwards a meeting of Communist geneticists was called, and at this it was explained to Haldane that a typographical error was the source of the *Worker*'s misrepresentation. There was considerable discussion of the line which should be taken, and J.B.S. pointed out that this was an opportunity for British Communists to be sympathetic but also independent and critical. This would show that they were not bound to follow the Moscow line—a proposal which illustrates the gulf which was now widening between J. B. S. Haldane the scientist and J. B. S. Haldane the dedicated Party member. This cautious and scientifically valuable proposal was brushed aside. Shortly afterwards Haldane, still Chairman of the Editorial Board of the *Daily Worker,* learned that an "Educational Commentary" on the subject—one of whose essential points he later described as "utterly untrue"—was to be issued by the paper. Many men would have resigned from the Board. Haldane wrote a reply to the Commentary, attacking it point by point, then had the reply cyclostyled and circulated.

Many top members of the Party realised by this time that however many efforts were made to justify the takeover of science by politics, the controversy was doing the Communists as a body considerable harm. A meeting of the Engels Society, which was used as a platform for the theoretical discussion of science, was therefore arranged. It was attended by Bernal, Haldane and about thirty or forty others, and it was apparently before this meeting that Haldane received a paper which was to be read. This contained, he wrote, "such a fantastically inaccurate set of statements concerning genetics that it can have no effect but to produce a row of the worst sort . . . We geneticists are not going to stand an indefinitely frequent repetition of these slanders against us . . . The first duty of Communist scientists in this country is to make data available on which Michurinism can be examined. This has not been done. The second is to examine these data, and to examine them critically. I certainly cannot support a resolution which calls for us to examine our own work critically, and not that of others. Nor can I support a statement that the Michurinist criticisms are based on dialectical materialism. Some are. In my opinion others are not. If ......'s paper is taken as 'Michurinist criticisms', it is clear that they are largely based on ignorance."

The meeting of the society was a curious affair and was opened by a biologist who read a prepared statement in favour of the Lysenko position. "It was agreed," according to one of those present, "that Haldane would reply. Before the old man could rise to his feet, someone whom none of us had ever seen before got up and began to explain elementary genetics to the boys. He appeared to be under a complete misapprehension as to the nature of the meeting, and obviously thought we were all convinced Michurinists in support of the Party line, which he believed to be wrong. We were all waiting to hear Haldane, and tried to shout him down. Eventually he sat down, protesting that he would take the matter up with higher quarters. Then Haldane got up and attacked the first speaker. Other people spoke and tempers ran quite high, but the position wasn't yet formalised. At the end of the meeting, Bernal made a soothing statement and intimated there would be further discussion."

The controversy was by this time having an increasingly divisive effect on the Party. At one end of the spectrum there were those members who still appeared to follow the Party line in humble obedience; at the other were members who resigned, deeply disillusioned. In between, Haldane stubbornly held on, insisting that he was still a good Marxist and, by implication, causing a great deal of trouble. One prominent Party member had by this time collected a minor dossier on Haldane and at a meeting of the Engels Society produced it to support an extraordinary theory: that Mendelism and the Nazi race theory had the same origin and that this explained why Haldane and other Party geneticists had failed to attack the Nazi theories with sufficient energy. Haldane was not present at this meeting. This, one must assume, was lucky for the Party member.

Any doubt about Haldane's attitude was ended by his "In Defence of Genetics", published in the *Modern Quarterly* in 1949. "It is of the utmost importance that biologists in this country should be able to appreciate both the positive and the negative elements in the views put forward by Lysenko and his supporters in the Soviet Union," this began. "Unfortunately, this has been made much more difficult by ill-informed criticism of genetics by supporters of Lysenko in this country." He took as his text, he said, the *Daily Worker*'s original Educational Commentary on Lysenko and he treated it as a kindly adult might treat a child's first steps in genetics. "I am," he said, nailing his colours to the mast, "a Mendelist-Morganist." He was sceptical of the claims that in general "acquired characters are inherited", and while he kept an open mind about some aspects of Lysenko's work and praised yet others, he left readers in no doubt of his position. "I believe that wholly unjustifiable attacks have been made on my profession, and one of the most important lessons which I have learned as a Marxist is the duty of supporting my fellow workers," he concluded. "We are not infallible, but we certainly do not hold many of the opinions which are attributed to us."

His attitude was underlined in a letter which he wrote later in the year to Dr. Lewis, *Modern Quarterly*'s editor who had sent him a manuscript. Publication, J.B.S. wrote, "would undoubtedly be an advantage to the supporters of Lysenko. But it would hardly improve the reputation of the *Modern Quarterly*."

At the time, the political and the biological issues of "Lysenko-ism" appeared inextricably intertwined. Years later, in February 1964, Haldane summed up the position rather differently, with what even the most committed might admit was considerable impartiality. "I am often asked what I think about Lysenko," he said. "In my opinion, Lysenko is a very fine biologist and some of his ideas are right. Curiously enough, they are much more often right for bacteria, in my opinion, than they are for larger organisms such as animals and plants with which we are familiar. But again, in my opinion, some of Lysenko's ideas are wrong and badly wrong, as, of course, some of mine or any other biologist may well prove to be. And I think it was extremely unfortunate both for Soviet agriculture and Soviet biology that he was given the powers that he got under Stalin, and that he used to suppress a lot of what I believe, and what most geneticists believe, to be valuable work, much of which has been started up again but with a considerable lag."

By the end of 1949, Haldane's disgruntlement with Lysenko-ism was beginning to show through. But it was not the only thing to which he objected in the Communist sphere. His position can be inferred from a letter written by the editor of the

Daily Worker, Bill Rust, excusing the action of one of his staff. "I can hardly call this Comrade a mental defective," he protested, "unless you will tell me what is wrong with the paragraph." There was a long line of grievances which was still being added to, and Haldane now began to use these in a process of disengagement from the Party. He still remained loyal to what he considered to be its principles. He still wished, as he had put it in his draft resignation letter a year or so earlier, to support its general policies. But it becomes clear from his correspondence that he now found himself increasingly placed in positions where to speak out would be disloyal and to remain silent would be to give his name to what he knew to be wrong. He intended to get out, but he intended to do so decently.

On March 16th he wrote to the new editor of the *Daily Worker*, John Campbell, complaining that his article in the previous Monday's issue—dealing with the trial of Cardinal Mindszenty under the title: "Should They Be Above the Law?" —had been altered without his consent. There had, he said, been previous occasions—"for example when an article on streptomycin was headed 'A cure for tuberculosis'"—but he had been promised that it would not happen again. "During the past few months a number of statements have been made in Party organs with which I am in disagreement," he continued. "As a Party member I have refrained from public criticism of them. But my position becomes completely impossible if my articles are to be altered without my consent. If I thought that you have been aware of the promise made to me, I should have no option but to resign my Party membership in order to be at full liberty to defend myself were such alterations made on matters which seem important to me, as they have been in the past . . . Were the articles anonymous the matter would be different. But I am not prepared on the one hand to admit to authorship of altered or curtailed articles, or on the other to attack the *Daily Worker* so long as I am a member of the Communist Party." His conclusion, "May I ask for an early reply" was very nearly a threat. Haldane had his reply, almost by return, but it is doubtful if he was satisfied with it. "With regard to Gallacher," he was told, "it is true that he has taken no oath of allegiance to Stalin, but he has a general allegiance to international Communism and this paragraph in question might be interpreted as meaning that we were denying it." And the second paragraph had been cut out because Campbell felt that it was contradictory to the general argument.

Haldane soldiered on. But the news of his attitude outlined

in the *Modern Quarterly* quickly spread. Had he been anyone other than Haldane, he would have been questioned more fiercely and sooner. Even so, more than one obedient *Worker* reader was beginning to have doubts about Comrade Haldane, and by December, J.B.S. felt constrained to write to Campbell pointing out: "From the two letters which I have received in the last week it is clear that I no longer enjoy the confidence of an important section of our readers. I am therefore no longer the right person to be Chairman of the Editorial Board, and I must ask you to put my resignation in its hands at the next meeting." There then followed the nub of his argument with the Communists. "It may well be that my opinions are incorrect," he wrote, "but I cannot change them unless arguments against them are produced. If there is general agreement that my proper function is not to try to refute false views on scientific grounds, but to explain the political and economic grounds on which people hold them, then someone else can do it better. If on the other hand it is still considered that the *Daily Worker* is a suitable place in which to describe the results of scientific work, I hope to continue to do so."

Off the Board, he continued his regular contributions. At least, he continued for six months. Then, in a way that only Haldane could have managed, he broke this link since, as he put it, "it becomes increasingly clear that my articles do not satisfy a number of readers". He pleaded increasing age plus decreasing energy and time, said that he would continue for another month and hoped to continue with the occasional article. Campbell pleaded for an article a month—but was successfully evaded or refused. Haldane's last article for the *Daily Worker*—"They Want to Sterilise the Poor"—appeared on August 9th 1950.

J.B.S. remained a convinced Marxist; but the marriage with the Party was over. Three months later it was widely reported that he had resigned from it. He was taking no part in the preliminary work for the World Peace Congress which was to be held at Sheffield; his name no longer appeared as a member of the *Daily Worker*'s Editorial Board; he was no longer contributing his regular articles. Haldane refused to comment. Instead he issued, through the *Daily Worker*, a statement that was a masterpiece of evasion.

"Professor Haldane considers that a very bad precedent would be established if university teachers were expected to state their membership or otherwise of political organisations when requested to do so by newspapers," this said. "He also considers that, when suffering from a broken leg (Pott's fracture of malleolus) he was under no obligation to ascend the staircase to answer a telephone call from a newspaper (the *Sunday Pictorial*) which refused to state the subject under discussion. He has not read the various statements made about him in newspapers and leaves it to their readers to speculate as to their truth or otherwise.

"For the guidance of such readers, he remarks that in view of the experience of 1914-18 and 1939-45, he regards the rearmament of Germany as a suicidal policy for Britain and that, as a doubtless old-fashioned believer in such notions as honour, he regards the wholesale massacre of civilians, whether by atom bomb or otherwise, as unworthy of a civilised people.

"In this respect he is in full agreement with the policy of the Communist Party."

Haldane kept what he would have been shocked to hear described as a stiff upper lip. The Cold War was at its height. Any stick was good enough to beat the Russians with, and his publicly announced defection from the Party would have made juicy anti-Communist propaganda. Instead, as he had proposed in his draft letter of resignation some while earlier, he remained silent.

After the death of Stalin Haldane commented, of a report that he had resigned because "he could not reconcile himself to the dogma of the infallibility of authorities outside the field of science in solving the problems of science", that the report was "not entirely correct". He later wrote to a colleague in the U.S. that "Lysenko was too dogmatic about his own results, and above all Stalin interfered unjustifiably with research as he did with other matters". And in 1963 he commented in a letter to a friend that he had resigned from the Party about fifteen years earlier, "because of Stalin's interference with science". Even so, his attitude both to Communism and to Stalin remained ambivalent. When he was asked by the Czechs in April 1952 for his "opinions on the bacteriological war unleashed against the people of North Korea", he replied that he preferred "to await the report of qualified bacteriologists and entomologists". Yet a year later he added his signature to a message of condolence on Stalin's death.

.   .   .

Haldane's links with the Communists had repercussions on two aspects of his life. One concerned his continuing work for the Services, the other his reaction to "the bomb". The Service

186

authorities had tended to look on his political views as a mere eccentricity while the Russians were engaging the main bulk of the German armies, but these became something different as the alarms and excursions of the Cold War increased. In March 1948, when the general question of Communists having access to official secrets was raised in the House of Commons, Haldane's reaction was open and truculent.

"I certainly am a Communist—as good a Communist as anyone," he said on March 15th 1948. "I am working on two Government scientific committees, one of which deals with under-water physiology. They don't pay me anything and they can throw me off them if they want to. But if they'd thrown me off six months ago, they might not have had certain increased efficiency in under-water craft. They can go on sacking people, but the only result will be that all sorts of people will be denounced as Communists when they are not. If I got orders from Moscow I would leave the Communist party forthwith. But sometimes I wish we did get orders from Moscow. I would like to know what they are thinking. The only group of people in this country who get orders from foreign powers are Roman Catholics."

This, as Haldane may well have suspected, poured oil on the fire, and the following month Sir Waldron Smithers wanted to know whether Haldane was, or was not, as he claimed, working on two Government scientific committees. By what was a lucky chance for the Government, both the committees came under the aegis of the Medical Research Council even though at least one was directly concerned with Service work for the Admiralty. Mr. Attlee was therefore able to allay fears that Communists might here be getting access to Service secrets. Professor Haldane, he replied, was working on two scientific committees of the Medical Research Council.

Here matters rested for two years. Then the strains which had been taken by the Admiralty in time of war, first under Chamberlain's government and then Churchill's, became too much for it in time of peace under Attlee's. On June 2nd 1950, Haldane received a letter from the Medical Research Council. The Board of Admiralty, Haldane was told, fully appreciated the services which he had given them in the past. But they now felt unable to pass on the information needed by the Underwater Physiology Sub-Committee of the R.N. Personnel Research Committee while Haldane remained a member. The only course, it was regretted, was for Haldane to cease to be a member.

Two years earlier, Mr. Attlee had been asked in the House to give an assurance that when anyone's reliability was in doubt the person concerned would be told the charge made against him and would be given an opportunity to answer it. "Yes, certainly," he replied, an answer that must have echoed strangely in Haldane's ears as he read what was, in practice, his dismissal.

Since his case had already been raised in the Commons it must have rankled that it should now be settled in secret. However, he accepted the official decision in a dignified letter which he wrote on July 19th.

"I have little doubt," this said, "that the Board of Admiralty has been misinformed concerning me. It is a fact that I disapprove of some aspects of the foreign policy of His Majesty's present Government, and make no attempt to hide this disapproval. If the Board has any other reason to suppose that I would divulge secret information imparted to me, I should be interested to learn it. The reasons which, as I suspect, they would give, would merely disclose the inaccuracy of the information on which their decision was made.

"I have, in the past, been particularly scrupulous in keeping my mouth shut on such matters, both as a matter of honour, and in my own interests. Other persons, of different political views to my own, have been far less so. If the Board of Admiralty desire it, which I doubt, I should be willing to describe three cases in which information which does not concern me, in one case as to radar, in two as to the utilisation of nuclear energy, was communicated to me before it reached the general public. In each case, I, at any rate, did not pass this information to others.

"In my own interests I do not ask the Board of Admiralty to reconsider their decision. But in the public interest they might well be better informed as to the probable sources of leakage."

When the Sub-committee met the following month all its members regretted Haldane's absence, although they felt it better that their feelings should not go on official record. Haldane, acknowledging this information, said that he was quite glad of the development since he did not like having information which he could not discuss freely. "I am only sorry," he added, "because I might perhaps have been instrumental in saving a few lives." Haldane no doubt put it all down to the Americans. He may well have been right.

So far as the atomic bomb was concerned, Haldane's attitude

had one similarity with his attitude to the Lysenko affair—it was split into political and scientific compartments and the first was a good deal less objective than the second. His initial reaction, pronounced in the columns of the *Daily Worker*, was: "To sum up, I welcome the atomic bomb." Soon afterwards, when it was realised that the Americans would have a monopoly of the weapon for some years, he believed that it would be a danger to peace until the Russians had it also. While by 1955 he had so far forgotten his welcoming of the bomb on Hiroshima that he could write: "I have received several invitations to visit Harwell in recent months, and refused them with some rancour, as I hope that, had I been a German, I should have refused invitations to visit Auschwitz or Belsen in 1942. I take the view that the mass killing of civilians is murder, whether it is done with gas chambers or atomic bombs."

By 1955 Haldane had finally split with the Communists, and the view that the morality of the bomb lies in the judgement of the user. On the purely scientific issue he never supported the more sensational statements of the genetic damage that would be caused by fall-out—"I am aware that . . . the probable genetic effect of atomic bombs has been considerably exaggerated," he wrote to a member of the M.R.C.'s Protection Committee on which he also served. When he gave grounds for suggesting that explosions up to the end of 1955 would cause about 30,000 deaths in India, he pointed out that this would be spread over "some thousand years". In a debate with Cockroft in the columns of *Nature* he suggested that Cockroft's estimate of the danger was too slight, but he suggested also that Linus Pauling's and Lord Russell's were too great. He did not scream about the bomb; his estimates of what nuclear fission might mean in terms of human mutation and the deaths of those still unborn carry all the more weight because of the fact.

Haldane realised that one by-product of the wartime work on nuclear fission was the creation of a new experimental tool. He himself might well have used this for genetical research but for a situation that could have developed only with Haldane. In the summer of 1946 it was proposed that he should carry out work for the M.R.C. which involved radiation protection and was of industrial and medical, as well as of Service, interest. Would he please, it was asked, sign a declaration that he had read the Official Secrets Act? Haldane's reply might have been forecast. He had worked on the most secret work throughout the war and he had at no time signed any such declaration. "I repeatedly requested to be shown the form in question during the war," he replied, "and was as repeatedly refused. With regard to my signing such a document now, I should first want a specific assurance in writing that no work on the genetic effects of radiation which I am to direct shall be deemed to be secret within the meaning of the Act."

This hurdle was cleared. Haldane would not have to sign the form. He then insisted that all rabbits to be used in the experiments should be available to him and his staff "without let or hindrance". This would be possible, it was suggested, by using thirty acres of ground—at Harwell but outside the restricted area. Haldane also insisted that all results should be freely published—and was assured that this would be so. However, he further insisted that neither he nor any of the staff involved in his work should be asked, in any way, to observe the Official Secrets Act. Here was a stumbling block. For while Haldane was free of the Act, and while his juniors would mainly work outside the compound, their laboratory space would be inside it; they would thereupon, inevitably, come within the scope of the Act. Haldane dug in his heels; his full participation in the scheme fell through.

CHAPTER

IO

"The Cuddly Cactus"

THE fact that Haldane was enmeshed at the heart of the
Lysenko controversy in the years which followed the war,
helped to turn him into one of the best-known—if notorious is
not a more accurate word—of the professors who worked in
University College. His fame as the geneticist who could be
relied upon to make the devastating comment, who was heartily
disliked by some of his colleagues and students and equally
loved by others, did not stem entirely from this, or from his
Daily Worker articles. He himself attracted attention since
time, instead of softening the points on which he differed from
the ordinary run of people, had tended to raise them into rugo-
sities. If he had always been outspoken he now became more so,
a living example of how to lose friends and influence people. If
he had always been ambivalent over money, this ambivalence
had now expanded into a meanness about small matters and a
generosity about large ones; he would fumble in his pockets
at tea-time until someone else paid for his penny bun but would
think nothing of paying a student's air fare to a scientific conference. And if he had always earned a reputation for casual
untidiness, this had now grown into a subject which genuinely
pained many of the staff at University College.

He was generous with his time and his experience to any
who he felt might make use of it, and became an Honorary
Member of the Cave Diving Group only on condition that the
Group would ask his advice when they needed it. They did so
on more than one occasion, and led Haldane to write a revealing letter after a fatal accident had taken place. "I am sure that
you are feeling that you neglected something or other," he wrote
to one of those involved. "If so, cut it out. One cannot possibly
think of all the things which might go wrong. If one tried to,
one would never get anything done. And one might always be
killed by a fall of roof . . . No doubt one or two people will
stop diving in consequence of the accident. One can only say
that if they thought it was as safe as bus travel they were some-

what unrealistic. On the other hand, it should be possible to make it as safe as rock-climbing . . . But allow an outsider to say that you have nothing to blame yourself for, except for undertaking a job which is bound to be dangerous, and if nobody did that, we should not get very far in any direction."

It was against a background of such work that J.B.S., Weldon Professor for a decade, worked on in London. His Biometry Department was still housed within the Department of Zoology, the head of which, Professor D. M. S. Watson, was succeeded in 1951 by Professor Peter Medawar. Haldane had managed to get on well with Watson and he and Medawar now became equally good friends who enjoyed each other's company. Due to Haldane's wartime injuries, which caused him regular and severe pain, a deckchair had replaced the armchair which had once stood island-like among the sea of papers in his room. Around it there lapped the waves of reports and articles and theses, their significance known only to Helen, by now his strong right arm in the daily business of work. Providing a secretary for such a man was a difficult task, and legend claims that at one period six left in tears in as many weeks. Yet when a girl could be found whose mind chimed in with his, the loyalty created was deep and lasting. The trouble was not his variability—the day's fortunes could be forecast when the secretary, putting her head round the door was greeted either by a "Good morning, Miss . . .", or by a hardly perceptible raising of the head and a "Ough!"—but his occasional failure to appreciate how other humans react. Thus on one occasion, told that the library did not have a book he required, he countered by: "We'll go along and see. I bet you £50 you're wrong." It was J.B.S. who was wrong—and who thereupon sat down and wrote a cheque for £50, insisting on acceptance until the girl collapsed in tears.

To junior colleagues he was almost unfailingly helpful. One had a particular problem which arose while he was working by day and Haldane mainly at night. The morning after he had mentioned the matter to Haldane he found on his desk three sheets of paper to which was attached a note from J.B.S. saying: "Here's a solution to your problem." The following morning he arrived to find a single sheet with an attached note saying: "Here's a better solution." The third morning he found a sheet of paper with a single equation on it and a note which said: "Here's a still better solution, and in future don't ask so many damned questions."

During the post-war years, Haldane produced a great deal of important work—"I have to do more and more as I grow older,

J.B.S. with three of the four members of the International Brigade who
worked with him on the *Thetis* investigation, George Ives, Patrick Duff and
Donald Renton

J.B.S. and his first wife, Charlotte

J.B.S. at an international conference, 1948

J.B.S. at the Indian Statistical Institute, Calcutta

J.B.S. at Bhubaneswar, 1963

J.B.S., a few weeks before his death, at Bhubaneswar with the members of his research team, Shastri, Hari, Suresh Jayakar and Helen Spurway

not less and less," he commented to his sister. This work was, even for Haldane, of an extraordinary variety. On one level he worked out a mutation rate for the gene for haemophilia, and its segregation ratios in males and females, as well as a more accurate estimate of the linkage between the genes for colour-blindness and haemophilia. He provided material for the quantitative measurement of rates of evolution and for the mutation rate of human genes, and he dealt with a number of the complex mathematical problems involved in such work. Yet this dogged pushing back of the frontiers of knowledge can be compared with broad surveys such as his Croonian Lecture to the Royal Society on the formal genetics of man, outlining the aim of human genetics as the building up of an anatomy and physiology of the human nucleus which might give mankind "the same powers for good or evil . . . as the knowledge of the atomic nucleus has given us over parts of the external world". In the United States he ranged at the Princeton Centennial over "Human Evolution: Past and Future"; and in Oxford he gave the Herbert Spencer lecture. He could hardly spare the time for its preparation "but in view of the totally anti-Herbert Spencer attitude of most of the lectures, I think I should . . ." he wrote to his sister. He rejected the idea of speaking on the philosopher's economic and political ideas since he would, he said, "have to choose Marx and Spencer as my title, which could have been misunderstood".

He wrote during these years on disease and evolution, on the mathematics of biology, on the origins of language, on the mechanical chess player. When his subject did not restrain him to scientific detail he utilised both his love of the classics and his accumulation of unexpected knowledge to illuminate, illustrate, point up his arguments, and it is typical that a paper on "Animal Ritual and Human Language" should be prefaced by a quotation from Dante's *Purgatorio*. In 1952 he received the Royal Society's Darwin Medal from Dr., later Lord, Adrian, who spoke feelingly of how "the conclusions derived from his research have permeated practically every field of evolutionary discussion [while] his ideas have fundamentally altered our knowledge of evolutionary change".

Later in the year Haldane celebrated his sixtieth birthday, a fortuitous visit from a group of Americans allowing him to explain how the students were celebrating it with fireworks as they always did. This year the event was remarkable not merely for Haldane's birthday but for the poems presented to him by students and staff, a *festschrift* he greatly appreciated. This

Cautionary Tales for Aspiring Species, or The Bad Beast's Book of Blunders was a glorious effort which included "Struthicmimus or The Danger of Being Too Clever", "Anomalus Obscurus or The Perils of Parthenogenesis", and "Triassochelys or The Effects of Excessive Specialisation", a collection from various hands quite up to the high standard which J.B.S. would have demanded of himself.

Cautionary Tales is not only intrinsically good stuff, it is also a pointer to the genuine affection which so many people felt for Haldane. When, after he had left University College, his sister Naomi was taken into University College Hospital and was asked her occupation, she answered "Novelist". That appeared to worry the young man treating her, so she added that she was the sister of J.B.S. "At that," she says, "he leaned with all his weight on my already suffering liver—and I had no clothes on—tears sprung into his eyes and he said: 'Oh do tell him how much we all miss him and Helen—the pub's just not the same.' I asked him for his name, which he didn't supply, saying only: 'It's the same for us all, we miss them so much.'"

This popularity was partly due to his own personal humanity, but another factor was the doggedness with which he would fight for his department and for his staff. The need for this was made greater by his own reluctance to work through the normal channels, while the methods he used were typical of the somewhat anarchic manner in which he regarded much of his own finances. But though constantly complaining that his department was under-financed, he made no claims for himself. The reverse was the case, and in March 1947 he wrote to the authorities saying, "the salary offered me by the College exceeds my present needs, the more so as I am constantly receiving money from the B.B.C., and other sources. I also find that I have somewhat underestimated the expenses of my department. I should therefore be very glad if you would see your way to transfer £100 from my salary for this year to the Departmental Account."

His casualness about his personal finances was startling. At times he mis-ordered his affairs so that his account was too small to meet his Standing Orders; at another, when he was able to claim his Post-War Credits, he ignored the necessary forms repeatedly sent to him by his Bank. While he could be mean over pence he was generous over pounds and was repeatedly diverting his own fees into other people's pockets. Thus he insisted that payment for the Bateson Lecture which he gave in 1956 should be "paid to an Indian worker whom I wish to subsidise". When he learned that he was to be paid £100 for "Is Evolution a Myth?" he asked that one half should be paid to a colleague, another half to his secretary. Penguin Books were instructed to pay the money for an article in their *Science News* to the Communist Party, while on another occasion they were asked to send the cheque to University College. "This is how I pay for some research expenses of my department," added Haldane. His motives were certainly mixed—"this seems to be the best way of escaping the payment of income tax", he wrote to one publication—but there is no doubt that a great deal of money earned by extra-curricular work was poured into his department. "I should like to obtain £50 towards the expenses of his work, otherwise the expenses will have to come from my own pocket," he wrote to one grant-giving authority of one of his students. In March 1953, he wrote to the College authorities saying: "I regret that during the next session I shall have to pay £300 out of my own pocket to keep my department going", and seven months later he wrote to the Secretary of the Agricultural Research Council: "In spite of the steady rise in prices and salaries, the grants available for my department from Univeristy sources have fallen and during the past few years I have had to contribute to them from my own resources. During the current academic year I have, in particular, to find the salary of my senior technician, which amounts to £395. I can, in fact, do so by writing a sufficient number of popular articles and books. But I can only do this by devoting less energy to research and teaching. I shall in any case contribute £200 or so from this source to University College."

Such pleas were not always answered. One reason is suggested by a letter that Haldane wrote to the same Agricultural Research Council saying that he had applied for a grant for one specific worker. "Today my secretary received a request for information as to her examination results," he continued. "I consider this to be a piece of blackmail on your part. As you know very well, the results of examinations are secret. I refuse to give you the information, and withdraw my request for a grant. I shall pay for her out of my own pocket."

The nature of genetics, which demanded animal stocks and simple equipment, made Haldane less dependent on hard cash than workers in other disciplines. He could, when necessary, provide from his own pocket the sums required—a circumstance very different from that of a man working in radio-astronomy or physics. Partly due to this, he was able to carry on, with the flow of his papers continuing throughout the 1950's. They ranged over most of the fields which he had traversed in the previous third of a century—those of physiology and bio-chemistry as well of genetics—but perhaps the most important was that on "The Cost of Natural Selection" which he read at the Sheffield meeting of the Genetical Society in 1957. Explaining its essence simply in a letter, he wrote: "Natural selection means that members of genotypes ill-adapted to the environment die prematurely or are partly sterile. The unit process of evolution is the replacement of one gene by another in a population. The total number of deaths involved in this process is independent of the intensity of selection when this is small. It depends on the rarity, before selection starts, of the gene selected, and on the degree of its dominance. A representative number of deaths is 30 times the number of individuals in a generation. Thus evolution at the rate of one gene substitution in 300 generations would lower the reproductive capacity of a species by about 10 per cent. This fact sets an upper limit to the rate of evolution." What Haldane did in fact do in this paper was to provide a quantitative explanation of the slowness with which evolution takes place.

He was also a much sought-after speaker at foreign Congresses throughout this period. He turned down more invitations than he accepted—"I am getting old, and find that I have already more work than I can manage," he wrote in refusing one. "As I can no longer comfortably travel third class, I find travel expensive, and as I have to pay for a certain amount of research out of my own pocket, I prefer to spend money in this way." But he did give a series of lectures to the Singer-Polignac Foundation in Paris. He travelled in India three times, spending some weeks there on each occasion, and forming links with the Indian Statistical Institute in Calcutta that were, as we shall see, vitally to affect his future. And in 1953 he attended the International Biological Union Symposium on Genetics of Population Structure in Pavia—astounding those present not only by his comments in the symposium itself but by the *tour de force* of his closing address. He had merely jotted down a few details on a dinner menu but he quoted Dante on the application of genetics to human affairs and Lucretius for the view that genes were immutable.

Preparation of the papers which Haldane read as a guest at foreign Congresses ate into the small amount of free time which he allowed himself. So did his regular appearance at public or private meetings—of the Hammersmith Peace Council, the

Socialist Medical Association, the Union Society of London and the South Place Ethical Society, to name a few at random. He was still driving himself hard and the love of clowning or buffoonery that never left him did not always make up for the annoyance with an audience which he sometimes betrayed.

When he came to London's Queen Mary College Debating Society to second the motion "This house has no need for a God", his back was troubling him badly and glaring at the chair set for him on the platform he commented: "I can't sit on that, it's much too severe." The President anxiously asked for another, but Haldane stopped him with: "Don't bother; I'll stand." He then noticed that the seats in the auditorium were of comfortable plush, left the platform, and sat down below it in one of them. Shortly afterwards, as the president was introducing the speakers he unwisely mentioned a piece of work which he believed J.B.S. had done. From the auditorium there bellowed up Haldane's voice: "That's not true. Withdraw that statement."

Later, J.B.S. spoke from the platform and, as might have been safely prophesied, commented on the doctors at Lourdes. One of his statements was then taken up from the floor, and to Haldane's "I never said that", there came a chorus of "Yes, you did; yes, you did."

"If I said that, I'll commit suicide," declared J.B.S. "I will I'll slit my throat."

At this he produced from his pocket an object which appeared to be an ordinary razor. However, the College Catholic Society had packed the meeting and Haldane's move was merely greeted with: "Well, go on then—because you did."

After order had been restored, a member of the audience began a series of questions—had Haldane not read so and so; had he never thought so and so. He replied with a deferential, "Yes, sir", "No, sir", "No, sir, I'm sorry, sir"—at each response meekly touching with his hand the place where his forelock had been forty years earlier. When the motion was announced as lost, he stalked out of the room without a word.

"One got the impression," said a spectator, "that it was one of his less satisfactory afternoons."

Haldane's irascibility, strongly denied by those who had experienced only his warm friendliness, was only one of the traits which had by this time turned him into one of the "sights" of University College. There was also his bluntness, shown at the end of his Karl Pearson Centenary address. "To me at least there seems to be an element of hypocrisy about the present celebrations," he said. "I believe that we should be honouring Pearson more effectively if, to take one example out of many possible, we ensured that the College library possessed copies of all his works, placed where students could consult them, rather than by making speeches and eating food." Haldane, being Haldane, refused to attend the dinner that followed the address.

His sincerity and his sense of humour helped to lighten his image. So did his facility for making these shine through his correspondence. "I do not know what the future of mankind will be, but I do not suppose that it will be one of which I should approve," he wrote. "Except that your letter to me refers to 'the new daft regulations' I can find nothing to criticise." Of his friend R. A. Fisher, he commented that he was "apt to regard any gilding of his lilies as an attack". Describing how he had helped one woman who sought advice on a family problem, he commented: "I ought, I suppose, to have told her to go to Heaven—but I feel some sympathy for the barmies." He insisted that "No Perfume" compartments on railways are much more necessary for comfort than "No Smoking"; and, asked by a students' union to oppose the resolution "This House believes in Western Democracy", he replied: "I am not prepared to support a motion so carelessly framed. I do not know what it means. It reminds me of the aged don at Cambridge who was heard to say in chapel: 'And I believe in Pontius Pilate—Oh no I don't.'"

The idiosyncrasies of which such letters were the outward sign tended to over-emphasise the extrovert side of Haldane's character, the side which tried to fight down the traditional feeling that publicity must always be in poor taste, which found the warmth of the limelight enjoyable if unpardonable, and which comforted itself with the thought that all such occasions might be turned to good use. Kingsley Martin's "Cuddly Cactus", driving his small Jowett through the Christmas crowds of Piccadilly with an impatient "Get out of my way", booming perpetual and uninhibited complaints about the coffee at University College, writing under black headlines in the *Sunday Pictorial* and still willing to give his opinions on any subject under the sun, made up a figure which was not only larger than life. It was also a figure which tended to obscure the other Haldane, a man as devoted to science as Galahad to pursuit of the Grail and one who found it impossible to fight against the demands of social conscience.

In 1948, the Lysenko affair had forced Haldane into a recantation which was no less searing for being private. Eight years later another twist of world events was to play its part in deciding his future. As before, he seemed—judged by the evidence of his papers—quite willing to let his own case go by default, as though he cared little whether or not he got the worst of both worlds. As before, the first rustles of the approaching storm came in the closed company of science.

In the autumn of 1956, Haldane was awarded the Huxley Memorial Medal of the Royal Anthropological Institute. On November 1, the Institute informed him that the 29th had been fixed as the date for his Huxley lecture, and that it would be followed by a dinner in the Peers' Dining Room at the House of Lords, arranged with the co-operation of Lord Raglan, the Institute's President. The letter giving the news could hardly have arrived at a less fortunate time, for on the evening of the 1st the House of Lords had voted strongly in favour of the Allied action on Egypt.

Haldane's reaction was predictable. "In view of the House of Lords' heavy vote last night in favour of British aggression, I do not propose even to appear to give countenance to so foul an institution by dining there," he replied to the Institute. "I would respectfully urge that by holding a dinner there the Royal Anthropological Institute is making things more difficult for British anthropologists throughout the world, whereas were it known that the Institute had refused, things would be made slightly easier for all British anthropologists. However that may be, I am sorry that I cannot accept your invitation."

The letter was passed on to Raglan who replied, more in sorrow than in anger, that unless Haldane thought better of his decision, and unless he withdrew the word "foul", the President would be unable to chair the lecture. Haldane, far from being driven into a corner by the suggestion, welcomed it. "I think your decision not to take the chair at my lecture is correct," he replied. "The people of this country are sharply divided into those who think that the present government is committing a crime under international law, and those who think otherwise. Some of the former are prepared to take all steps to which they are legally entitled to express their abhorrence of the government's action. It is inevitable, and in my opinion desirable, that their opponents should be annoyed by such steps. I think that your action will help to demonstrate the depth of division which exists in this country [as it exists in the British Commonwealth] on this important moral issue. I therefore welcome it, and thank you for your letter." Raglan did his best, sending a placatory note and suggesting that substitution of "deplorable" for "foul" might remove the impediment to his presence. Haldane stood his ground, and the dinner was cancelled.

The argument was a pale shadow of events to come.

PART
IV

THE GREEN FIELDS BEYOND

I I

The Great Decision

ON the morning of July 24 1957, Haldane and his wife stood on the apron at London Airport, ready for the final stage of emigration to India. He was going, he confirmed once again, because he did not wish to live in a police state, in a criminal state such as the one which had attacked Egypt. For full measure, and the benefit of any American reporters present, he added: "I want to live in a free country where there are no foreign troops based all over the place."

Thus Haldane supported the myth that he was leaving London solely as a result of the Anglo-French aggression against Suez, a reaction which drew the ideological sympathy of many, but which few had either the chance or the courage to emulate. During the preceding nine months he had encouraged the story, fuming to his friends at the slightest opportunity and delighting newspaper reporters with his statements that he was leaving his native land because of the mass murders of civilians in Port Said. Yet only part of this was true. Haldane felt as strongly about Suez as many other decent men. But now, as at so many other critical moments of his life, he could not help trailing his coat and helping to build up a picture of himself that was in some ways grossly distorted. The whole truth was less emotional and more complex than a reflex reaction to Suez, less worthy of the headlines but vastly more interesting. Haldane had in fact been considering emigration to India years before the Anglo-French aggression. In October 1956, he had written to a friend: "I also am to retire in two years, but I propose to retire to India, and pass the rest of my life there. It seems reasonable. Climate grand, living cheap, great demand for teachers." In fact, by November 1st 1956, the day of the British ultimatum to Egypt, Haldane was actually writing to the Director of the Indian Statistical Institute in Calcutta, accepting the offer of appointments there—not only for himself, but for his wife. "Helen is overjoyed at the offer of a full-time post," he added. "There is no question of her wanting to go anywhere else, though she thinks that she might perhaps want in future to ask your leave to do some teaching in Calcutta University, to go to international congresses, and so on."

This decision of Haldane's to emigrate to India, was not only taken before the Anglo-French attack on Egypt but had been maturing over a number of years. He had been invited to the Indian Science Congress early in 1952, and had then spent six weeks in the country, giving thirty-five lectures during this time, notably a series of twelve at the Indian Statistical Institute in Calcutta, run by another remarkable Fellow of the Royal Society, Professor Mahalanobis.

On his return, Haldane had written to Nehru outlining his ideas for developing Indian biology, and adding: "If it were considered that either or both of these lines of work should be encouraged, I should be glad to assist in their development in any way in my power, if only because I feel an obligation to a country whose government is doing as much for world peace as the present Indian Government."

He visited the Indian Statistical Institute again in 1954, and on his return wrote revealingly to his old friend, Dame Janet Vaughan of Somerville. Professor Nirmal Kumar Bose, the editor of *Man in India*, and formerly Gandhi's secretary, was planning to write the history of Gandhi's forty campaigns, a project which would involve him in extensive travels and in interviewing many thousands of people. "He estimates the cost of his research at about £800," Haldane wrote. "I cannot imagine a more fruitful way of spending such a sum on sociological research, and am quite prepared to back my opinion with a contribution of £100. The suggestion would be opposed by those who find Gandhi much more useful in heaven than on earth, and by those who genuinely think he never made a mistake and by those who think he was a dangerous revolutionary or a dangerous reactionary."

His thoughts were increasingly turning to emigration, as he had hinted to many of his friends. In 1955, he put his position to Mahalanobis. "I shall be superannuated in 1958," he wrote. "I have already an offer of part-time employment in Britain after this. But I should prefer an unpaid post in India provided there were opportunity for research. Helen has a paid post here and it would be hard to settle down in India unless there were some provision for her to do research and perhaps some teaching. Of course your own country needs work on 'pure' animal genetics and behaviour, and this does not demand expensive apparatus.

"I am personally no longer much attached and could work anywhere, given sources of data and library facilities. She on the other hand says that she is 'homesick for India', and would be happy to work at Calcutta or Santiniketan."

A few months later, early in 1956, he wrote to one friend that he hoped "to leave for India this summer and settle down there", and shortly afterwards he wrote that he was trying to get a post in India. "The conditions for work in such a place as Calcutta are somewhat more favourable than in London," he added. In fact, there now came two offers. One was from the Vice-Chancellor of Banaras University, the other was from Mahalanobis, who said that whatever happened he would be glad to have Haldane and his wife for a four-month visit to the Institute in 1957, and then added: "I should also take this opportunity of getting the record straight. We should be very glad to have you in the Institute, on a full-time or part-time basis, on such terms and conditions and with such designation [for example, Research Professor or Visiting Professor, or Research Director] that you may consider suitable. We have already agreed to give a full-time teaching post to Helen and it was my intention to send her informally the terms and conditions for her consideration."

It was to this letter which Haldane replied on November 1st, stressing the pleasure that it had given him and his wife. Helen would be delighted to work in the Institute. "As for me, if it is possible to get the *Journal of Genetics* printed at Baranagar, I shall have all the money I want (and India will have another export)," he added. "If not, I shall, of course, have more time to spare, but would like some remuneration for working in the Institute." Thus by the time of Suez Haldane's plans for emigration were already settled.

His reasons for dragging up his roots were varied and complex, although the operation was simpler for him than it would have been for most men; his roots were short. Since his departure from Cambridge almost a quarter of a century previously, he had failed to settle down as part of any community. At University College he tended to be the eccentric outsider, much feared or much loved according to circumstance but the centre of only a group within a group. He had been a member of the Communist Party, had sympathised with much that it did, had given it the benefit of his superior wisdom, yet had not been fully of it. Whatever the magnetism of Scotland and the Scots, it was not enough to hold him. He entertained respect for his aged mother, affection for his sister and for his brother-in-law. Yet he was a man with many acquaintances but few friends. As for the word "home", as most men understand it, there had perhaps been no real home since the days of Roebuck House which he had left more than three decades before. Emotionally, he could afford to pack his bags and go.

The attractions of India for J.B.S.—and also for Helen— were numerous and compelling, even though he himself was apt to camouflage them. "One of my reasons for settling in India was to avoid wearing socks," he once insisted. "Sixty years in socks is enough." The truth was that by the later-1950's Haldane was profoundly pessimistic about the future of Europe, which he saw as becoming increasingly anti-socialist. This was in one sense a reason for remaining—and he later wrote from India that "I might have done better to stay in England and be a nuisance like Russell". But this was only a passing regret. Despite all his strong feelings, Haldane was not a political animal. He had no passion for the complicated play and counter-play which can be described as dishonesty or manoeuvre according to taste but which is the stuff of politics. He did not agree with it all and he was both pleased and proud to get out.

In addition, he had both liking and respect not only for Nehru's international stance but for his personal record, and the same was true of Mahalanobis. To these general attitudes there were added practical reasons for a move. Haldane was due for retirement in 1959, while Helen's appointment as Lecturer ran only to September 1957, and while he could no doubt have acquired an Emeritus post without undue trouble, the eccentricities of greatness were tolerated more readily in India than in the West. In addition, Haldane had strong feelings about his wife being given a post in conjunction with himself, a factor which further limited the possibilities. There was, moreover, his continuing belief that work was being unnecessarily held back at University College. "I believe that the opportunities for biometric research are now better in India than in Britain," he stated at the Karl Pearson Centenary celebrations in May 1957, "and for this reason among others I have thought it my duty to emigrate there."

Overshadowing all these considerations were three others. One was the fact that both Haldane and Helen had been over-whelmed by the richness, the variety, the attraction and the beauty of India's animals and plants, and the prospects of biological investigation which they held out. Here was exciting virgin country, and its exploration demanded not expensive equipment but the exercise of human observation and a stretching of the human mind.

To this professional magnet there was added something both stronger and more subtle; the attraction of the Hindu philosophy of life towards which Haldane had been increasingly drawn during the years that followed the end of the Second World War. His second thoughts on "the bomb" had driven him to the belief that now, more than ever before, the policy of non-violence was both practically wise and morally compulsive. He was drawn on to consider, in more detail than during his first days in India, the complexities of Hindu beliefs, whose eternal "endure" was so comparable to the "Suffer" on the walls of "Cherwell". Hinduism, with its progress and regress of the soul worked out like a game of snakes and ladders, continuing until lucky competitors reached the hundred mark and attained a lasting salvation, was a game he understood. There was thus a number of logical reasons whose combination induced Haldane to pull himself up by the roots. There was also one other. It would be easy, he realised, for his enemies to claim that he was planning emigration to avoid payments to his first wife, because he found it difficult to get a post for his second, because he was becoming too cantankerous to hold down an appointment equal to his intellect, or because his Marxism would no longer let him live in a land of Conservative aggressors. He knew these dangers; they must have seemed irresistible. When all sane men knew that, for his reputation it was suicidally dangerous to leave for India, Haldane made up his mind. No man can escape his own demon; Haldane's forced him to emigrate.

Thus an amalgam of motives had driven him to decide on emigration some while before the Suez crisis. That they were to be obscured was due only partly to his forceful condemnation of the British attack. Almost as important in creating the public image was the purely fortuitous incident, on Monday November 5th, of the police dog and its tail.

By this time Britain was split down the middle on both the morality and the wisdom of the Suez adventure. Passions were inflamed, Haldane's as much as any man's. On the 2nd he had written a blistering letter to the *Manchester Guardian* suggesting that William Blake had been correct in his statement that "The whore and gambler, by the state Licensed, build that nation's fate". It was not, he suggested, a coincidence that on the night preceding the first day on which premium bonds were sold, British bombs were dropped on Egypt. "I suggest that Mr. Macmillan, in the interests of consistency, should put a heavy tax on the earnings of prostitutes to defray some of the expense of the present operations. Such a measure would command quite as much public support as the present Government policy." Those who objected to the Government's policy were vociferous. Those who doubted its legality possibly remembered Lord Kilmuir's comment on the Nuremburg Trials— "It is a point from which we must not flinch that henceforth, if a General is conscious that the plans are the actual, practical, and proximate plans for aggressive war, he becomes criminally liable if he takes part." The authorities were edgy, and as November 5th arrived with its enlarged possibilities of disturbance the police were also edgy.

That evening Helen Spurway met a young American, William Clarke, then working as a research assistant in University College. They had a drink in the Marlborough Arms, a favourite haunt of the Haldanes, and after she had introduced him to several other members of the University staff they began to walk back to University College where Haldane, on his 64th birthday, was still at work.

"On the way to the college," Clarke has written, "we approached two policemen and their police dog. The dog was sitting on the pavement with its tail straight out behind it. As we passed the police and the dog, Mrs. Haldane put her foot on the dog's tail. She did not stamp on the tail, but only lightly rested her foot on it as she walked by. The dog did not appear to be hurt at all. When Mrs. Haldane stepped past, the dog stood up and wagged its tail."

There are varying versions of what happened next, but it appears clear that the police questioned Helen, that Helen thumbed her nose at them and gave them her own considered opinion of policemen in general. The couple were arrested, and shortly afterwards Mrs. Haldane was charged with being drunk and disorderly and with assaulting a police officer, while her companion was charged with obstructing the police.

Long before the couple appeared in court the following morning it seemed likely that they had been mistaken for skylarking undergraduates, that no one had really intended to arrest a University Lecturer and a visiting American, and that the authorities might be heartily pleased if the whole affair could be forgotten in the presence of a small fine. Any hopes of this in the case of Helen Haldane bordered on fantasy.

In Court the following morning she resolutely refused to pay the fine imposed and was duly told that in lieu of the cash arriving within the stipulated time she would be committed to prison. She was later warned by the Provost that if she insisted on going to jail she would have to resign her post, a suggestion that produced a picturesque verbal response. In due course, on the 13th, she was taken to Holloway—where, she later said, she found treatment and staff considerably better than she had been led to expect.

Haldane himself, now confirmed by the Suez events in his worst suspicions of what a Conservative Government could do, had his feelings compounded by Helen's misfortune, and sent his own formal resignation and hers, to University College.

"On October 28th in view of the news of British military actions, I wrote to India asking whether it would be possible for my wife and myself to obtain employment there next year," he wrote. There was, he went on, "no alternative in view of my wish no longer to be a subject of a state which has been found guilty of aggression by the overwhelming verdict of the human race. I believe that we shall find in India opportunities for research and teaching in a country whose Government, by its active work for peace, gives an example to the world." This was certainly the truth, but it was by no means the whole truth. Suez was not the spur which was sending him east; it was, instead, the unexpected mast, arriving suddenly before him, on to which he quickly nailed his colours.

On the day that he wrote to the Provost, Haldane wrote also to the University of Amsterdam where he was to lecture, saying that he now refused to travel under the auspices of the British Council who were arranging his visit, since he was "not prepared to come as representative of a state which has been adjudged criminal by the vast majority of other states". However, he did not wish to break his promise; he would come at his own expense.

Meanwhile, after he had written with some pride that his wife had been arrested and was now in Holloway, he received a telephone call. It came on the evening of November 16th, from Helen herself who indignantly reported that a Mr. Waller had arrived at the prison and paid her fine. He had offered her a lift home which she had refused. And having been photographed, first on leaving prison and then again as she telephoned J.B.S., she assumed that she had been freed by a newspaper in hope of an interview. If so—as seems likely—the paper was disappointed.

With Helen now out of prison, Haldane's resignation lying in the Provost's office and Helen's own confirmation of her resignation now on its way, J.B.S. officially announced that he

209

was emigrating to India because he considered Britain to be a "criminal state". The decision, he added, had been made because of the "mass murders at Port Said". His attitude formed a useful prop to the Left. But the fact that he had not publicly dissociated himself from the Communist Party made Haldane's response to Suez little more than might have been expected. He had always been a man of bomb-like utterances and this, in itself, diminished the impact—so that "British Scientist Emigrating Over Suez" seemed less startling when one learned that the scientist was J.B.S.

In University College there was genuine regret that the Haldanes were leaving. There were also pinpricks, of which he made the most, and in April he wrote to the Provost complaining that he had been turned out of his room by the Works Department. "My secretary was in the building but was not consulted," he added. "It is, of course, only twenty years since I was promised another and larger room. It may be that something is now being done about it. I reserve the right to claim damages, as my belongings have been moved in a totally chaotic manner."

Three months later, as J.B.S. and his wife were preparing to go, he wrote: "We are leaving here amid mixed emotions of others. Some are genuinely sympathetic. They have painted my portrait, given us dinners, and so on. Others regard my leaving here three years before my superannuation as an insult to themselves and their culture. They would not feel so strongly were I going to America. But there is a very real prejudice against India."

Prejudice there might be, but there was also affection, and an appreciation of what he had done for University College over the years. In July, Haldane learned that the Senate had decided to confer on him the title of Professor Emeritus. He pointed out that if he had been consulted in advance he would have refused, and he added that he had not been superannuated but had resigned to take up another chair, and wished the conferment to be withdrawn. For one thing, he did not think it was usual for such a title to be given to a professor taking up an appointment in Oxford, Cambridge or McGill. "The Indian Statistical Institute to which I am going, has a higher standard of research and teaching than these universities," he replied, "and it seems somewhat discourteous to it to suggest that I can in any sense be said to be retiring on accepting a post there." In addition, he went on, he was leaving London prematurely because, as he put it, "promises made to me over the last twenty years both by the administrative authorities of the University and of this College, have been systematically broken", although he knew that this was partly due to promises broken by Government officials. "Further," he continued, "in the past, the University systematically behaved as if it found me an embarrassment, which may well have been the case. To take one example, a colleague junior to myself was chosen as its official representative at the last International Genetical Congress. The University had a perfect right to do this, but as it did so it appears inconsistent to confer a title on me on my departure." The University appears to have noted Haldane's objections. Six years later he received University College's Annual Calendar. He immediately wrote to the College, protesting that he was not listed as a Professor Emeritus.

By midsummer 1957, J.B.S. had bundled up most of his journals and scientific papers, the accumulations of a lifetime. His schoolboy diaries, the drafts of unpublished papers on his father and on various aspects of his own life, family correspondence going back deep into the 19th century, details of his Army Service in the First World War and the records of his work for the Admiralty in the Second—all were boxed and finally despatched to follow the Haldanes to India by sea. At least, almost all of them were despatched. Years later, after Haldane's death, further files were discovered in University College, including his own copies of the minutes circulated after the meetings of the *Daily Worker* Editorial Board.

At the end of July the Haldanes left England. Less than twenty-four hours later they were descending across the sprawling outliers of Calcutta to Dum-Dum Airport where an official reception committee awaited them. To the Indian authorities, the settling in their country of such a distinguished biologist as J.B.S. was an accolade; he was different, a distinguished white man who had chosen them. However much Haldane wanted to merge himself into what was to become the country of his adoption, this was a fact they would never let him forget. It is doubtful if he would, wholly and unreservedly, have wished them to.

The Institute into whose life Haldane and his wife now prepared to settle down—a heterogeneous collection of dusty buildings lying eight miles from the heart of Calcutta on the dusty road leading through the suburbs to Barrackpore—already occupied a key position in the new India which was struggling up in the aftermath of Independence. It had been founded as a learned society in 1932, largely a crystallisation of ideas discussed by the group of young men who had gathered round

Professor Prasanta Chandra Mahalanobis. Although technically Professor of Physics in the Presidency College, Calcutta, Mahalanobis was already a statistician of international fame, and the rooms where his colleagues met regularly became known as the Statistical Laboratory. Why not, it was asked, apply statistical methods to the multitude of problems, both government and private, which cried out for solution in the awakening sub-Continent? The Institute was then formed to foster such applications, a modest enough project to begin with and one which during its first year of existence employed a single, part-time worker.

One of the first problems tackled by the Institute was that of flood-control in Bengal and Orissa—the results being both short-term in the form of better control and long-term in the shape of such enterprises as the Hirakud Dam Project which in Haldane's day was to involve the building of the biggest earth dam in the world. Another set of problems centred round agricultural field trials, a subject on which Mahalanobis worked with Haldane's colleague R. A. Fisher. Work flowed in from private companies and from Government agencies, and by the 1950's the Institute employed a staff of nearly 2,000 and had grown tentacles which reached out into many aspects of Government work. In 1949 Mahalanobis had been appointed Statistical Adviser to the Indian Cabinet, and five years later Nehru inaugurated studies at the Institute from which the draft of India's Second Five Year Plan was prepared. By 1957 preparations were already being made for the Act which was to empower the Institute to confer degrees in statistics. Thus the scientists, projects and plans among which the Haldanes were now to find themselves working were deeply responsible both for such economic order as existed across the developing nation and for the failures which still periodically racked it.

Haldane's work as Research Professor was to be mixed. Within his first year he gave some fifty lectures, mainly on genetics but also on general statistical investigations. He started work on a number of problems in mathematical statistics, but his main occupation was, as he himself put it, "assisting others in research". This was helped by the glamour with which his name was surrounded in India; for he was not only a scientist of world-wide fame—he was one who had chosen to uproot himself and take to the Indian way of life, and the more able and the more ambitious wrote asking to study under him in Calcutta. What happened to one student is typical. "I first read of Haldane's migration to India in the Sunday issue of a Delhi newspaper," he has said. "Having received some earlier training in genetics I immediately wrote to him asking for facilities for research in genetics under his supervision at the Indian Statistical Institute. A reply soon came from him asking me three questions in plant genetics with permission to use the local libraries to consult references and so on. I found out later that this habit of prompt reply was characteristic of him."

In Calcutta, the Haldanes lived initially in a flat on the fourth floor of the Institute, an ideal arrangement as far as J.B.S. was concerned since he had always tried to mark as thin a line as possible between his professional working life and what for most other men would be called "spare time". His new home was small, and made smaller still by the packing cases of books and papers which eventually arrived from England. "Our flat is certainly in a mess by European standards, though not, I think, by Indian standards," he wrote to one prospective visitor. "You may find our simplicity, or squalor, trying."

One part of this simplicity was Haldane's adoption of Indian dress which he found cheaper and more comfortable than English clothes. "Indian dress is so practical," he once commented. "No braces, no belts. It's cheaper, and poor people can afford to have a clean change of clothing every day." He owned two hats, "one of more or less European type, a kind of deer-stalker made of stout cotton, which is very light, and a heavy conical straw one of rather Chinese appearance, as worn in the local country-side". He rarely wore either and the hugeness of his frame, unusual in an Indian, frequently suggested that the impressive advancing figure might be that of a Parsee. In food, also, he largely adopted Indian customs, a move made more pleasurable by his belief that while France and China provided two of the world's great cuisines, South India provided the third. As for drink, he missed English beer, and was shocked at the cost of the local variety; but, he wrote to a friend, "we make gin, whisky and several other liquors a good deal better than imported stuff". In externals, therefore, he now became three-quarters Indian and only one-quarter European, an attitude which enabled him to live comfortably within his means, and whose minor disadvantages he felt to be no great hardship. More important still was his fascination with, and sympathy for, Hindu philosophy. Many of the incongruities of Indian life dissolved as one remembered that "Suffer" on the "Cherwell" wall and related it to the Hindu "endure".

The Haldanes settled in well, and more quickly than many friends thought would be possible. One reason was the genuine feeling behind Helen's "homesickness for India". Another was Haldane's ability to teach without preaching. "I am not going to India to 'enlighten' you or 'elevate you in the field of science'," he had written to an Indian acquaintance while still in England. "You will have to do that for yourselves. I am going because I like India and a great many Indians. If they choose to use what few accomplishments I possess, they are welcome. If not, I shall be quite happy to contemplate nature."

A month after his arrival, Haldane noted that he did not feel at home anywhere, "at least in this present world", but he expected to be happy in Calcutta. As for his wife, she had no doubts, no qualifications, no regrets. She had not adopted Indian dress, but she had adopted most other things Indian. "I personally feel at home here as I never felt at home at University College, London, where I could never recover from having been a student," she wrote a few months later. "There is plenty of evidence that we are collecting enemies, and our tranquillity puzzles us somewhat."

Enemies maybe, but friends as well, and by the autumn of 1957 the Haldanes' home with its flat roof—the best room in the house as Haldane called it—was a regular meeting-place for the staff of the Institute, for the students, and for the friends, both European and Indian, which they collected with speed and in number. The roof is one of those features of the Haldanes' Calcutta life that has lodged most securely in the mind of many who knew them—for here, after the work of the day, something of the best in Haldane's character would rise to the surface.

"It is only fair to warn you that you should probably avoid being on the roof with me at night," he wrote to the young fiancée of his secretary, who was coming to stay at the flat. "This is not for the reason which you might guess, for I am sixty-five years old, and love my wife; but because I am liable to start talking about the stars, and many people find this very boring. I personally think it most exciting that Vega is a main sequence star of type A, and only about 10 parsecs distant. But most people are unwilling to learn the very simple ideas involved, though many of them could be understood by an intelligent child of six, and are therefore within your professional sphere."

If some were bored, many were intrigued. Sitting in a deck-chair and sipping his tea, Haldane would point out the prominent stars and planets; he would identify them by their Greek and their Sanskrit names, expound on their positions and importance, and explain how the industrial smog of European cities, and their blaze of lights, made such observations more difficult than in the velvet night of India.

If Haldane explaining the stars provides one typical picture of his life in Calcutta, another involves the watertank of the Institute's grounds, eighty yards by thirty and, as Haldane described it to a friend, "more suited for an old man of sixty-six like me than for yourself". Here Haldane swam regularly, by himself, with the students, with the staff, and sometimes with his sister's grandson, Graeme, whose father worked for a while in India—a young boy in whom J.B.S. espied the makings of a mathematician. Sometimes, as in the Cam of earlier years, he swam smoking a lighted cigar. "I remember one Sunday morning in the grounds trying to trace a voice which said 'Good morning' to me," says one of his former students. "I finally spotted his lighted cigar, his head and his submerged body."

It was the same Haldane. The transplantation to India had been successful.

12

Aiding India

FROM the late summer of 1957 Haldane began to exert a grow-ing influence from his position in the Indian Statistical Institute. He taught, he carried out his own research, he quickly became the man to whom Indian scientists almost automatically appealed for advice, whether they worked for Government or University. Invitations to lecture poured in, notably from All-India Radio, for whom Haldane in December 1957 gave the third series of Patel lectures, a notable discourse on "The Unity and Diversity of Life", based on "a study of biology over some sixty years, largely a study of what a philosopher might con-sider minor details, such as the shapes of bones of extinct animals, the chemical composition of my own blood, the inherit-ance of flower shape in primroses, and the ascents of fish for air."

He received, also, an almost ceaseless flow of invitations to appear as a guest of honour, or to say a few words on a public platform, a form of appearance which he ranked with the British equivalent of foundation-stone laying and church bazaar-opening. Haldane's reactions on such occasions were as unquali-fied as they would have been in England. He thought it wrong in principle to attend events where he could neither learn nor teach—he was, after all, well into his sixties and had reached the age where it was fatally easy to cease research, work and, as he put it, "appear on public platforms to utter pomposities". He became, as he said, peevish when forced to meet Chief Ministers and their wives when he could be looking at crabs and flowers. His attitude was summed up in one letter describing how a colleague had turned to Helen and said: "Oh, Mrs. Hal-dane, these hens are not interesting. They only belong to poor men. If I had known that you were interested in poultry I would have taken you to see a flock of White Leghorns five miles away." He and his wife demanded, J.B.S. went on, "the right to stop to look at rice, coconuts, cows, hens, etc. belonging to poor men, and even at lizards which are nobody's property."

Official visits, Haldane quickly learned, had the same drawbacks in India as they had in England, and this could be as true of the Services as of the civilian authorities. He himself discovered this, since although India's peaceful intentions had been one of the magnets which had drawn him, he had for long been concerned with defence science. And just as he had served the Royal Navy while chairing the Editorial Board of the *Daily Worker*, so did he now find himself advising the Indian Services while advocating some of the policies which came under the heading of non-violence. One of his first contacts ended on a note of typical Haldanism.

It was natural that J.B.S. should, with his great experience of diving, be invited to inspect the Indian naval diving school at Trivandrum in Southern India; it was natural that Helen, herself greatly experienced in under-water work, should be invited to accompany him; and it was a kindly thought of Admiral Kotari, Chief of Naval Staff, that both should then be taken on to visit the Laccadives. However, when J.B.S. received his programme for the proposed visit, he found something very different from what he had expected. "Of three days, only 105 minutes are devoted to the visit to the diving school, which is our purpose in visiting Cochin," he objected. Neither he nor his wife knew anything about gunnery, signalling, the manufacture of aluminium or the separation of rare earths, all items on their itinerary. Since Helen could not be accommodated at the naval base, the Haldanes were to be separated from their Indian colleagues, and made the guests of an European. J.B.S. commented that he would probably find his luxury embarrassing "and his food inedible". He was expected to speak at a Rotary Club. Finally, Helen would not, because of her sex, be allowed aboard the naval vessel which was to take them to the Laccadives. "I fully understand that the programme was intended to be complimentary to me," Haldane concluded, "and thank you for your kind intentions. But unless it can be revised completely, I have no option but to refuse your invitation." Refused it was.

Later, as the authorities appreciated Haldane's reluctance to be treated as a V.I.P., he helped more than one of the Service authorities, advising the Defence Ministry's Chief Psychologist on mental tests for troops, discussing human resistance to cold and oxygen want—"For example, is it practicable to cover metal parts of weapons (including the trigger) which may touch human skin, with non-conducting films?"—lecturing Indian Air Force cadets on life at high pressures and attending a symposium on high altitude problems at the Himalayan Mountaineering Institute, Darjeeling.

Such activities had to be fitted as well as possible into the routine of teaching at the Indian Statistical Institute. "My most important work there," J.B.S. subsequently wrote, "was beyond doubt starting S. K. Roy, K. R. Dronamraju, T. A. Davis, and S. D. Jayakar on their scientific careers, which are likely, in my opinion, to be illustrious. At least twenty of my pupils have become Fellows of the Royal Society, so I can probably judge fairly well."

Each of these young men—as well as others less notable—he managed to fire with the excitement of detailed observation he regarded as the groundwork of so much scientific research. More than one produced, from the work that followed, results which could vitally affect the future of India. Roy, for instance, told Haldane how, years previously, his father had refused to take part in the sacrifice of goats, then even more common in India than it is today, believing that this would affect the mother of the kids that were usually slaughtered. "I put the notion into Roy's head," Haldane later wrote, "that rice plants have certain needs which are not obvious to us but require a little imagination." After due thought Roy proposed a series of experiments involving different strains of rice. Haldane thought that the main experiment would fail—which it did; but against his advice Roy continued. The result was what may yet turn out to be a major discovery. For Roy found that some pure lines of rice produce substances which act on other strains of rice and stimulate greater production of seeds. The substances are soluble in water, in which rice grows, and all that is required to increase yield is to plant alternate rows of the two strains; yet the marginal addition of labour required was found to produce as much as a 26 per cent increase per acre.

Roy's initial work was carried out on very small plots. When it was found difficult to enlarge the experiments, Haldane came to the rescue and helped to finance further work on about twenty acres. Roy himself deserved about 95 per cent of the credit, according to Haldane. "The other 5 per cent may be divided between the Indian Statistical Institute and myself," he added. "I deserve credit for letting him try what I thought was a rather ill-planned experiment, on the general principle that I am not omniscient." But he had little hope that credit would be given that way. "Every effort will be made here to crab his work," he wrote. "He has not got a Ph.D. or even a first class M.Sc. So either the research is no good, or I did it."

Roy also found that if the heads of one particular line of nearly pure rice are pulled off the plants, these produce after forty-five days or so a second crop almost as big as the first. Haldane was pessimistic as to how long it would be before such ideas would be tested on a really large scale or, if found successful, put into operation. But he was in no doubt about Roy's potential worth. "It is my considered opinion," he wrote to Roy's father, "that your son may be the most important person in India today. As you know, he has rather more than doubled the yield of rice from three small plots. It is clear that if his method will raise the yield over the whole rice-growing area by even a half, he will have solved the food problem for India, East Pakistan, and Indonesia for a generation to come. I find it very difficult to believe that he will not raise it by 20 per cent. If so his achievement will only be comparable to that of a man who built the dam and dug the canal for the irrigation of Rajasthan with his own hands."

The practical outcome of exploiting an idea and observing the results excited Haldane almost as much by its scientific beauty as by its possibilities for good in a country as short of food as India. So did what he described as the "fantastic discovery" about coconut palms made by one of his workers. The palms have their leaves arranged in either right-handed or left-handed spirals, the numbers being roughly equal—50 per cent right-handers among 7,000 or so trees—although the characteristic does not appear to be inherited. But T. A. Davis, a young man almost obsessed by his interest in coconut trees, discovered that the right-handers gave about a fifth more nuts than the left-handers. Here again there seemed to Haldane to be a remarkable fact of nature, newly discovered, which could surely be turned to economic use.

Davis and Haldane had first met casually at the Central Coconut Research Station in Kerala. "If you are interested in chimaeras in other plants, and have the possibility of working on them [even in your own garden], I should be glad to make some suggestions as to what would be interesting," J.B.S. wrote soon afterwards. "I know very little of plant physiology and can give you no advice. [But] . . . if you like I will write to some colleagues in Europe who might help you . . ." The friendship flourished and Davis wrote later that he had been impressed by Haldane's "innate urge to drag youngsters to science". Eventually Davis decided to resign from his post in Kerala and join Haldane in Calcutta. "It is not easy to give you advice," Haldane wrote when he heard the news. "If I knew that I should live for another five years, I should certainly back your decision. But I do not. If my wife and I are both killed, you will have enough money to go abroad. But if I die and she does not, your situation will not be so good. So I enclose a note which you may care to keep in case of an emergency."

Such attitudes personally encouraged both his students and his fellow-workers at the Institute. So did his continuing advice that they should first look around at the enormous biological laboratory presented by an India in which field research had, judged by European standards, barely begun. And by observing, by drawing deductions, by asking themselves questions and then seeking the answers, they would be able to accustom themselves to the scientific discipline; at the same time they might possibly ease the enormous problems that their country was facing. This incentive to look and think for themselves, to break away from what he derided as the parrot-like learning so often demanded by the Indian authorities, was one of the things which Haldane brought to India. Another was the encouragement of non-violent biology.

He and Helen were, he wrote of a famous Indian ornithologist, "particularly keen to help Salim Ali and a few others to start again the tradition of non-violent research on animals". He had written in *Mankind*, before his emigration to India, "Some Reflections on Non-Violence". Now he spoke on "The Non-Violent Scientific Study of Birds", and he encouraged such attitudes among his students, among his casual acquaintances, whenever he spoke or wrote or discussed the methods of science. This was part and parcel of his developing vegetarianism, which with the encouragement of non-violent methods of research increasingly became an essential factor in his outlook. The two things grew together, and they can be ascribed to a mixture of causes. His father had always refused to utilise one of the "lower" animals if a man would do. J.B.S. himself had become increasingly attracted by the Hindu philosophy of non-violence. And close contact with the unthinking cruelty so often shown by Indian practice merely reinforced his already strengthening feelings.

Haldane's vegetarianism, which steadily became stricter throughout his years in India, was certainly not based on dietetics—"the food faddists tried to get hold of him and were sent away with a flea in their ear", his wife said. Writing to a friend he stressed that from the physiological point of view he did not think that a vegetarian diet was "good enough for growing children, pregnant or nursing mothers, or men going into training and developing muscles, unless supplemented with milk more heavily than is possible for most people in India". His point of view rested simply on what some people would call humanitarianism and what he himself called animalitarianism —"because," as he put it in a letter describing his and his wife's feelings, "we take the higher animals seriously." At first he was not particularly rigid about it, and could sometimes be tempted, so that when he wrote to the General Secretary of the World Vegetarian Congress in 1957, he said: "I regret that I am not a vegetarian. I prefer vegetarian food when I can get it. But, like the Lord Buddha, I will accept meat rather than insult my host." Nevertheless, he increasingly objected to causing any animal pain; he objected more to eating domestic animals which had learned to trust humans than to eating wild animals which had been caught by luck or cunning; and he quickly developed a repugnance to eating meat, fish or crustaceans. About some he felt strongly, and on being asked during his last visit to England in 1963 whether he would eat lobster, he replied: "No, it is an animal with noble limbs." Among the molluscs, mussels were edible, since J.B.S. did not believe that they suffered when killed. As in so many other things, his reasons were a mixture of the complex and the basically simple. "Once you try to teach evolutionary biology to people with the Indian ideological background, the distinction between eating goats and cannibalism appears rather thin," he wrote to a friend in London in 1960. Basically, the matter was even simpler: "I think other peoples' dinner is as material as mine, and that my claim to a more immortal soul than a goat is not strong enough to justify me in eating the goat."

This attitude to food was a reflection of his changing attitude to methods of research. But the attitude appears to have been changing long before he settled in India; the contrast between the sub-Continent and the laboratories of England only speeded the process. In the 1920's Haldane could write merely that "it is probably right that some control should be kept over experiments likely to involve severe and prolonged pain in animals". Immediately after the Second World War he was writing that he could "see no more objection to painless experiments on animals than to eating meat"—a rather different attitude. Two years later he wrote of experimental work in general that "you have got to try these things on 'the weak and helpless' including human babies, whose lives you hope to save. I wish the world were not so constituted that this was not necessary"—a slip of the pen which leaves no doubt in the reader of his still changing attitude.

It is certainly true that long before Haldane left University College he showed a greater awareness of the situation than he is sometimes credited with. In a paper on the estimation of mutation rates produced by high energy events in mammals, of which a summary was published in the Indian *Current Science* in March 1956, he pointed out that while the effects of man-made fission products could not be experimentally studied in men, they could be so studied in mice. "It can be argued," he concluded, "that the suggested experiment is cruel to the mice concerned. However, irradiation is painless, and most of the lethal genes will probably act before birth or immediately afterwards. It is certainly less cruel than the destruction of mice by many of the types of poison and trap which are in common use, or even by cats, which seldom kill mice quickly. Nevertheless I must admit that some mice will be born with potentially painful diseases. I can only say that, perhaps wrongly, I prefer to contemplate such conditions in mice than in men." The paragraph would not satisfy everyone. But it is refreshing to have the pain honestly admitted; quite apart from the "perhaps wrongly".

In India, as one example from many, Haldane took infinite trouble to advise the University Federation for Animal Welfare on the method of destroying unwanted dogs in Tokio that would cause the animals the minimum pain or distress. He wrote that he specially prized his recognition of the presence of cytochrome oxidase in plant seedlings, moths and rats, because it involved neither killing nor cutting up. And of non-violent biology he wrote: "It is my experience that if one watches an animal for eight hours or so daily for over a week, noting down its behaviour, this has effects on the observer which could be described by such a phrase as spiritual enlightenment." One example which he was fond of quoting concerned three *koi* fish which he and Helen had studied when they had visited India in 1954. When the fish are put in foul water containing little oxygen they swim up to the surface and make up the deficiency by breathing air. Haldane and his wife altered the composition of the gases dissolved in the water and of the air above it; then they took careful notes of the fish's reactions. "I don't say these fish never suffered at all," Haldane said. "To judge from my own experience they may have had severe headaches for some minutes." But they were not seriously injured, and it would have been unthinkable for the Haldanes to have handed over the fish for killing and eating. "We became so fond of them that we took them back to England, and two were still alive when given to a friend on our departure this year," Haldane wrote in 1957.

It would, of course, be totally wrong to suggest that India drove J.B.S. into the anti-vivisectionist camp. But all life consists of a choice between evils, and the choice is rarely more difficult than when the honest scientist is faced with experiments on living creatures. "It is our duty, as far as possible," Haldane had agreed in the 1920's, "to diminish the amount of pain in the world." He never tried to dodge this duty. What he did do, as he grew older, was to draw up a new profit and loss account in such matters, to shift the line demarcating what was acceptable to a position he considered more fitting. Both anti-vivisectionists and many scientists would object to it—although for different reasons.

In discussing the non-violent study of birds before the Bombay Natural History Society in 1959, and the problems of finding out what certain birds ate, Haldane said: "One can of course kill parents and examine their crop contents. Apart from ethical consideration, this means . . ." In an article on non-violent biology for the *Visvabharati Quarterly*, he said that he did not wish to suggest that all zoology should be non-violent. "But," he went on, "I can state that, though I have killed a few insects in the course of forty years of scientific research, I have never killed a vertebrate nor mutilated it in any way, save for a few mice and kittens which were clearly dying, through no intervention of my own, and whose further suffering I wished to spare. I think that a similar attitude to animals could be practised at Santiniketan, and that so far from sterilising research, it could guide it into channels of the greatest value." To the students of the Gandhi Medical College in Hyderabad he stressed that they should avoid causing suffering to others unless they volunteer for it and added: "That is why I do not recommend you to experiment on dogs or rats."

This developing attitude to animals as objects of scientific interest had similarities to his regard for them as food. He thought in terms of limitations rather than in terms of absolutes, as when he wrote in "Some Reflections on Non-Violence": "I sympathise with, but do not share, the Hindu practice of non-violence to insects. They will die in any case, but they need not suffer. I am ashamed if I cause an insect suffering, but not if I kill it painlessly."

He was glad that his subject of genetics demanded little

violence to animals, and that his reputation in India enabled
him to "try to do a little to abate cruelty to animals". This
attitude is well illustrated by two letters which he wrote to
friends in the U.F.A.W. in 1963. "The beasts here are mostly
harmless to men, if not to plants," he wrote in one. "Even
mosquitos are rare. It is probably worth while persuading my
servants that a four foot long Varanus in the bathroom is unlikely to bite them, and won't hurt them much if it does. They
now bring us all sorts of animals, and the example may spread."
In the second letter he pointed out that "One of the things
badly needed here is a picture book of non-poisonous snakes,
with names in various local languages. I am afraid that in view
of the large number of barefooted people here, I could not con-
scientiously save the life of a Russell's Viper near my house.
Send us 400 million pairs of shoes, and I will found a Society
for the Protection of Poisonous Snakes and Scorpions."

The essential Haldane came out when Helen one day discovered a young injured bird, a *Milvus migrans*, defying a
crow in the middle of the road. Haldane himself carried out
the necessary operation on its seriously injured left wing, set
about discovering whether a false wing-tip could be made for
the bird, and wrote to a friend in England, asking if he had the
information required. "If not," he continued, "I will try to get
someone from the local Indian Air Force Medical Service on to
the job. But I rely on you for the scientific literature. I can
supply the unscientific. At present the bird is called Jatayu,
after a valiant vulture in the Ramayana which lost its wings in
battle. If it turns out to be a ♀ it will have to be called Cressid,
I suppose, in view of Shakespeare's line (Pistol in 'Henry V',
probably misremembered):

> No, to the spital go
> And from the powdering tub of infamy
> Fetch forth the lazar kite of Cressid's kind
> Doll Tearsheet she by name, and her espouse.

However if it can be got airborne again he or she must be called
Bader."

Despite translation to India this essential Haldane remained,
stepping from science to the classics with enviable ease, subtly
cantankerous when he wished, as outspoken as ever, and successfully carrying the *Journal of Genetics* over the crisis involved
in printing in Calcutta. Other problems were solved and the
Journal was soon bringing an annual 60,000 Rupees of foreign

currency into the country. Haldane took particular pride in the book reviews, to which he added his own characteristic headlines: "The Harmless Atom Bomb?", "Sympatrick's Day No More We'll Keep" and—of a book which consisted "of twelve chapters, mostly, in my opinion, very bad"—"A Parade of Ignorance".

As he went about his work, perpetually interested in the animals and insects, the flowers and the birds, all presented in a profusion unknown in England, Haldane quickly became a figure slightly different in kind from the one he had appeared to be in Europe. There, a common impression was of the crank —to which he had no objection since "cranks make revolutions". In India he appeared as a more distinguished mixture of sage and scientist, counsellor, adviser and enquire-within-upon-everything, a personage both on a higher pedestal than the one he had occupied in England yet one just as accessible to the multitude.

He had a handy objection to most things of which he disapproved, and a cunningly effective method of discouraging those who he felt dropped below his own high standards. Thus he not only protested to one Indian Academy about misprints and mistakes in the reprint of a lecture he had given its members. He proposed as follows if it were not withdrawn: "Whenever I am asked by an Indian Institution to give a lecture for publication, I shall normally refuse, and send them one of the reprints received from you, in order to show why I am refusing."

He still rode his hobby-horses in splendid style, writing to Krishna Menon that "in general you may take it that a biologist once granted a knighthood will do no further work of value, even if he did any before, which is by no means always so"— and then listing the scientists of both categories who he felt illustrated his belief.

However, both J.B.S. and Helen had re-established themselves in their new habitat. It is difficult not to feel that both were finding themselves emotionally rooted in a way that neither had felt in England. The transplantation, like the marriage, had worked in a way that discredited the prophets. However, Haldane had been in his mid-sixties when he had emigrated, and in August 1960, he wrote significantly to a friend at the Calcutta Medical College. He wondered whether he would be able to take students round the College hospital. He wanted to be immunised against a number of common snakes. And, he added, he would "like to make arrangements for the disposal of [his] corpse, should Yama see fit to keep his appointment with [him] in Calcutta". He then listed sixteen different varieties of injuries or operations to which he had been subjected, ranging from his hernia at the age of ten months to a fracture of the right malleus in 1950. "I have probably forgotten a few episodes, and omitted sprained ankles, possibly pulmonary lesions from chlorine etc.," he concluded. "However, I hope you will agree that my corpse may be worth looking at. If you want it, keep the list."

Despite his age, which seemed to trouble him singularly little, Haldane continued to travel a good deal more extensively than his programme of work in Calcutta might suggest. In 1958 he and Helen visited Singapore and Malaya—"a perfect police state. It has, however, some pleasing plants and animals"—and he lectured at the University of Singapore. In the last two months of 1959 they managed to visit Gauhati in Assam, where in the Zoo "Helen was patted on the leg by a tiger while an elephant trod on her toe" and where in the forest they had "to beat a swift but not disorderly retreat from an elephant of alleged roguish tendencies". They flew across country to Bombay, visited Ajanta to inspect the cave paintings, Ellora to see the sculptures, and Allahabad where the pilgrimage to the holy river was taking place. Haldane was now enjoying the Indian past much as he had previously enjoyed the British past of Avebury or Ely. He had arrived in India with a considerable knowledge of India's history and culture—and had in fact lectured on this at University College in the early 1950's. Now he was learning Bengali, and studying the Indian past in the same methodical yet enthusiastic way that he had studied the classics almost half a century earlier.

The following year the Haldanes were invited to Ceylon for the sixteenth annual session of the Ceylon Association for the Advancement of Science, and within a few days J.B.S. exhibited all those traits and tendencies for which he had become famous. The visit might almost represent a microcosm of his life. He began by insisting that he had booked into Colombo's eastern-style hotel and not into either of the western-styled hotels at which his hosts at first tried to accommodate him. He was sincerely honoured by Sir Oliver Goonetilleka, the Governor-General, who described him as "a world leader whose judgement comes from deep convictions", and who added that there were not many who had, like Haldane, "a broad understanding of how the world has got the way it is". He gave three lectures to packed audiences—typically enough, on biological research with simple apparatus, on the physical chemistry of enzyme action, and on the study of human heredity. In the Colombo Museum, when told that the only place for tea was a kiosk patronised by the workers, he exclaimed: "What on earth's wrong with that?" and forthwith joined them. Taken round the coral reefs by a young biologist, he commented: "The only way to see fish is under water," and having stripped to his trunks, dived in without further argument. "We couldn't get him away from any animal or bird or insect," says one guide who showed him round—and who still remembers how J.B.S. and Helen sat down in his kitchen as friends, charmed the children, and explained how they could tell whether a pet tortoise was male or female.

Haldane trying to crawl into a culvert in pursuit of a lizard, or running to identify cows and making his colleagues pant with the effort, are some of the pictures that remain. Another is of his asking why work on one famous temple should have Hindu rather than Buddhist characteristics. "The point goes unnoticed by most visitors, even the Ceylonese," says his guide. "Haldane had spotted it, and we explained that when the temple was built no local labour could be found and Southern Indians were brought in." Towards the end of his visit, J.B.S. slipped while visiting one of the buildings. "I tried not to make too much fuss," he later wrote from Calcutta to one of his hosts, "but on return here an X-ray examination disclosed two broken ribs and a broken metatarsus. This has diminished my capacity for work."

By this time, January 1961, he was approaching a climax in his relations with the Indian Statistical Institute. Before this was reached, however, he was, incongruously enough, asked to advise on the Queen's visit to India, and was also drawn into a public avowal of his strong anti-Americanism.

When Her Majesty's visit had first been mooted, Haldane had been asked what the Queen should see in India. "If Her Majesty were allowed to choose her own programme after consultation with Mr. Salim Ali, our greatest naturalist, she would perhaps visit Chilka lake [Orissa, world's finest duck habitat]. Kaziynanga [Assam, wild Indian rhinoceroses] and Sambal Lake [Rajasthan, rare species of flamingo], preferably not killing any animals," he replied. "She would at once acquire popularity with the hundred million or so Indians who take animals seriously, as Jehangir acquired it." Now, in January 1961, on the eve of the visit, a mutual friend of Haldane and the Governor of Bengal explained that the Governor was worried as to what to discuss with the Queen. Haldane again advised wild life, and suggested that Her Majesty might be presented with a bound copy of Salim Ali's Book of Indian birds. "The ideal gift, were it available," he added with a typical Haldane touch, "would, I believe, be a Mugul or Rajput picture of a polo match."

One result of the advice was that Haldane and his wife were invited to meet the Queen when she visited Calcutta in February. He asked to be excused since he was still recovering from his fall in Ceylon. "Neither my wife nor I possess clothes suitable for such a reception," he went on. "My European tail coat was bought before 1939, and looks it. My Indian clothes come from the Gram Khadi Udyog, and look it. My wife has also no formal evening dress, jewellery and the like. One reason for our coming to India is that the Gandhian tradition makes such simplifications of life not only practicable but respectable. On the other hand they might be regarded as insulting to the Queen of England, and we have no wish to insult her." Everyone would therefore be satisfied by his non-appearance—"I have no burning desire to grasp a glove containing Queen Elizabeth's hand," he commented later to a friend, "and she can survive without my grasp."

While preparations for this Royal visit were continuing, J.B.S. embarked on his much-publicised one week fast, undertaken mainly as a protest against what he considered a gratuitous insult by the American authorities to three Indian biologists but partly, as he said in a letter to Linus Pauling, "to get down my fat". His initial anti-Americanism had been caused partly by the slightly hysterical wave of legislation passed in the early days of the Cold War. When asked to become a member of the American Ecological Society, he had been forced to reply that "unfortunately, recent legislation by your Congress would prevent me, along with many other Europeans, from attending its meetings. Persons who state publicly that they object to the use of atomic bombs are now classed as dangerous revolutionaries [as Washington, Paine and Jefferson were in their time]". Another was his fear that the America which he admired and respected would not only make itself the most detested country in the world but would do so by repeating Britain's errors. "Arm by all means," he wrote to one correspondent, "and ally yourselves with other nations if their freely elected governments ask for such an alliance. But don't think that you can assure peace by having airfields all over the globe. The British thought this about their naval bases up to 1914."

At times his attitude was understandable enough, as when he wrote of "the keen business methods adopted by some American firms, which do so much for the spread of Communism in Asia". At others, it had a paranoic ring, as when he wrote to a U.S. Correspondent who had questioned a statement of his given in an *Encyclopaedia Britannica* article. "I know nothing about any article on Heredity in the *Encyclopaedia Britannica* which purports to be by me," he said. "I wrote them one some time before 1930. I cannot prevent them reprinting it without payment or revision. But this is the kind of action which makes the name of America stink throughout the world. I am here as a refugee from the American occupation of my country. American soldiers have turned my home town into a brothel. I am not surprised that American publishers sell thirty-year-old stuff of mine as science. But I do not feel any compulsion to answer questions about it." This strength of feeling was further increased by the supply of American arms to Pakistan, and when Haldane wrote to President Eisenhower in August 1959, on behalf of 100 teachers and researchers in California who had been summoned before the House Un-American Activities Committee, he described such arms as "weapons which would be useless against Russian missiles or aeroplanes but very useful against the forces of the Indian Republic".

Haldane rather enjoyed his anti Americanism. He therefore relished an invitation to speak at a conference of genetics to be held in the University of Utah. "I should particularly like to visit Utah," he wrote in reply. "I cannot share the theological views of the first settlers. But I can, and do, admire their heroism." There was, however, an impediment. When he asked for the necessary visa he received a form from the Consulate-General in Calcutta on which he was asked to state the names of all organisations of which he had been a member since his sixteenth birthday, together with dates of membership. He could, of course, have lied; but he had, he said, "a professional prejudice in favour of truth".

"I regret that I cannot answer this question," he wrote to his prospective hosts in Utah. "I am now sixty-seven years old, I do not, for example, know in what year [?1921] I became a member of the Genetical Society, and in what year [?1922] I became a member of the Association of Scientific Workers. I have been a member of various political organisations, mainly of an anti-fascist nature, but cannot remember them all, and have no idea how long they lasted. The number of organisations must exceed fifty. As however I am liable to penalties under U.S. Law if I make a false declaration, and I doubt if I can avoid errors [especially as before leaving England I destroyed many old papers] I have no option but to decline your kind invitation. The whole document seems to me unworthy of 'the land of the free and the home of the brave', whose government is apparently afraid that I may try to subvert it."

Haldane was still a Communist in spirit, if no longer a Party member. Yet few men can better have illustrated the absurdity of the rules which were to keep him from the U.S. for a number of years. "If I wished to blow up the Empire State Building or subvert the Republican Party I should doubtless be willing to sign false statements," he wrote to Senator Humphrey. "And it seems to me ridiculous that a great country like yours [or rather its government] should be so frightened of what I can do as to make such demands. If I came I should certainly annoy some powerful people in your country. I should state for example that I had not met a Fulbright Fellow who was not making the U.S.A. respected and even loved in India, nor a Technological Co-operation Mission [part of I.C.A.] member who was not making it hated, at least by some Indians. No doubt my sample of both is small. Such comment, even if it is biased, would do your country no harm."

Haldane was saying no more than many other Europeans in India felt, but he can hardly have been regarded with kindly eye by the U.S. authorities in Calcutta whose task it was to spread U.S. propaganda. However, he was still the man best fitted to help visiting biologists or prospective biologists, and on January 13th 1961 he received a letter from the U.S. Deputy Scientific Attaché in New Delhi. Would Haldane help two High School students, both potential biologists, both picked for their ability, who would be visiting Calcutta. Haldane helped. He invited them to lunch and he arranged for them to dine with three prominent Indian biologists. However, when arrangements were complete the American authorities in Calcutta announced that the two visitors were to dine with an official of the U.S. Information Service, and the two visitors—through no fault of their own—failed to turn up for the carefully-arranged meeting. In the subsequent exchange of letters, the head of the Information Service described the affair as "a mix-up", while Haldane, confident that a successful attempt had been made to shield the visitors from all contact with heretical thoughts, declared it to be "a matter of deliberate policy".

As a protest he insisted on fasting for a week on coffee and water, going as usual to the Indian Statistical library in the evenings to work and, with his ankle still in plaster from his Ceylon fall, making an impressive figure of a martyr. The fast, much publicised, at least showed that not all white men in India were of one mind. But Haldane wrote to New Delhi, "you may as well know that three fairly good Indian biologists will think more kindly of the U.S.S.R. as the result of the activities of the U.S.I.S.". Honesty forced him to add: "Luckily for you, one of the three has been let down by Soviet officials!"

The minor flurry of the protest-fast came as Haldane's relations with Professor Mahalanobis were reaching breaking-point.

It was now three and a half years since he had arrived in Calcutta with high hopes; many of them had been fulfilled. He had found his bright young men, and he had set a number of them on the right lines. He himself had done a good deal of useful work. He continued to produce papers, and the *Journal of Genetics* was not only lively but was beginning to illustrate one of Haldane's particular traits—his ability to read someone else's paper and to see in it some important significance of which the author had been unaware. In a number of cases, the *Journal* would contain not only a paper but a consequential paper or note by Haldane re-analysing the data presented and, in many cases, showing that the data was really far more exciting than the author had realised. "This," says one biologist, "was an obvious aspect of Haldane's unusual scientific ability. He was someone who could see the connections between quite disparate types of scientific knowledge and could thus produce results which were beyond the scope of other people."

Despite all this, Haldane was increasingly unhappy at the Indian Statistical Institute. Perhaps this was inevitable. Perhaps any man—and particularly a Haldane—who had enjoyed the assurance of Oxford, ten years of Cambridge under Hopkins, and then almost a quarter-century of undisputed if complaining rule at University College, was bound to feel confined by an Institute being steered into a position of power in a State with little more than a decade of independence behind it.

The difficulty sprang not so much from the organisation of the Institute itself as from the framework within which it was forced to operate. After a member of the staff had been sacked for smoking in front of a worker senior to himself, Haldane commented: "It appears that some persons in the Indian Statistical Institute wish to model it on the court of a British Viceroy rather than on a scientific laboratory. If they succeed they will certainly make original work there impossible, and this may well be their aim." He noted that in the Indian bureaucracy, which spread out round research workers like all-enveloping glue, "incompetence is pretty well organised to protect itself".

And at times he felt forced to dig into his own pocket and pay air fares for scientists to save them time.

There was also a haziness about his formal relations with the Institute. Although he had been working there three years by the summer of 1960, Haldane had received no statement of his duties or powers. "For some purposes," he wrote on July 27th 1960, "I am treated as head of a department, for others as a subordinate." There was also the business of signing on daily in the book—the equivalent of the humblest factory worker's "clocking-in". Two of Haldane's colleagues were forced to sign twice daily. Inevitably, Haldane said that as long as that went on he too would sign; but it seemed a poor recommendation for the way the Institute was run.

These points were merely indicators of what Haldane considered to be the poor conditions within the Institute for carrying out "open" as opposed to "closed" experimental work. In the latter, where, as an example, it was known what it was proposed to measure or estimate, one kind of organisation was required. In "open" work, where the emphasis was on watching for the unexpected, a totally different kind of organisation was needed—that of an army rather than of a post office.

It was encouragement of this "open" work at which Haldane excelled. From his early days as a don at Oxford he had emphasised the value of looking for unexpected results, reactions, correlations; the significance of such things was more likely to be realised in the atmosphere of communal interchange, of cross-fertilising ideas, which Haldane encouraged—even though he himself might get little or no credit for the ideas which finally emerged. Significantly, such a policy had a marked resemblance to that of A. P. Rowe's wartime Telecommunications Research Establishment which fostered the ramifications of radar—and where the weekly interchanges were known as the Sunday Soviets. Such free-and-easy exchange of ideas between all levels would have been difficult in any Indian establishment. It was made no easier in the Statistical Institute by the multiplicity of its director's duties and interests. Haldane continued, after his break with the Institute, to have the highest regard for Professor Mahalanobis, but felt that he was "an impossible boss. He does not realise," he wrote to Isaiah Berlin, "that from the age of sixty one should contract one's activities."

Yet the fact that something deeper lay behind Haldane's disagreements at the Institute is clear from a letter which he wrote to Mahalanobis after he had, in the October of 1961, been offered an Honorary Doctorate. He declined because he felt that the Institute authorities had made it abundantly clear that he was "not considered fit to teach in it". He detailed other complaints. But whatever the individual rights or wrongs of each point raised, his letter made on thing clear: there was no room in the same Institute for John Burdon Sanderson Haldane and Professor Prasanta Chandra Mahalanobis.

The break came in February 1961, and it came, as might have been expected of Haldane, over a matter of principle, and in a somewhat spectacular way. Quite as typically, Haldane himself neither said nor wrote much about the incident. He believed that his Director was in the wrong; loyalty prevented him from publicly announcing the fact as he might well have done.

Late in February Mr. Kosygin, later to become Prime Minister of the U.S.S.R., paid an official visit to Calcutta. It was arranged that he should be shown the work of the Indian Statistical Institute, and the more important members of the staff were told to prepare exhibits which would illustrate the work going on. This was natural enough and usual enough. Haldane duly arranged what was available, including the research material of two junior Indian colleagues who were absent on work elsewhere.

The day before Mr. Kosygin was due to arrive in Calcutta, Professor Mahalanobis returned to the Institute. In Haldane's subsequent words, "he countermanded these arrangements without consulting me, and asked me to rearrange my colleagues' research material according to a plan of his own".

This was the spark which set off the dynamite, and with Haldane there was always dynamite to spare. He refused to rearrange the exhibits, standing firm on the ground that however distinguished a visitor was, he should not be allowed to interrupt the scientific work in progress—which would, he implied, be inevitable if the Director's orders were carried out.

When Mahalanobis refused to budge, Haldane resigned; on the spot, and in no uncertain terms. Helen, standing by, did the same. Principle and instinct united them, and both confirmed their resignations despite pleas to do otherwise.

Both also held good strategic ground. More than a month previously Haldane had been told by the Indian Vice-President, S. Radhakrishnan, that the proposed National Laboratory for Biological Science might be ready within the year. "Possibly you and Dr. Helen Spurway may be enabled to work there according to your own likes," he added.

The interaction of two such strong-minded and individualistic men as Haldane and Mahalanobis may well have made inevitable Haldane's eventual resignation from the Indian Statistical Institute. Yet the impediments of bureaucracy, which tended to entangle the Institute, even though it was not an official limb of the Government, had tended to exacerbate the situation. Haldane was well aware of this, and at first it seems strange that he was so willing to move from the Institute into the red-tape thickets of Government service. He was in no desperate financial need. His reputation gave him the pick of the available posts, and more than one academic institution in India would have been willing to create posts specifically for J.B.S. and his wife.

Before any Government appointment was finally settled, he did, in fact, receive an offer from the Vice-Chancellor of the Panjab University in Chandigarh, the new Corbusier-planned State capital, of the Chair of Genetics which had just been created. Haldane was greatly attracted, particularly as he saw the university "as a bastion of Indian culture near a frontier, comparable with the French university of Strassbourg, which perhaps is only second to Paris". "If I come," he added, "I shall not want a great deal of laboratory space, but I shall want accommodation for my wife's and my library, consisting of about 60,000 volumes and their equivalent in pamphlets and reprints. They will be available to the staff and selected students of the university, as they are here. Most of the books are biological, but many of the others [e.g. Greek, Latin and English poetry] can be of use in a university. I shall want four or five acres of ground on which to keep plants and animals. I shall want very little imported equipment. However, for research I shall need one desk calculating machine, and fairly soon, one good microscope with accessories. For teaching, apart from a lantern, I shall want one binocular microscope with lamp, costing about Rs.700, for each student taking practical genetics."

The demands were modest enough. The opportunities were considerable enough. And there seems little doubt that Haldane would have been happy at Chandigarh. Yet by the time that the offer was made he already felt himself morally committed elsewhere. For when his resignation from the Institute had become known, Dr. Thacker, head of the Council for Scientific and Industrial Research, had begun to follow up the Vice-President's offer. Haldane soon found himself agreeing to start a Genetics and Biometry Research Unit in Calcutta. Buildings, laboratory and ground would follow in due course, he was assured; so would the details of his status and the manner in which he was to fit into the official machine. Meanwhile he could begin work in his own home, where the unit would formally come into existence, if no other accommodation had been provided, on November 1st 1961. It was perhaps significant and certainly ominous that as details were being arranged Haldane should write to his old friend, Professor Bernal, and say of the post that: "I expect it will be so tied up by Government regulations as to render research very difficult."

The hiatus until the autumn was necessary since Haldane was planning to leave India at the end of May for an important four-month journey to Europe. He had been invited to Oxford for the meeting of the Physiological Society being held to celebrate the centenary of his father's birth. He had been invited to the International Congress on Human Genetics at Rome, and that on Social Insects at Pavia. He and Jayakar were to prepare a paper for Rome, his colleague Dronamraju was to read two there, and his wife and Dronamraju were to read a joint paper in Pavia. "Beside this," he had already written to Mahalanobis before resigning from the Institute, "we have informal invitations to Poland, Scotland and France, and I should like us all three to go to England by way of Moscow."

In addition, he now learned that he had, as he wrote to Dr. Salim Ali, "received a monstrous prize of about Rs.160,000 from the Italian Accademia dei Lincei . . . Probably you deserve this prize more than I. It was difficult for you to become a biologist. It was difficult for me not to become one, with my father's example before me." On first hearing news that he was to receive this Feltrinelli prize Haldane had been sceptical of its value, which turned out to be greater than the cash value of a Nobel Prize. "I have offered to sell it for £5,750, but can find no takers," he wrote to a friend.

When he left India in May on this long round tour of scientific activities Haldane travelled, for the first time, on an Indian passport. He had not renounced his British citizenship on leaving England for India in 1957. But when making arrangements for his visit to Ceylon during 1960 he discovered that his existing passport would expire before the end of the year, and the need for renewal gave him cause for thought. He and Helen had already spent nearly three years in India, they had resolved to settle permanently, and they had decided that it was "only common courtesy in such a case to apply for citizenship, as we would if we intended to settle down in Australia".

J.B.S. wrote to the local passport officer in Calcutta, was referred to the West Bengal authorities, and received no reply to his application. "No doubt if I knew whom to bribe at a low level, or to ask to dinner at a high one, the thing would go through smoothly," he wrote in a note to Krishna Menon, asking whether he could pull any kind of string. "But I don't . . . You will perhaps appreciate the reasons for my desire to become a citizen of the Indian Republic rather than a subject of Queen Elizabeth II. They do not include a blind admiration of everything Indian, but my admiration of some of them is sufficient to make me feel it worth while to criticise some others. In England at present I doubt if this is worth while!"

Shortly afterwards he made formal application for himself and his wife on the correct pieces of paper that had by this time been blown along the official corridors to his address. Apart from the common courtesy he had written of there were other reasons for their actions. "We approve of the present foreign policy of the Government of India and find it vastly preferable to that of the British Government," he added. "We also prefer the declared policy of the Government of India in internal affairs to that of either of the principal British parties." The formalities took some time but in April 1961, the Haldanes signed their nationalisation papers, formally cutting the link which had been cut in practice more than three years previously.

Thus fortified, they set out for Europe the following month. Before they left, Haldane sent a revealing letter, plus cheque, to his friend Nirmal Bose. "If during my absence in Europe, any one for whom I am partly responsible needs money, e.g. Subodh Roy is run over and his sister is destitute, please use the enclosed cheque," he said. "Be generous to X rather than just to me. One cannot go through life without being swindled; one may escape neglecting one's more obvious obligations. These are of course more in India than England. There no one goes without food and shelter. I pay taxes, and can recommend people who would be my dependents here to apply for state assistance. This is better for the poor, but not perhaps so good for the rich. A few of both are however recognising some of their remoter obligations, which I think are infinite." Bose was given instructions as executor—"But in principle let the boys have what they like (after you have taken up to 100 books) and stop them quarrelling." And if his Feltrinelli Prize was in fact worth the suggested £11,500, "please ask the legatees to spare a few hundred rupees for persons not named in the will who have worked for me, e.g. my servant Gyan and one sweeper." The extent of the Feltrinelli did seem to worry him. "The sum seems to be very large," he wrote to Davis. "If it really is so, I will be able to leave enough in Italy to pay for a visit by yourself and family to Rome . . . I left my will in the bottom drawer of the left-hand *almirah* in my bedroom. Don't open it unless both my wife and I are killed, in which case you will benefit financially, if not in other ways."

When it came to the things that mattered, J.B.S. could be big and generous. This is not only the impression that wells up from his correspondence but the impression he left during his four-month journey round Europe. He spoke to a packed audience in Oxford on how his father's views on the relation between quantum mechanics and biology might be developed and subsequently accepted both an Honorary Doctorate of Science and an Honorary Fellowship of New College. "If, as I hope, it is possible for me to receive the degree," he had written to the University Registrar, Sir Folliott Sandford, "I shall have to re-read the chapter of St. Thomas Aquinas' Summa beginning, if I remember, *Utrum doctori sureola debetur*. I am already, like him, a Doctor of the University of Paris, and should certainly wish to obtain a second doctorate which he would have recognised as a qualification for a halo."

As an Honorary Fellow he was particularly delighted by one privilege of which his sister reminded him—that he was now allowed to walk up the Mound, which they had both done secretly as children. "Yes," he replied, "but now we are ghosts." In Rome he accepted the Feltrinelli and in Pavia gave a statistical analysis prepared with Jayakar on ant and wasp behaviour.

Haldane returned to India in September 1961, having visited Israel *en route*. He had been back in Calcutta only a few weeks when he received the expected news of his mother's death. In Oxford, where he had seen her during the meetings in honour of her husband's birth, he had found her confused and not always clear about his identity. "It was a real sorrow to see her in this state, but a formal break rather than a sorrow to learn of her death," he now wrote. "At our age one should be rational about such matters, and not wish a condition in those one has loved which one would not wish for oneself . . ." His mother had bequeathed her body to the Anatomy Department at Oxford and J.B.S. wrote to Professor Sir Wilfrid Le Gros Clark, the University Professor of Anatomy. "I shall be most interested to learn what changes had taken place in her brain," he said, adding: "My own is beginning to deteriorate, in that I find it hard to learn [e.g. a new language] and need to be reminded of day-to-day duties. However, I can still do original work and, what is more important, help others to do so . . ."

And with his mother's death he could at last help others as generously as he had often wanted to help them. Of the £30,000 and more which now came to him he had £5,000 transferred to the Royal Society as a fund on which he could draw—largely for aid to others, it appears. To Helen, Mrs. Haldane left "Cherwell".

Haldane's feelings about his own inheritance were qualified. "Its total value may not be much more than the proceeds of what I have spent on scientific research during my lifetime, had it been intelligently invested," he wrote soon afterwards. "However, my father told me not to save money. As a result I was able to save some years which I should otherwise have spent in getting to know influential people and cadging for research grants. I am therefore not quite so ashamed of inheriting the money as I perhaps ought to be as a scientist."

On his return to Calcutta, J.B.S. knuckled down to the task of working with the C.S.I.R. He was still, fundamentally, an "against" man—against the stupidities of officialdom, against the lumberingly large organisation, against the deadening effects of bureaucracy. He still, at the age of sixty-eight, refused to acquiesce. He still tried to train an organisation the way he felt it should go, and if the organisation was the C.S.I.R.—the Council for the Suppression of Independent Research, as he was soon calling it—so much the worse for the C.S.I.R.

A number of colleagues had come with him from the Indian Statistical Institute to the new unit. One was Dronamraju. Another was Suresh Jayakar, who had taken an M.Sc. in Statistics in Lucknow, had come to the Institute in 1958, and who had for a year studied genetics as an additional subject under J.B.S. A gentle kindly man with much the same feeling for animals as Haldane, Jayakar was considered by him as one of the stars which would soon be rising in the Indian scientific firmament. There was also Ramaswamy Shastri Mangipudi, who had first been brought into the Haldane circle by Dronamraju when the latter was working on colour-blindness in Vizagapatam. Shastri, self-schooled to the level where Haldane had been happy to put him in charge of his library, had first helped on the colour-blindness tests and had then come to Calcutta to work in the Institute library. Haldane and Shastri were mutually impressed; and when J.B.S. had left for Europe with Helen in the spring of 1961, Shastri had been left in complete charge of the ever-growing library in the Haldane home. Now, on Haldane's return, he began to play an increasingly important role in the work of the new unit.

Little progress appeared to have been made in finding accommodation for it, so Haldane began such work as was possible in his own flat. His programme was ambitious, and the outline which he drew up for the authorities later that autumn gives a good idea of the research which he thought was necessary. In plant genetics, Roy and Davis were to follow up their discoveries with rice and palm trees. Dronamraju was to start work on various problems in human genetics—on simple morphological and physiological characters whose genetics and geographical distribution in India had been neglected; on genetically determined biochemical abnormalities which might cause mental defect; on the effects of inbreeding in Andhra Pradesh, in one area of which 7 per cent of all marriages were between uncles and nieces and 16 per cent between first cousins. Jayakar would concern himself with animal biometry, while Haldane himself would concentrate on animal genetics, and in particular on those of poultry. "Apart from the 'pure' interest of such work," he said, in outlining what he intended to do, "there is a possibility that these wild species may be resistant to some of the common poultry diseases, and that such resistance may be transferred to domestic poultry."

As usual, his own money was to go into the work. He was planning that part of the Feltrinelli Prize would support an Indian worker in Italy and hoped that out of the same award an Italian could be brought to work in collaboration with the new unit in Calcutta. To the Home Secretary of the U.S. National Academy of Sciences, which had recently given him the Kimber Award, he wrote: "Let me give you one example of what we propose to tackle. Most of the local ducks lay white eggs. A few lay blue, like European and, I suppose, American breeds. How is the egg colour determined? Is there a metabolic difference? Can we, for example, find a porphyrin in the blood of blue-egged ducks which is absent in the white-egged? Anyway we will buy the birds from the Kimber money, and the first drake shall be called Kimber."

By the end of the year, 1961, no accommodation for the unit had been provided by the authorities. In his own flat, Haldane had converted the bathroom into a laboratory, while balcony and dining-room, where he himself normally worked, were both stacked high with books and papers. Shastri also worked in the dining-room between meals. This was the Indian Government's "Genetics and Biometry Research Unit", and as late as the following April Haldane was writing: "I have no reason to believe that I shall receive the laboratory on any assignable date. So reprints pile up in my bedroom."

It soon became necessary for him to find another assistant. What he wanted was a secretary, but he wanted, at the same time, a man of many parts who could drive his car when necessary, would not be bound by unnecessary rules of convention or caste, and who could be relied upon to use his own initiative. He wanted an exceptional man; he got one. When Shastri heard of the requirement he remembered a friend working in Vizapatam. Haldane, enquiring further, was told that this friend spoke excellent English and had a large variety of experiences. He had been a cycle-repairer; he had spent six months in the Army; he had become an electrical wire-man; had become first secretary and finally president of the relevant union; and had a multitude of abilities which would prove of use in unexpected situations. This was Sri P. Srihari Rao, known as Hari, who came to Calcutta and was engaged by Haldane in March. Two years later Haldane was able to write that his "knowledge of English scientific terminology is much superior to that of many Indian university graduates, and on several occasions he has helped my colleagues in scientific observations in the field. He conducts much of the administrative correspondence of the laboratory without troubling me, and is most reliable in financial matters." Hari quickly became both invaluable and irreplaceable.

Haldane's exasperation with the authorities was heightened in early 1962 by a number of pin-pricks. He discovered that he was forbidden to speak in support of a Congress candidate in the elections; Government employees, and that included Haldane, were forbidden to take part in politics. The ban ruled out any co-operation with the various anti-nuclear bomb movements which were growing up in India, and in wishing one of them good luck, Haldane felt forced to add "—if this is not a breach of my contract with the C.S.I.R."

He no doubt remembered how he had earlier written to a friend: "We are to be called a Research Unit (how I hate that word, it suggests that we shall have, as Blake put it in his able anticipation of totalitarianism (1st Bk. of Urizen):

One command, one joy, one desire,
One curse, one weight, one measure,
One king, one god, one law)

for genetics and biometry. Almost anything can be biometry."

240

Even this might have been taken as no more than the customary growl of complaint from a man deeply immersed in his work. But the extent of the network in which he had now become entangled was being continually stressed. Haldane was asked to sign a document underlining the fact that as a member of the C.S.I.R. he could be ordered to any part of India at a month's notice. Then, in June, it was announced that no such employees should approach any foreign organisation for help in travelling abroad without first obtaining official approval. Haldane, outlining in great detail to the authorities his connections with foreign scientific organisations, protested: "I claim the right to approach these bodies for assistance to myself and others without the sanction of officials who know no more about scientific research than I know about Indian music. If, by continuing service under the C.S.I.R., I forfeit this right, I wish to resign in order to regain it. An early reply will oblige."

By this time the contentious matter of accommodation was coming to a head. Work on the quarters which Haldane had expected to be ready so much earlier was now started; furthermore, he was provided with what he called "half a table for our administrative officer". The result was that when Haldane's position was raised in June in the Lok Sahba—the Indian equivalent of the House of Commons—a small peg existed on which the authorities could hang the claim that all was going as Haldane desired. They had not studied their man carefully enough.

The day after the statement had been made in the Lok Sahba, Haldane issued a 300-word statement to the Press. "In view of the false statements made about me . . . I have given notice of my resignation from the services of the C.S.I.R." this began. "It is not right that Rs.1,800 a month of the tax-payers' money should be spent on my salary if those who pay it are misinformed."

The letter of resignation was a blistering outline of Haldane's grievances since he had returned to India from Europe some nine months previously. "This is entirely typical of the official treatment of scientists in India," he concluded. "It is the intolerable conditions imposed by bureaucrats, and not the low salaries or the lack of equipment, which cause so many Indians to take up posts abroad. I hope that my resignation may do something to draw public attention to these conditions."

Attention was certainly drawn, but one conclusion, a false one, was that Haldane was about to leave India. His real attitude was very different. "Please don't think I am fed up with this

241

country," he wrote to Florey at the Royal Society, "Some of the people at the top should be liquidated (though not the President, Nehru, Krishna Menon, and Jagjivan Ram, to mention no more). But the young men are grand; and so are a lot of the plants and animals."

Studying the bulky files of correspondence which arose from Haldane's nine-month liaison with the C.S.I.R., one feels that here, however great his ability to build a minor grievance into a major issue, he had the perfect case. He wanted to get on with his research, and he had money enough to start his own laboratory; but he also sincerely wanted to give young Indians the encouragement he felt would best be given within a Government organisation. Instead of that he had been forced to waste a year. He did not intend to waste another.

13

A Brief Look at Paradise

HALDANE'S letter to Florey restating his enthusiasm for India, was written on June 15th. Within a fortnight he had signed a contract which was to take him out of Calcutta to a town where he was to set up his own laboratory, and to work under conditions which satisfied all—or at least nearly all—of his own exacting demands. The town was Bhubaneswar, the new "garden city" capital of the State of Orissa. Haldane's movement there was the result of a series of lucky chances.

Carved from East Bengal, and stretching down the coast some hundreds of miles south-west of Calcutta, Orissa covers much of the ancient kingdom of Kalinga and it was as the Kalinga Prize that a notable Indian businessman and politician, Biju Patnaik, had in 1952 founded an annual award for popular science writing. In 1960 the Kalinga Prize was awarded to Ritchie Calder, and early in 1962 Calder visited India on a lecture tour. In Calcutta he met both Dr. Thacker and Haldane. Both were old friends, but Calder was unable to resolve the argument then raging between them. Haldane was now determined to leave the C.S.I.R., and with this fact clear in his mind Calder travelled down to Orissa.

By this time, Patnaik was Chief Minister of the State, a powerful position made more so by his personal drive and ambition. "Patnaik had told me that he wanted to raise the status of science in his State and to make it something more than applied research," says Calder. Both men knew and admired Haldane, and during Calder's stay in Orissa there was talk of the possibility of providing Haldane with facilities there. On March 8th, Haldane wrote to Patnaik in Orissa. "I know that you take science seriously, and are one of the few people in Indian politics who do so," he began. "I am therefore writing to ask whether you can offer any opportunities." He outlined his troubles at the C.S.I.R. and went on: "I am paid Rs.1,800 per month by the C.S.I.R. I am quite willing to give this up, as I own securities valued at about five lakhs. I should be willing to act as unpaid adviser to an Institute in which the following had security of tenure and of research, with salaries round Rs.1,000 per month"—and he went on to name his wife and certain of his colleagues.

"I could, I think, trust these three to run such an institute," he went on. "I should prefer to be on a footing of equality with them, but do not ask for this. I see no reason why I should be better paid. I could of course give university lectures if desired, but they might not fit into the curriculum. We would need a house and land, but not much imported apparatus. Anyway I can buy this, if I get import permits, so no foreign exchange is needed. Of course we would want the salaries of malis, clerks, and laboratory assistants, and a little for animal food and housing, and so on. A motor-car would be very useful. And of course we would want to take on young people. It will be hard to make exact estimates, but not impossible."

Thus began negotiations that continued for three months. Haldane and Helen visited Orissa. They liked, and were liked by, the people they saw. And while Haldane's relationship with the C.S.I.R. was drawing to its close, the final details of his new post in Orissa were being settled. Eventually only two points remained at issue. One was that Haldane insisted on security of tenure—not for himself, but because, as he pointed out, if work could be stopped at a month's notice, this would be a discouragement to genetic work which was essentially long-term. Secondly, he insisted that those who came with him to Orissa should be colleagues rather than assistants—just as he disliked the proposed term "Unit" since it suggested "a lot of people obeying my order when I shout at them, which is not what I intend". He was confident that at Orissa a lot of his work would come to fruition, and he perhaps saw there, at the age of seventy, some hope of achieving a life's ambition. "I should like," he wrote, "to be remembered as the man who in his last years founded the famous Bhubaneswar school of biology. You can't do that by ordering people about."

The difficulties were overcome. By June 1962 the final amendments were being made to the agreement which was to take Haldane and his colleagues out of Calcutta. As a P.S., Haldane wrote to the Chief Secretary: "Unless I can resign quickly from the C.S.I.R. I may not be able to accept employment on July 1st." However, the question in the Lok Sabha came like a question from the Gods. The answer gave Haldane his excuse for resignation and a fortnight later he was able to cable Orissa. "Agreement accepted." Within little more than a month, Haldane and his wife and colleagues were moving to a new life in Bhubaneswar.

This new capital of the state of Orissa had been designed and brought into being when, after Independence, it had been decided to abandon as a capital the old city of Cuttack, largely pinched as it was on an island site between two branches of the river Mahanadi. Even when the Haldanes arrived in the summer of 1962, Bhubaneswar still had the unfinished air of a frontier-town, with semi-laid-out roads leading off into the wilderness. Neat boards standing solitary in grass plots still announced future buildings, as though prospectors had staked their claims to the future. With the bulk of its 38,000 inhabitants members of a burgeoning bureaucracy, there was some truth in the local saying that in Bhubaneswar there were no people, only Civil Servants; no homes, only quarters. Yet after the dusty suburbs of Calcutta, there was a relief in the green rice-fields that spread from the outskirts, across the delta to the white breakers of the Indian Ocean, interspersed with low crinkled hills and the intervening forest.

"This is a lovely place," Haldane wrote soon after his arrival to the latest of the English children who wrote to him about "Mr. Leakey". "About two hundred egrets fly over my house every evening, going to bed. They spend the day with cows and buffalos. When a cow walks through the grass, grasshoppers and other insects jump away, and the birds catch them . . . Elephants live in the woods round here, but they don't come out of them much. The biggest animal who has trespassed in to my house is a green lizard about four feet long, who got into a bathroom."

At Bhubaneswar, nature was pressing in and around all the time. On the horizon, almost seen from the balcony of the house, were the two distant hills of Udayagiri and Khandagiri with their cave-cells carved for ascetic priests and the twin temples of the Jains, that sect for which Haldane had much respect. While only a mile or so from the house, clustered round the sacred lake of Old Bhubaneswar, were the remains of some 7,000 shrines and temples, including Lingaraja, "perhaps the finest example of a purely Hindu temple in India". In a curious yet purely fortuitous way, Bhubaneswar seems to have offered Haldane more of the things he wanted than any place he had ever known.

After the first visits to Bhubaneswar, he and Helen moved into a Grade One official bungalow, only a mile or so from the buildings in which Haldane was to set up Orissa's

Genetics and Biometry Laboratory. With them came Dronamraju, Jayakar, Shastry and Hari. This team—and its members always thought of themselves as a team—had come with Haldane from Calcutta partly out of personal loyalty, partly out of personal affection. But they had been initially chosen by Haldane because in some ways he saw them as typifying India's scientific potential. None of the four then had a doctorate but all four were "as good as my post-graduate students in Cambridge, and well above the level in London". What is more, they were particularly good in the kind of work which Haldane believed to be necessary everywhere and particularly necessary in such countries as India—observation and deduction.

Work began in August 1962, and it is significant that within a year this newly-created laboratory, consisting of four rooms with the minimum of equipment, had attracted visitors from the Universities of Paris, Poitiers and London, from Columbia University, Berkeley University and the Rockefeller Institute. Within the year Haldane and Jayakar had completed a number of theoretical investigations in population genetics and statistics, Dronamraju, investigating colour-blindness in Orissa, had discovered why this was rarer in India than in Europe; Jayakar and Helen had discovered a new type of sex determination in wasps in which all male progeny arise from eggs laid before any giving rise to females. And the influence of time of sunset, weather, and various other factors on the 200 egrets which flew over the house every evening on their way from feeding to roost was being worked out from the records of their flights, an example of the work which Haldane hoped would make Bhubaneswar one of the world's standard localities for such studies.

But he also encouraged observation of animal behaviour along revolutionary lines, typified by Helen and Jayakar's minute-by-minute record of how wasps built nests, a record in which every visit of the builder to the nest was timed and recorded and the work done was described. Such work was reported in a number of papers. "I wish to emphasise," said Haldane in a report to the Orissa authorities, "that these papers are not merely an extension to India of studies now being conducted elsewhere. They are the first serious attempts anywhere in the world to apply various statistical methods in this field, and I do not doubt that they will influence science throughout the world."

But there was more to it than that. "I think we can still learn a great deal from observation," he wrote to Radhakrishnan, the Indian President, about the beginnings of such work. "For three months S. D. Jayakar and my wife have been watching a wasp's nest throughout the hours of daylight. When alone they merely record flights to and from the nest, with loads carried, and unusual events, such as egg-laying. When together [for about eight hours daily] they try to record every activity of each wasp [all marked with spots of lacquer]. Nobody has ever done this before. We shall have a history of this little animal community better than that of many human communities. And neither observer will ever be the same again. I do not say that neither of them will ever kill an insect. But if they do so they will regard it as an act comparable, if remotely, with killing a man, and therefore requiring moral justification. This is the negative side. The positive one is more important. It is the development of a respect [not necessarily love] for animals."

Reading such words in Haldane's massive correspondence, in the torrent of letters to Indian friends and to former colleagues in England, the advice, the comments on politics and art, it is difficult not to feel that while still absorbed by the world of science, he was now operating on a more Olympian, perhaps less scientific level. "The fact about science," he wrote to Robert Graves, "is that everyone who has made a serious contribution to it is aware, or very strongly suspects, that the world is not only queerer than anyone has imagined, but queerer than any one can imagine. This is a most disturbing thought, and one flees from it by stating the exact opposite . . ."

To Fred Hoyle, whose *The Black Cloud* fascinated him—"The scientists behaved like scientists, not like magicians, politicians or capitalists. This fact alone justifies your writing it"—J.B.S. commented that the disappearance of the Clouds which attained knowledge of the unlimited intelligence was good Hinduism. "One of the most pleasing myths of our religion," he told Hoyle, "is that whereas one can hope to attain deliverance after seven lives spent in loving this intelligence, one can do so after only three of consistently hating it, and acting accordingly. One learns more about the nature of another being by fighting it than by obeying it. But of course the three lives are somewhat stormy, and end in violent death, probably followed by a sojourn in hell. So this method is not recommended."

He still continued to give much thought to the way in which Marxism might be worked out in practice, and a letter to an old friend at University College illustrates his attitude both to the Sino-Soviet split and to Stalin. "The Chinese thesis is more attractive to workers here than to those in, say Italy, who have a fair lot besides their chains to lose," he wrote. "Those in the

Soviet Union have a very great deal to lose, and would lose much of it in a thermonuclear war. But workers in southern Asia have very little to lose, so naturally many of them find the Chinese point of view attractive. I certainly don't go all the way with Kruschev. As you know, I disagreed, during Stalin's lifetime, with some of his actions. But I thought, and think, that he was a very great man who did a very good job. And as I did not denounce him then, I am not going to do so now . . ."

Haldane's ideas continued to proliferate—for recording Indian bird-song, for carrying out fresh genetic surveys in specified parts of the country, for bringing to India "a few hundred young British people, preferably under thirty-five, who will settle down somewhere for at least a year, and do research, teaching or both". In an attempt to gain support for this last scheme he wrote to Lord Salisbury, in an effort to "retrieve some of the mistakes of British policy in the past. You and I disagree strongly as to what these mistakes were," he said, "but we may find some area of agreement." Haldane's distress was that while there were only British business men in Bhubaneswar the place was, as he put it, "lousy with Americans". He wanted to renew the Anglo-Indian links that had been broken at the time of Independence and believed that "you won't remake broken contacts merely by sending out high R.A.F. officers and high-brow poets. What is needed is young people who will get to know their opposite numbers here by working with them."

It was natural enough that Haldane should want to encourage young Englishmen out to India, for he had somehow become seized of the country during the five years he had spent in it. It is clear that he was happier at Bhubaneswar than he had been for many years. He felt that those under his influence were doing good scientific work. He was building up what he hoped would be a research centre whose activities would be discussed throughout the scientific world. He was comparatively untouched by bureaucracy, working as he did in his own small unit and in practice responsible only to the Chief Minister. Somehow, in a way which those of strong national loyalties will find it difficult to comprehend, he had struck down roots here between the mountains and the sea.

In the autumn of 1962 Haldane started his seventy-first year. He was beginning to feel his age, "not so much directly," as he wrote to his old friend, Sir Robert Davis of Siebe Gorman, "as by constantly having slight accidents leading to fractures or sprains because I have not learned to move slowly and quietly." These minor impediments did little to hamper his physical activities and nothing to limit his mental work—"I am ordering a copy of the new edition of *Astro-physical Quantities*, which I find a pleasing bedside book," he wrote to its author, Professor C. W. Allen, Professor of Astronomy at University College. "I am sorry you have not extended it to the 200 brightest stars. I don't suppose they would represent any more types, but I get a certain satisfaction from knowing the natures of the more obvious stars."

That he was happy in Bhubaneswar was underlined in a letter to Martin Case whom he now learned was working as a Government biochemist in Wormwood Scrubs Prison. He no doubt delighted in addressing the letter to "The Condemned Cell"—where the laboratory had in fact been set up—hoped that Case would remain there "for longer than the usual period of three weeks", and went on to describe his work. "I have settled down here, I hope for the term of my natural life," he went on. "This place has a very pleasant climate, and the people are highly civilised, though so easy-going that I can be a nuisance by working a little too hard for them at the age of seventy . . . I live here in astonishing luxury, the house being provided with fluorescent-tube lamps, fans, whisky, and gin, all made in India. We don't need mosquito nets or air conditioning. My car, a Fiat made in India, is quite efficient, though not as big as I could wish . . . People here tend to be rather unadventurous. However, some go in for flying, Communism, and mountaineering, not to mention dangerous driving of mechanically-propelled vehicles, which seems to be one of our leading national sports. Failure to acquire a driving licence adds to the fun . . . Some of our local temples are decorated with amorous couples or trios in remarkable attitudes. I am too old to attempt such novelties, many of which involve heavy muscular effort; but it is alleged that the tradition still persists. Kinsey's institute should send a team of Americans of both sexes here to verify this."

He was happy and he was still working hard. Moreover, in a curious way his life now seemed to be swinging round full circle. On the fundamental level, he was coming back to the nature of reality itself. In 1934 he had speculated on quantum mechanics as a basis for philosophy. Now, in "Life and Mind as Physical Realities"—the essay could be regarded, he concluded, as a piece of pretentious nonsense or the key to dark mysteries—he appeared to wrap up the lessons of his life, at least synthesising some of his own and his father's views and postulating the existence of "only one science, of which physics, biology, and psychology are different aspects". This speculation on the unity of existence, published in Penguin Science Survey, was one of the most remarkable of Haldane's *tours de force*. It also provided a faint indication of a new flutter in his thoughts; for here Haldane began to hint at an order and a unity in the universe which he had hardly before suspected; like T. H. Huxley he began to feel the "limited revelation of the nature of things which we call scientific knowledge".

It was not only in this field that he began to synthesise his experiences. He had worked in genetics for half a century, with a part of his mind forever watching the human implications of what he and his fellow-workers were doing. Now he was to produce a characteristically controversial paper summing-up his lifetime of knowledge—"The Implications of Genetics for Human Society". The same was true of his long interest in the origin of life. For now he was to become the honoured guest at an international symposium on the subject, to prepare a new paper giving the "Data needed for a Blueprint of the First Organism", and to meet A. I. Oparin who had provided the first half of what had been known for thirty years as the Oparin-Haldane theory.

These two papers were to be given during an autumn of travel. Earlier in 1963, Haldane had received a number of invitations to visit the United States, including one from the Kaiser Foundation Hospital in San Francisco and another from the University of Miami which was organising a conference on the origins of life. At first, Haldane was cautious. He had already experienced enough frustration with American visa problems. So at first he declined—on the grounds that he would have to detail all the organisations to which he had belonged. "I do not suppose that I should be sent to Alcatraz for stating that I resigned from the Bald and Beard Club [a pigeon fanciers' association] in 1926, when it was 1924. But I have a quaint professional respect for truth," he wrote. However, he finally decided to apply.

This time he won, being informed that "a visa to visit the United States will be given to you without question about your personal or professional history . . . You have made a significant gain for dignity, and as I wrote earlier, your request was sympathetically received by our Government." When he went to Calcutta to pick up his visa he found that the Consul there "was most polite, asked no questions, and was told no lies". It is difficult not to believe that Haldane was faintly disappointed.

However, before he set out for the United States he was to

receive a shock. It came not from the Federal authorities but from North Carolina, at whose Institute of Biological Sciences he had been asked to deliver a series of lectures. Was he, it was asked, a member of the Communist Party? The reason for the question was simple. Academic freedom meant one thing to the U.S. Government, but it meant something different to the State legislature of North Carolina—since members of the Communist Party were barred from speaking at State-supported functions. Haldane, predictably enough, absolutely refused to answer the question, pointed out that the Soviet Union did not ask whether visiting scientists were members of the Conservative Party, and suggested that it was a curious question to be asked in "the free world". He went on to say that he would try to arrange his visit to the United States without visiting North Carolina. "I shall however," he went on, "use the incident for propaganda against the present set-up in your country, which is, of course, in flat contradiction of the principles laid down by your Founding Fathers in the Declaration of Independence and other contemporary documents." The University authorities may well have agreed.

Meanwhile, Haldane and his wife completed their preparations. First he was to go to The Hague, where the Eleventh International Congress of Genetics was to be held, and then to Frascati for a conference on the teaching of science and mathematics. Then Haldane was to leave for the conference on prebiological systems, to be held in Florida. At The Hague, where he spoke on the implications of genetics for human society, he commented that it was "impossible to speak on the applications of human genetics without giving offence to someone. I hope I shall give it impartially." In this paper, which caused something of a stir even outside scientific circles, Haldane ranged across the possibilities and the impossibilities of genetics, puncturing fallacies and starting hares with comparable ease and frequency. The socially innate characters of the Danes and Norwegians had been transformed in 1,200 years: pulmonary tuberculosis was more likely among those with certain rare recessive genes which might contribute to poetic powers—and "if so, I hope that the fact that pulmonary tuberculosis is now rapidly curable will allow such genes to become common once more"; these were merely some of Haldane's statements which raised eyebrows during a paper in which he noted: "Plato, in his Republic, first formalised the ideal of a hereditary class, with occasional rejection of unworthy members, and recruitment of worthy ones from the ruled . . . As a geneticist I agree with

Plato in theory." As if this was not enough, he added: "I believe that any satisfactory political and economic system must be based on the recognition of human inequality"—and quoted Stalin in support of his belief.

After the visit to Frascati, J.B.S. set out for the United States, going first to New York, where he met his old friend Professor Dobzhansky of the Rockefeller University, and where he was asked if he would read a paper at the University of Wisconsin. "That would depend on the extent of your honorarium," he replied. "I have to pay about $2,400 [two years' salary] for expenses of a research in India nominally run by the W.H.O. who, however, will only pay part of the cash. So I want to bag all the dollars I can." Three weeks later, he flew down to Florida.

For nearly forty years both Haldane and Oparin had been developing, along independent but parallel lines, their theories of how life had began on earth. They had corresponded with one another but they were to meet for the first time only now, towards the end of their lives. There was something slightly ironic in the fact that they were doing so not in one of the world centres of science but in Wakulla Springs, fifteen miles from Tallahassee, a remote spot in rural North Florida. An added piquancy was provided by the fact that the conformist but Communist Russian had been allowed into the United States after little more than a mere formality. Haldane's request for a visa had accumulated a thick file.

On the first evening of the meeting Haldane, in the chair, introduced Oparin as the opening speaker. "I suppose that Oparin and I may be regarded as ancient monuments in this branch of science, but there is a very considerable difference," he said; "that whereas I know nothing serious about it, Dr. Oparin has devoted his life to this subject." Ancient monuments maybe, but for many of those present an intriguing question concerned their relative antiquity. Who, in fact, had first put forward the Oparin-Haldane theory? Oparin was tactfully asked at what point he had decided that the synthesis of complex organic molecules could come from methane, ammonia, water and hydrogen. "Almost forty years ago in 1924," he replied, "in the book published at that time, I was led to this view by Mendeleyev."

Haldane himself then confirmed the position—and more than one observer noted that he was as willing to turn his bitter sarcasm on to himself, as on to others. "I have very little doubt that Professor Oparin has the priority over me," he said. "I am ashamed that I haven't read his early work, so that I don't know. As far as I know, I didn't publish until 1927, and he did so in 1924, and there was precious little of my small article which was not to be found in his books. I think if his first book was in 1924 the question of priority doesn't arise. The question of plagiarism might."

The conference was a great success, and it was made so largely by the presence of Haldane and Oparin. It was across this visit to Florida, however, that the future threw its shadow. During an early stage of the conference Haldane told Professor Fox, who had organised the symposium, that he felt he should see a doctor. He was suffering from rectal bleeding and he wanted to discuss a possible recurrence of an earlier amoebic dysentery.

Few people in the hospital to which he now went knew who Haldane was. But both his appearance, and his way of speaking, were impressive and long remembered. He was told that he should spend several days under observation, and that a careful diagnosis should be made; he might have cancer. His hosts and colleagues repeated the advice.

It would have been possible, with safety, to have made a large bet on Haldane's reaction. He felt that the conference was of the utmost importance, and he had come half-way round the world to attend it. If attendance and discussion at it proved to be his last principal activity—well, that was the sort of thing he would wish to be doing at the end of his life. He would get on with the job in hand; if he had to sink into hospital he would wait until he arrived back in England.

14

Goodbye to All That

HALDANE returned to London during the first days of November. Rather reluctantly, he entered University College Hospital where, shortly before the arrival of his wife cancer of the rectum was diagnosed. An operation was necessary, and the arrangements were now made.

While J.B.S. was awaiting the future in hospital he received a letter from a B.B.C. producer, Philip Daly. Daly was preparing a series of films in which well-known scientists discussed their most important work, and he suggested that Haldane might like to speak of his researches over half a century. In addition, he suggested, might J.B.S. not like to record his own obituary at the same time? The suggestion was a daring one, even though well-judged and well-timed, and Daly must have been in some doubt as to Haldane's reaction. It could hardly have been better.

"A goodbye to all that from a hospital bed would be an excellent idea," replied J.B.S., stipulating only that it would not be used in any way before his death. Perhaps he was throwing down the gauntlet; perhaps he was merely tickled by the idea. Certainly the letter of consent that he wrote on November 19th was vintage Haldane. The following day the operation took place.

At the very least, some weeks of convalescence were now necessary, and J.B.S. resigned himself to them with as good a grace as possible. He was, surprisingly perhaps, an ideal patient, amenable to hospital routine and winning the respect of the staff by his clinical interest in his own condition and the details of post-operation progress. "The removal of some feet of gut, and readjustments following, are more of a shock at seventy-one than they would have been at thirty-one," he wrote to Jayakar in Bhubaneswar. Nevertheless, he was already planning for the future with a vigour that would have done credit to a younger man. "I am still pretty well incapable of constructive thought," he wrote four weeks after his operation. "However, I am not so dull that I find fiction preferable to scientific or historical reading. In about a week I hope to start on mathematics again." His letters were full of instructions about work in progress and about what should be done with the *Journal of Genetics*—useful practice for Jayakar, he suggested, since he might take over the journal in about five years. "I say five years because the outlook for me is rather good," J.B.S. added. ". . . About 1969 I expect to be 'running down' in any case."

Early in January another minor operation, the first of two, had to be performed. When he recovered consciousness from the anaesthetic, Haldane later wrote to Arthur Clarke, the noted writer of science-fiction, he became aware of three tubes which had been inserted into him. "I was fed through one into a vein, another 'Ryle tube' went *via* my nose to my stomach, roughly speaking to keep my gut dry. The third was a urethral catheter, which I considered a great luxury. To judge from some S.F. this is a foretaste of the future. What little is left of our natural bodies is to be attached to a variety of gadgets. Things may go that way, or a very different one. We shan't live to see which. The present trend may be more transitory than the medieval exoskeleton for males partly symbiotic with perissodactyles. It will be if biology catches up with physics."

By mid-January Haldane was getting back into his old form. "I am at the mercy of nurses and visitors," he wrote to Jayakar. "The moment I try to think seriously they try to take my temperature, or someone wants to visit me. But even if left alone I dry up after an hour or two. However I have worked out the general equilibrium for a single gene under selection and mutation. I may be wrong. You should check and extend my algebra."

He was already becoming more mobile, and now agreed that he would give his auto-obituary before the TV cameras—not in University College Hospital but in his old room at University College, now occupied by his friend John Maynard Smith. Here he now appeared, dressed in his flowing Indian robes, leafing through the series of notes he had made, and puffing away at one of the Siebe Gorman pipes, its bowl shaped like a diver's helmet, which the firm sent him regularly.

"It is now February 1964, and this is supposed to be my own obituary," J.B.S. began, "so I hope it won't be shown, say, until 1975, when I shall be eighty-two years old, which is perhaps old enough. However, I have just been operated on for cancer, and if the operation has not been successful, you will be seeing and hearing me a lot sooner.

"I am going to begin with a boast. I believe that I am one of the most influential people living today, though I haven't got a scrap of power. Let me explain. In 1932 I was the first person to estimate the rate of mutation of a human gene; and my estimate was not far out. A great many more have been found to mutate at about the same rate since." He then went on to recapitulate his most important achievements—his early experiments into human biochemistry and his formulation of the Mathematical Theory. He looked back to defend some but not all of Lysenko's theories, and to attack the political use which had been made of them by Stalin—although for Stalin himself, whose roughcut brutality he may have seen as in line with the natural order of things, he still kept a soft spot.

He spoke, intermittently, for between two and three hours, good-humouredly repeating some sections at the request of the film-men, sweating under the hot lamps, but not visibly worried by the proceedings. At one point Daly saw that Haldane was doodling on the desk in front of him; looking over his shoulder he saw that the doodles were in Greek. More than once, as the cameras moved nearer, Haldane's hands slipped down over the pencillings—so that Daly finally suggested he should keep his hands away and let the doodlings be shown. "Don't worry," he added, "it will be all Greek to most people." Haldane smiled: "Maybe it's Greek to you," he said, "but it's still obscene to those who understand it."

Eventually the interview was finished. Haldane returned across Gower Street to hospital; and here he now put the finishing touches to a short poem that stirred up as much controversy as anything he had written. "It is to be published in the *New Statesman*," he wrote to Jayakar. "It is unusual to start being paid as a poet at the age of seventy-one. I think a case can be made out for encouraging people not to take cancer too seriously."

The poem—it's title of "Cancer's a Funny Thing" taken from W. H. Auden who "put these words into the mouth of a doctor in his poem on Miss Gee and her sarcoma"—brought him a large post-bag composed of letters, which in almost equal numbers, complained at his lack of feeling or praised him for his courage. "This 'poem' has involved me in so much correspondence [and would have involved me in litigation if I were that sort of fool] that I wish I had never written it . . ." he subsequently wrote.

This was the poem:

I wish I had the voice of Homer
To sing of rectal carcinoma,
Which kills a lot more chaps, in fact,
Than were bumped off when Troy was sacked.
I noticed I was passing blood
(Only a few drops, not a flood).
So pausing on my homeward way
From Tallahassee to Bombay
I asked a doctor, now my friend,
To peer into my hinder end,
To prove or to disprove the rumour
That I had a malignant tumour.
They pumped in Ba S O₄

Till I could really stand no more,
And, when sufficient had been pressed in,
They photographed my large intestine,
In order to decide the issue
They next scraped out some bits of tissue.
(Before they did so, some good pal
Had knocked me out with pentothal,
Whose action is extremely quick.
And does not leave me feeling sick.)
The microscope returned the answer
That I had certainly got cancer.
So I was wheeled into the theatre
Where holes were made to make me better.
One set is in my perineum
Where I can feel, but can't yet see 'em.
Another made me like a kipper
Or female prey of Jack the Ripper.
Through this incision, I don't doubt,
The neoplasm was taken out,
Along with colon, and lymph nodes
Where cancer cells might find abodes.
A third much smaller hole is meant
To function as a ventral vent:
So now I am like two-faced Janus
The only* god who sees his anus.
*In India there are several more
With extra faces, up to four,
But both in Brahma and in Shiva
I own myself an unbeliever.

257

I'll swear, without the risk of perjury,
It was a snappy bit of surgery.
My rectum is a serious loss to me,
But I've a very neat colostomy,
And hope, as soon as I am able,
To make it keep a fixed time-table.
So do not wait for aches and pains
To have a surgeon mend your drains;
If he says "cancer" you're a dunce
Unless you have it out at once,
For if you wait it's sure to swell,
And may have progeny as well.
My final word, before I'm done,
Is "Cancer can be rather fun".
Thanks to the nurses and Nye Bevan
The NHS is quite like heaven
Provided one confronts the tumour
With a sufficient sense of humour.
I know that cancer often kills,
But so do cars and sleeping pills;
And it can hurt one till one sweats,
So can bad teeth and unpaid debts.
A spot of laughter, I am sure,
Often accelerates one's cure;
So let us patients do our bit
To help the surgeons make us fit.

J. B. S. Haldane

The poem, which was reprinted in a number of countries, brought great praise, caused great offence, and in some ways crystallises both Haldane's attitude to the world and the world's reaction. "I certainly intended to help others as well as myself," he later wrote. "I am a good enough Marxist to think that every poem should have a social function, though not a good enough one to think that it must. The main functions of my rhyme, to induce cancer patients to be operated on early and to be cheerful about it, would have been better served had it included the following lines after the fourth:

Yet, thanks to modern surgeon's skills,
It can be killed before it kills
Upon a scientific basis
In nineteen out of twenty cases.

"This appears to be about the correct figure for early operated cases of rectal cancer. Unfortunately my muse is now rather a slow old lady, and only produced these lines after publication. A second function, and not I think a negligible one, is to express the very genuine gratitude which many patients feel, though all of them do not express it, to the medical and nursing staffs of our hospitals."

J.B.S. had often imagined what his behaviour would be if informed that he had an inoperable cancer, and the "message" in his lines was not basically altered by the fact that he believed his operation had been successful. "The poem might still have been written if he had known that the operation had been unsuccessful," Helen wrote later, "but even so, involving a strong emotion, it might have been better, more of a poem and less witty verse."

"Cancer's a Funny Thing" had been published only a few weeks when, in mid-March, Haldane was discharged from University College Hospital. One of his first actions was to write a typical letter to the hospital authorities, making some minor suggestions about treatment and singling out "the psychological efficiency" of someone who he felt had been an outstanding hospital worker—"Staff Nurse Dear, who gave me just what I needed, the maximum of encouragement and the minimum of sympathy. Doubtless her ration for other patients was a little different."

Late in March Haldane flew back to India in the belief that he could plan ahead, that there was no desperate need to put his affairs in order under the threat of approaching death.

Within the month he was working up to six hours a day. "I hope to do more when the air is a bit cooler," he wrote to Staff Nurse Dear. "My colleagues are finding a lot of facts about birds, and some about men and other animals. I find that the mathematics which I did in hospital had numerous mistakes. This suggests that my brain is beginning to function." If she wanted to visit India he could, he wrote, provide the fare. "However, it might take me a month to raise the needed foreign exchange, so give me plenty of notice," he added.

Haldane appeared to be recovering quickly. It is true that his right hand was still weak from his war wound of 1915. The lesion in his spinal cord which he suffered on his submarine work for the Navy gave him a chronic itch whenever he sat, while there were occasional effects of other injuries suffered in the same cause. He had occasional pains from two broken ribs and a knee damaged in a car accident, as well as "normal" rheumatism. "These," he commented to a correspondent, "provide a kind of orchestral background to the various themes provided by my recent operations. I am only worried when they overlap."

He had soon not only resumed a good part of his normal work, but was planning ahead. In June, he was asked to preside over the Third International Congress of Human Genetics to be held in Chicago in September 1966, and he immediately wrote to the Governor of Orissa to enlist help in taking Indian scientists there. He felt lazy and sleepy during this hottest part of the year but, as he wrote to the Warden of New College when congratulating the College on its decision to admit women students, had managed to get one good bit of research done. "Now the monsoon has reached us we are much cooler, and [I] hope to increase my output," he added.

Early in August he had a slight relapse. He sometimes slept for twelve hours and did not feel energetic while awake. However, as he wrote to Sister Dear on August 17th, he had been examined twice by a British surgeon in Calcutta who told him that there was no sign of the cancer having moved from one part of his body to another.

And to the same correspondent he wrote with pride that henceforth his telegraphic address at Bhubaneswar would be "Elah". During their visit to Israel he and Helen had visited this brook from which David had taken the sling-stone which killed Goliath. When it came to choosing a word for the telegraphic address, J.B.S. had convinced the authorities that "Elah" would serve—"for we don't like giants". To another correspondent he explained that "most Christians and Jews say they believe in the bible, but don't take it seriously. I am a heathen, and don't believe in the bible, but do take it seriously. I carry round a small stone from this brook in my pocket. Call me a fetishist. There is something, but not much, to be said for fetishism. I agree with Lenin that the religions are sterile but genuine flowers on the tree of human culture."

He was taking his time on recuperation, indulging in what he called the mild luxury of reading fiction instead of getting through urgent work, planning ahead for 1965 and 1966. He still believed that he had time to take.

Now, during the first week in September, the whole situation was transformed. During the last days of August Haldane had visited Calcutta and had been X-rayed once again. The information revealed by the plates was sent to Jayakar.

"My news to you is, however, not good," said the accompanying letter. "His cancer has recurred in his abdomen and liver and, short of a miracle, his days are numbered. This must have been known in London when he had his first operation. He was not told about it then and I see no good reason to tell him now. I do not know whether his wife knows. If she does not, I must leave it to your good judgement to inform her or not, as you think fit."

Jayakar knew Helen's quality. There was no question of hiding the facts from her. She in turn knew Haldane's. She went to him, told him that she had a letter which contained bad news about the persistence of his cancer, and handed him the letter.

Here was the ultimate test. There had been times in Haldane's life when it had been difficult to know how closely the front which he presented to the world was linked to the man within. He had been a competent dissimulator for good causes. At times he had felt it a duty to appear larger than life, to impress by exaggeration, to overwhelm by flamboyance. At times this image had almost become part of the man himself. Now, and in the next few weeks, it would be clear whether greatness belonged to the man or the image.

Haldane read the letter and handed it back. Then he set himself to the task ahead.

He had much to do, and he was shocked by the statement that he could have been warned of his condition before he left London. "I am sure," wrote his sister Naomi in the British Medical Journal, four months later, "that the surgeon behaved absolutely correctly. But I must add that before my brother went into hospital it was particularly brought to the notice of the hospital authorities that he was the kind of person who ought to be told what was happening to him. Several responsible people tried to find out, but the pattern of medical hierarchy prevented this."

Haldane himself was a good deal more outspoken. "There are three very good reasons for telling me," he wrote to his friend Professor Medawar. "Had I been told in 1963, I should have tried one of the 'crank' cures, such as the high pressure O_2 at Barts. Here negative information can be quite useful. Had I known when I arrived here, I should have known not to make certain plans which turned out over-ambitious. I could have completed several bits of work which I may not [have time] to do.

"Thirdly, my wife, who showed me the letter, which she said contained bad news about the persistence of my cancer, is

261

a good biologist, but not, alas, good enough to take my pulse before and after I read the death sentence. I don't think my pulse rate changed by five per minute."

The results of this adherence to medical etiquette are clear from the letters that Haldane wrote during the next few days, including one to a friend to whom he quoted Nehru's favourite lines from Robert Frost:

> The woods are lovely, dark and deep.
> But I have promises to keep,
> And miles to go before I sleep,
> And miles to go before I sleep.

In his own case, Haldane commented, "one must substitute 'run' for 'go' in the last lines".

"I don't mind dying," was his summing-up. "I mind dying with unkept promises." To Professor Pilcher of University College Hospital he wrote saying: "It might be reasonable to keep the facts from me till I was leaving hospital. The result of longer concealment has been disastrous. I have been making rather elaborate plans for the future and several young men will be let down. I have now to get less elaborate plans approved, in a desperate hurry . . . I must now spend the rest of my life in a frenzied attempt to get various papers ready for the press. I daren't relax." And he concluded by asking: "Why cannot people learn to speak the truth? I have, I think, taught two, perhaps three, Indian colleagues to do so. It will probably wreck their careers."

He had a great many personal affairs to settle. The record from his files of how he did so is impressive. "I fear you will have to pick another president for Chicago," he wrote to Professor Steinberg who was organising the International Congress in 1966 ". . . I am in fact dying. Please do not sympathise. I am in no appreciable pain, nor, I think, emotionally disturbed. Unfortunately, my wife and friends here are so, and I cannot blame them." To Professor Medawar he wrote in the course of a long letter: "I have a fight ahead, and if I can do even an hour's work in the last twenty-four hours of my life I shan't feel too ashamed", while to Dr. Leakey he wrote that he preferred dying in Bhubaneswar, "escaping rheumatism among other things, surrounded by flowering trees at all times of the year, with no winter, and with plenty of friends, apart from my wife . . ." To Biju Patnaik, now Chairman of the Orissa State Planning Board, he wrote urging that the work of the laboratory should be carried on. "I shall die very happily if I can see some document giving its use to Jayakar and the others for five years," he added. "They will, I honestly believe, be world-famous by then, but as field workers rather than laboratory workers. About thirty of my pupils are now Fellows of the Royal Society, so I know what I am writing about."

An added personal problem was presented by his sister Naomi, and he asked more than one friend to keep the news of his condition from her family. "If asked, you may say I am not feeling quite so well, which is true and is all that yet appears on the surface," he wrote to one of them. "But if it gets round, I fear my sister will want to do all kinds of things, perhaps even to come here. Whereas I wish to die in peace, preferably on an easy chair or even a jointed bed, on my verandah, looking at flowering trees and birds in the sunshine."

To Naomi herself he wrote that while he was not very well, the cause was being treated. "If I am in better shape next autumn," he added, "we shall be delighted to have you stay."

While J.B.S. was thus prepared to dissimulate as far as his sister was concerned he had no qualms about protesting, in the strongest terms, about what he described as the "pack of lies" he had been told in London. However, he did not despair. If the surgeons could no longer help him he would turn to others. Before the end of September he had put himself in the hands of a Calcutta doctor who was also, Haldane believed, a good biochemist. "He does not claim to cure cancer," he wrote to Medawar, "But he is treating several allegedly inoperable cases with a drug which he makes himself synthetically, and they have shown remarkable improvement. If he can give me another year of life, the world shall know about it. If not, I shall be a minus sign in Table 3, which will at least be a fact to add to his still rather few data."

He had a good deal of faith in the treatment, and told some correspondents that his situation was better than he had feared. To the Governor of Orissa he wrote on October 10th that he hoped to live for two or three years. "Tell Brain I am not depressed or worried, as he says a lot of cancer patients are," he wrote to another friend. "I take it out in anger, which is more likely to keep me alive." There were minor, but what were at first thought to be significant improvements, in his condition. His weight, which had dropped more than four pounds in two weeks, went up three pounds in seven days. Whether he was really getting stronger was uncertain; he was certainly fighting hard, and taking deep interest in the battle.

Then, towards the end of October, a highly revealing incident took place. On the morning of October 24th, Haldane heard, over the wireless, the news that Kruschev had resigned and that Kosygin had stepped up to become Prime Minister of the U.S.S.R. He knew that he did not have long to live; but he wished to set the record right on one matter. "Dear Prime Minister," he wrote on a sheet of lined paper, in a hand that grew increasingly shaky as it continued, "This letter will not reach you, but might reach one of your subordinates who can convey some of its contents. In 1961 you visited the I.S.I. I had made rather full arrangements for you to see the work my colls were doing. Prof. M. arrived on the previous day, countermanded the arrangements without consulting me, and asked me to arrange my colleagues' research material according to a plan of his own. Two of the three were absent taking students round an agri. exhibition. My wife and I instantly resigned. However, during the visit I was in the Instt. as I should have been [as] an Academic of the Sov. Union. However, Prof. M. did not think it fit to inform you of my presence. I must therefore have appeared extremely impolite, if not worse. Yours sincerely." It was in character that one of the last letters written by J.B.S. should be to a new head of the U.S.S.R.; it is ironic that it should be a letter of apology for impoliteness.

He now visited Calcutta again and here, in a nursing home, he was called on by, among others, T. A. Davis. "He felt very miserable both in mind and body," says Davis. "He didn't allow me to leave his room even long after the bell announced visitors to leave. For three full hours, keeping me very close to his pillow, he went on talking, though feebly, on topics ranging from Christianity in his family through generations, his personal admiration for Christ who, he said, was much nobler than what we are told through the Bible, about his operation . . . about the merits of a shower over a bath-tub etc. During most of the time I was dumb, fully overtaken by emotion, but he didn't expect me to talk much either."

By the beginning of November he was very weak, and confined to his bed or a chair for most of the time. He still came out on to the Bhubaneswar verandah, sitting in one of his long low chairs in the warm air that follows the monsoon and looking south-west across his garden towards the low hills which with their temples rose above the fields of the delta. He still took care to ensure that none of the regular observations being taken by Helen or his colleagues were missed on his behalf. He was still ministered to by his devoted colleagues, Hari and

264

Shastri, who in the closing days massaged his feet, chose his food, vetted his visitors, so that to many suggestions J.B.S. responded only with: "Has it the approval of Hari or Shastri?"

Towards the end of the month he became rapidly weaker. He was unable to stand on the scales to be weighed. He began to be confused in his thoughts. On the evening of November 30th he gradually became worse and during the night his breathing became obstructed. On the morning of December 1st he was taken out on to the verandah as usual. He requested that some bougainvillaea from his garden should be sent to the wife of a neighbour who had called to see him. It was clear that he was dying but two of the best-liked local doctors who had also arrived dashed to the local hospital for a cardiac stimulant. Before they returned Haldane was dead.

A few months earlier, when he was recovering from his operation in London, he had written his last article for the *Rationalist Annual*, entitled "On Being Finite", suggesting that he might have only a year to live "if the cancer has sent a colony of cells to another part of my body". He ranged across his experiences and the lessons they had taught him, and he ended by saying: "I doubt whether, given my psychological make-up, I should have found many greater thrills in a hundred lives. So when the angel with the darker drink at last shall find me by the river's brink, and offering his cup, invite my soul forth to my lips to quaff, I shall not shrink." He did not shrink. Had there been any watchers in those Elysian fields whose existence Haldane placed far beyond reality, they might have discerned the trace of a smile.

Haldane's contributions to science had been extensive, and they had been so in the three different fields of physiology, biochemistry and genetics. It is still too soon after his death to speculate on which of his achievements will be considered most important to the long glance of history, yet it seems certain that his work on the mathematical theory of natural selection will be high on any priority list. He did not work alone, it is true, but even to have shared in providing numerical chapter and verse for Darwin gives him a niche among the great. At Cambridge under Hopkins, where he began to investigate the biochemical nature of fundamental gene activity and the genetic control of enzyme actions, he started to force a door which has now been pushed wide open. And from this to the mathematical study of the genetics of the evolutionary processes was but a natural step for a man of Haldane's ever-questioning mind.

In all these subjects he did more than postulate the theories, and carry out the researches, which are detailed in his scores of serious papers. He also sparked off other men—and women—so that many can trace their success back to the stimulus of J.B.S., to the suggestion that they should "try it" for themselves, to the insistence that there was no substitute for personal thought and careful experiment.

Yet Haldane's achievements in his own chosen fields are perhaps less important than other things which he did, even though they are more easy to pin down, to illustrate, and to docket by reference to his papers in the learned journals. For he made science comprehensible and he made it exciting. In an age when it was still on the defensive, he showed that it could be humane and that it could be motivated by the most impeccable of moral justifications. He fired his listeners, moreover, with what could be called, if the gilt had not been rubbed off the phrase by over-use, the romance of science. He really did feel that a greater knowledge of the physical world—like a greater knowledge of the classics—could make every day more stimulating and every life more worthwhile. Listening to him, one could see Tennyson's "fairy tales of science" turning into reality before one's eyes.

This ability to entrance was partly due to his own humble wonder at the world around him—a humility which at times embarrassed him so that he would tend to hide it with arrogance and bluster. It was also due to his facility for linking the facts of one science with those of all the rest, the result of intellectual omniscience and an optimistic Victorian belief that all was possible to those who worked hard, thought straight, and feared neither man nor Devil. Thus there was more than one factor in his make-up which made him appear as a direct descendant of that strong company which had included Hooker and Tyndall, Maxwell and Rayleigh and the J. J. Thomson whose life linked the worlds of the Prince Consort and of Adolf Hitler. Haldane might indulge in showmanship and in occasional posturing but beneath this there lay, and clearly lay to those with eyes to see, the touchstones of personal integrity, honesty and courage.

It was perhaps these qualities above all which throughout a long life enabled him to exhibit the qualities of the *guru*. When he said in his own way, "rise and follow me", men did, as his sister once wrote, give up safe and comparatively lucrative jobs and follow him. They followed him because he was intensely aware of the human predicament and because, despite his need for affection, he remained a fundamentally lonely man; like all leaders, he led because of the aura of isolation which he retained, not despite it. He came to his years of strength and influence when the bell tolled for those of the political Right and when many decent men came to the aid of the Communist Party. To the Comrades he remained loyal, if not to all of their beliefs; he could be shocked by them but not intimidated. And at the end of the day he continued to give the impression of the man too big in spirit for the age into which he had been born, the man who when events tried to thrust greatness upon him, would push it aside to get on with the job in hand.

In death, Haldane was true to his life. It had finally been arranged that his corpse should be sent for medical research and teaching to the Rangaraya Medical College, Kakinada. "My body has been used for both purposes during my lifetime," he wrote in his will, "and after my death, whether I continue to exist or not, I shall have no further use for it, and desire that it shall be used by others. Its refrigeration, if this is possible, should be a first charge on my estate."

The ever-competent Hari accompanied the body 400 miles south to Kakinada, waited until dissection was complete, and then drove back to Bhubaneswar. Here Helen, who had been almost besieged by the crowds who arrived on hearing of Haldane's death, issued a statement to the Press, announcing his death, criticising the lack of information in London a year previously, thanking those who had helped. "I am aware that by Indian manners I may have behaved rudely today, but the preservation of the corpse in the best condition for research was by his standards the only consideration," she added. "That students of any subject, let alone science, should wish to take a holiday from their studies because of his death would have disgusted and angered him."

In London, the auto-obituary which had been filmed in University College ten months earlier was shown as a nine-minutes wonder, and viewers watched J.B.S. explaining that he might be remembered not for one of the things he had mentioned, but for some now-forgotten remark or idea. "But I don't really very much care what people think about me, especially a hundred years hence," he concluded. "I should not like them to be too critical of me as long as my widow and a few friends survive me. But the greatest compliment made to me today, I believe, is when people refer to something which I discovered—for example that eating ammonium chloride causes acid poisoning in men—as a fact the whole world knows—to quote good old Aunt Jobiska in Lear's poem about the Pobble

—without mentioning me at all. To have got into the tradition of science in that way is to me more pleasing than to be specially mentioned. But what matters, in my opinion, is what I have done, good or evil, and not what people think of me."

The Times accorded Haldane a double column, three-quarters of a page deep. Elsewhere he was recalled variously, for his genetics, for the *Thetis* investigations, for his wartime work. The ghost of Lysenko was raised although it was rather grudgingly admitted that Haldane had eventually resigned from the Communist Party. But he had, of course, failed to join the Establishment and the odour of this lay over more than one obituary.

A different feeling was shown by the letters which during the following weeks arrived in Bhubaneswar. One came from a minute mountain hamlet in New Guinea, whose inhabitants had seen their first Europeans only eight years previously. "The news reached me *via* a two-week old *Manchester Guardian Weekly* carried for a day over forest trails by native cargo boys from the nearest bush airstrip," said the writer, who had immediately sent his condolences by the same route. Alex Comfort noted that Haldane "would be a little indignant to be lamented", and another friend said how impossible it was "to suppress thoughts that J.B.S. would regard as maudlin, emotional and irrelevant". With all this, Haldane would no doubt have been gruffly pleased. He would have enjoyed, too, the comments on his multitudinous virtues, the statement to Helen that "to live on equal terms with a man of J.B.S.'s calibre is an enterprise not to be lightly undertaken or ended". He would have enjoyed it all; though he might have been disappointed that those who criticised him while he was alive had now become less vocal.

But among the comments which arrived as the work of the laboratory went on and the future was faced, he would have been proud of one above all others: "Not only an eminent scientist," it ran, "but also a humanitarian and a great Indian."

Bibliography

(Compiled by N. W. Pirie, and printed with his *Biographical Memoir of J. B. S. Haldane* published by the Royal Society.)

An effort has been made to include in this bibliography all Haldane's scientific papers. Some unpublished work is being prepared for the press by S. D. Jayakar. Several popular articles are also listed, they have been selected because they contain ideas, comments or suggestions that are not so clearly or emphatically put in the more serious papers. Haldane also contributed 345 articles to the *Daily Worker* and 100 or more to *Reynold's News* and other papers and magazines.

1912 (With C. G. Douglas & J. S. Haldane) The laws of combination of haemoglobin with CO and oxygen. *J. Physiol.* **44**, 275.
The dissociation of oxyhaemoglobin in human blood during partial CO poisoning. *J. Physiol.* **45**, xxii.

1915 (With A. D. Sprunt & N. M. Haldane) Reduplication in mice. *J. Genet.* **5**, 133.

1919 The probable errors of calculated linkage values, and the most accurate method of determining gametic from certain zygotic series. *J. Genet.* **8**, 291.
The combination of linkage values, and the calculation of distances between the loci of linked factors. *J. Genet.* **8**, 299.

1920 Note on a case of linkage in *Paratettix*. *J. Genet.* **10**, 47.
Some recent work on heredity. *Trans. Oxford Univ. Jr. Sci. Club*, Series 3, **1**, 3.
(With H. W. Davies & E. L. Kennaway) Experiments on the regulation of the blood's alkalinity, I. *J. Physiol.* **54**, 32.

1921 Experiments on the regulation of the blood's alkalinity, II. *J. Physiol.* **55**, 265.
(With H. C. Bazett) Some effects of hot baths on man. *J. Physiol.* **55**, iv.
Linkage in poultry. *Science,* **54**, 663.

1922 (With M. M. Baird) Salt and water excretion in man. *J. Physiol.* **56**, 259.
(With H. W. Davies & G. L. Peskett) The excretion of chlorides and bicarbonates by the human kidney. *J. Physiol.* **56**, 269.
Sex-ratio and unisexual sterility in hybrid animals. *J. Genet.* **12**, 101.

1923 (With M. M. Baird, C. G. Douglas & J. G. Priestley) Ammonium chloride acidosis. *J. Physiol.* **57**, xli.
(With R. Hill & J. M. Luck) Calcium chloride acidosis, *J. Physiol.* **57**, 301.
Daedalus, or Science and the Future. London: Kegan, Paul, Trench, Trubner.

1924 A mathematical theory of natural and artificial selection. Pt. I. *Trans. Camb. Phil. Soc.* **23**, 19.
A mathematical theory of natural and artificial selection. Pt. II. The influence of partial self-fertilisation, inbreeding, assortative mating, and selective fertilisation on the composition of Mendelian populations, and on natural selection. *Proc. Camb. Phil. Soc.* **1**, 158.
Über Halluzinationen infolge von Änderungen des Kohlensauredrucks. *Psychologische Forschung.* **5**, 356.

(With J. H. Quastel) The changes in alveolar carbon dioxide pressure after violent exercise. *J. Physiol.* **50**, 138.

(With H. D. Kay & W. Smith) The effect of insulin on blood volume. *J. Physiol.* **59**, 193.

(With C. P. Stewart) Experimental alterations in the calcium content of human serum and urine. *Biochem. J.* **28**, 855.

(With V. B. Wigglesworth & C. E. Woodrow) Effect of reaction changes on human inorganic metabolism. *Proc. Roy. Soc.* B, **96**, 1.

(With V. B. Wigglesworth & C. E. Woodrow) The effect of reaction changes on human carbohydrate and oxygen metabolism. *Proc. Roy. Soc.* B, **96**, 15.

The possible existence of a growth regulating substance in termites. *Nature, Lond.* **113**, 676.

1925 (With G. Bourguignon) Electricité Physiologique—Evolution de la chronaxie au cours de la crise de tétanie expérimentale par hyperpnée volontaire chez l'homme. *C.R. Acad. Sci. Paris.* **180**, 321.

The production of acidosis by ingestion of magnesium chloride and strontium chloride. *Biochem. J.* **29**, 249.

(With G. E. Briggs) Note on the kinetics of enzyme action. *Biochem. J.* **29**, 338.

On the origin of the potential differences between the interior and exterior of cells. *Proc. Camb. Phil. Soc. (Biol. Sci.)*, **1**, 243.

(With F. A. E. Crew) Change of linkage in poultry with age. *Nature, Lond.* **115**, 641.

Callinicus—A Defence of Chemical Warfare. London: Kegan, Paul, Trench, Trubner.

1926 A mathematical theory of natural and artificial selection. Pt. III. *Proc. Camb. Phil. Soc.* **23**, 363.

1927 A mathematical theory of natural and artificial selection. Pt. IV. *Proc. Camb. Phil. Soc.* **23**, 607.

A mathematical theory of natural and artificial selection. Pt. V. Selection and mutation. *Proc. Camb. Phil. Soc.* **23**, 838.

The comparative genetics of colour in rodents and carnivora. *Biol. Rev.* **2**, 199.

Carbon monoxide as a tissue poison. *Biochem. J.* **21**, 1068.

Carbon monoxide poisoning in the absence of haemoglobin. *Nature, Lond.* **119**, 352.

Biological fact and theory. *Nature, Lond.* **119**, 456.

(With J. S. Huxley) *Animal Biology.* Oxford: Clarendon Press.

Possible Worlds and Other Essays. London: Chatto & Windus.

1928 (With G. C. Linder, R. Hilton & F. R. Fraser) The arterial blood in ammonium chloride acidosis. *J. Physiol.* **65**, 412.

Pituitrin and the chloride concentrating power of the kidneys. *J. Physiol.* **66**, 10.

The affinity of different types of enzyme for their substrates. *Nature, Lond.* **121**, 207.

The Universe and irreversibility. *Nature, Lond.* **122**, 808.

1929 Natural selection. *Nature, Lond.* **124**, 444.

The species problem in the light of genetics. *Nature, Lond.* **124**, 514.

(With A. E. Gairdner) A case of balanced lethal factors in *Antirrhinum majus. J. Genet.* **21**, 315.

The scientific point of view. *The Realist*, **1** (4), 10.

The place of science in western civilisation. *The Realist*, **2**, 149.

Genetics of polyploid plants. In *Conference on Polyploidy*. John Innes Horticultural Institute, p. 9.

The origin of life. *Rationalist Annual*, p. 3.

1930 *Enzymes.* London: Longmans, Green & Co.

A note on Fisher's theory of the origin of dominance and on a correlation between dominance and linkage. *Amer. Naturalist*, **64**, 87.

La cinétique des actions diastasiques. *J. Chim. Phys.* **27**, 277.

A mathematical theory of natural and artificial selection. Pt. VI. Isolation. *Proc. Camb. Phil. Soc.* **26**, 220.

Theoretical genetics of autopolyploids. *J. Genet.* **22**, 359.

Genetics of some autopolyploid plants. *Rep. Proc. 5th Int. Bot. Congr.* Cambridge, p. 232.

The principles of plant breeding, illustrated by the Chinese Primrose. *Proc. Roy. Inst.* **26**, 199.

Origin of asymmetry in gastropods. *Nature, Lond.* **126**, 10.

Natural selection intensity as a function of mortality rate. *Nature, Lond.* **126**, 883.

1931 A mathematical theory of natural and artificial selection. Pt. VII. Selection intensity as a function of mortality rate. *Proc. Camb. Phil. Soc.* **27**, 131.

A mathematical theory of natural selection. Pt. VIII. Metastable populations. *Proc. Camb. Phil. Soc.* **27**, 137.

(With D. De Winton) Linkage in the tetraploid *Primula sinensis*. *J. Genet.* **24**, 121.

(With C. H. Waddington) Inbreeding and linkage. *Genetics*, **16**, 357.

Embryology and evolution. *Nature, Lond.* **126**, 956; **127**, 274.

Oxidation by living cells. *Nature, Lond.* **128**, 175.

(With R. P. Cook & L. W. Mapson) The relationship between the respiratory catalysts of *B. coli*. *Biochem. J.* **25**, 534.

(With R. P. Cook) The respiration of *B. coli communis*. *Biochem. J.* **25**, 880.

The molecular statistics of an enzyme action. *Proc. Roy. Soc.* B, **106**, 559.

Prehistory in the light of genetics. *Proc. Roy. Inst.* **26**, 355.

The cytological basis of genetical interference. *Cytologia*, **3**, 54.

1932 A note on inverse probability. *Proc. Camb. Phil. Soc.* **28**, 55.

On the non-linear difference equation. *Proc. Camb. Phil. Soc.* **28**, 234.

A mathematical theory of natural and artificial selection. Pt. IX. Rapid selection. *Proc. Camb. Phil. Soc.* **28**, 244.

Discussion on recent advances in the study of enzymes and their action. *Proc. Roy. Soc.* B, **111**, 280.

The time of action of genes, and its bearing on some evolutionary problems. *Amer. Naturalist*, **66**, 5.

Note on a fallacious method of avoiding selection. *Amer. Naturalist*, **66**, 479.

A method for investigating recessive characters in man. *J. Genet.* **25**, 251.

Genetical evidence for a cytological abnormality in man. *J. Genet.* **26**, 341.

Determinism. *Nature, Lond.* **129**, 315.

The hereditary transmission of acquired characters. *Nature, Lond.* **129**, 817, 856.

Eland-ox hybrid. *Nature, Lond.* **129**, 906.

The inheritance of acquired characters. *Nature, Lond.* **130**, 20, 204.

Chain reactions in enzymatic catalyses. *Nature, Lond.* **130**, 61.

The Inequality of Man and Other Essays. London: Chatto & Windus.

The Causes of Evolution. London: Longmans, Green & Co.

1933 The part played by recurrent mutation in evolution. *Amer. Naturalist*, **67**, 5.

Two new allelomorphs for heterostylism in *Primula*. *Amer. Naturalist*, **67**, 559.

(With D. De Winton) The genetics of *Primula sinensis*. II. Segregation and interaction of factors in the diploid. *J. Genet.* **27**, 1.

(With A. E. Gairdner) A case of balanced lethal factors in *Antirrhinum majus*. ii. *J. Genet.* **27**, 287.

The genetics of cancer. *Nature, Lond.* **132**, 265.

The biologist and society. In *Science in the Changing World*. (Ed. Mary Adams.) London: Allen & Unwin.

1934 Quantum mechanics as a basis for philosophy. *Phil. Sci.* **1**, 78.

A contribution to the theory of price fluctuations. *Rev. Econ. Stud.* **1**, 186.

(With M. S. Bartlett) The theory of inbreeding in autotetraploids. *J. Genet.* **29**, 175.

Anthropology and human biology. *Man*, **34**, 142.

Anthropology and human biology. *Man*. **34**, 163.

A mathematical theory of natural and artificial selection. Pt. X. Some theorems on artificial selection. *Genetics*, **19**, 412.

The attitude of the German government towards science. *Nature, Lond.* **132**, 726.

Science and politics, *Nature, Lond.* **133**, 65.

(With C. D. Darlington & P. C. Koller) Possibility of incomplete sex linkage in mammals. *Nature, Lond.* **133**, 417.

Science at the universities. *Nature, Lond.* **134**, 571.

Methods for the detection of autosomal linkage in man. *Ann. Eug.* **6**, 26.

Human biology and politics. *The British Science Guild: 10th Norman Lockyer Lecture*, p. 3.

Race and culture. *Proc. Royal Anthropological Institute and the Institute of Sociology*, p. 8. London: Le Play House Press.

The relative efficiency of two methods of measuring human linkage. *Amer. Naturalist*, **68**, 286.

Genetika i sovremennye sotsyalyie teorie. *Usp. sovrem. Biol.* **3**, 426.

(With J. R. Baker) *Biology in Everyday Life*. London: George Allen & Unwin.

Fact and Faith. London: Watts.

1935 Genetics since 1910. *Nature, Lond.* **135**, 726.

(With L. S. Penrose) Mutation rates in man. *Nature, Lond.* **135**, 907.

Blood group inheritance. *Nature, Lond.* **136**, 432.

Human genetics and human ideals. *Nature, Lond.* **136**, 894.

(With D. De Winton) The genetics of *Primula sinensis*. III. Linkage in the diploid. *J. Genet.* **31**, 67.

The rate of spontaneous mutation of a human gene. *J. Genet.* **31**, 317.

(With M. S. Bartlett) The theory of inbreeding with forced heterozygosis. *J. Genet.* **31**, 327.

Contribution de la génétique à la solution de quelques problèmes physiologiques. Réunion Plénière, de la Societé de biologie, Paris.

Some problems of mathematical biology. *J. Math. & Phys.* **14**, 125.

The Outlook of Science. London: Kegan, Paul, Trench, Trubner.

(With A. Lunn) *Science and the Supernatural*. London: Eyre & Spottiswoode.

Science and Well-being. London: Kegan, Paul, Trench, Trubner.

1936 A provisional map of a human chromosome. *Nature, Lond.* **137**, 397.

Carbon dioxide content of atmospheric air. *Nature, Lond.* **137**, 575.

(With J. Bell) Linkage in man. *Nature, Lond.* **138**, 759.

(With E. Ashby, F. A. E. Crew, C. D. Darlington, E. B. Ford, E. J. Salisbury, W. B. Turrill & C. H. Waddington) Genetics in the universities. *Nature, Lond.* **138**, 972.

Natural selection. *Nature, Lond.* **138**, 1053.

Linkage in *Primula sinensis*—A correction. *J. Genet.* **32**, 373.

The amount of heterozygosis to be expected in an approximately pure line. *J. Genet.* **32**, 375.

Some natural populations of *Lythrum salicaria*. *J. Genet.* **32**, 393.

Some principles of causal analysis in genetics. *Erkenntnis*, **6**, 346.

A search for incomplete sex-linkage in man. *Ann. Eug.* **7**, 28.)

Is space-time simply connected? *The Observatory*, **59**, 228.

A discussion on the present state of the theory of natural selection. Primary and secondary effects of natural selection. *Proc. Roy. Soc. B*, **121**, 67.

1937 Physical science and philosophy. *Nature, Lond.* **139**, 1003.

Genetics in Madrid. *Nature, Lond.* **140**, 331.

The position of genetics. *Nature, Lond.* **140**, 428.

The exact value of the moments of the distribution of χ^2 used as a test of goodness of fit, when expectations are small. *Biometrika*, **29**, 133.

(With H. Gruneberg) Tests of goodness of fit applied to records of Mendelian segregation in mice. *Biometrika*, **29**, 144.

Some theoretical results of continued brother-sister mating. *J. Genet.* **34**, 265.

The effect of variation on fitness. *Amer. Naturalist*, **71**, 337.

(With J. Bell) The linkage between the genes for colour-blindness and haemophilia in man. *Proc. Roy. Soc. B*, **123**, 119.

A probable new sex-linked dominant in man. *J. Hered.* **28**, 58.

L'analyse génétique des populations naturelles. *Réunion internat. de Physique-Chimie-Biologie. Congrès du Palais de la découverte, Paris,* **8**, 517.

Science and future warfare. *J. Roy. United Services Inst.* **82**, 713.

Dialectical account of evolution. *Science & Society,* **1**, 473.

Biochemistry of the individual. In *Perspectives in Biochemistry,* p. 1. (Eds. J. Needham & D. E. Green.) Cambridge University Press.

My friend Mr Leaky. London: The Cresset Press.

1938 The first six moments of χ^2 for an *n*-fold table with *n* degrees of freedom when some expectations are small. *Biometrika,* **29**, 389.

The approximate normalisation of a class of frequency distributions. *Biometrika,* **29**, 392.

Heterostylism in natural populations of the primrose. *Biometrika,* **30**, 196.

Social relations of science. *Nature, Lond.* **141**, 730.

Mathematics of air raid protection. *Nature, Lond.* **142**, 791.

(With S. Bedichek) A search for autosomal recessive lethals in man. *Ann. Eug.* **8**, 245.

The estimation of the frequencies of recessive conditions in man. *Ann. Eug.* **8**, 255.

A hitherto unexpected complication in the genetics of human recessives. *Ann. Eug.* **8**, 263.

The location of the gene for haemophilia. *Genetica,* **20**, 423.

Indirect evidence for the mating system in natural populations. *J. Genet.* **36**, 213.

The nature of interspecific differences. *Evolution* (ed. J. R. de Beer) Oxford, p. 79.

Blood royal. A study of haemophilia in the royal families of Europe. *The Modern Quarterly,* **1**, 129.

Congenital disease. *Lancet,* ii, 1449.

The Chemistry of the Individual. 38th Robert Boyle Lecture (1938). Oxford University Press.

Forty years of genetics. In *Background to Modern Science.* (Eds. J. Needham & W. Pagel.) Cambridge University Press, p. 225.

A.R.P. London: Victor Gollancz.

The Marxist Philosophy and the Sciences. London: George Allen & Unwin.

Heredity and Politics. London: George Allen & Unwin.

1939 The theory of the evolution of dominance. *J. Genet.* **37**, 365.

(With U. Phillip) The daughters and sisters of haemophilics. *J. Genet.* **33**, 193.

(With U. Phillip) Relative sexuality in unicellular algae. *Nature, Lond.* **143**, 334.

Speculative biology. *The Modern Quarterly,* **2**, 1.

Protoplasm. *The Modern Quarterly,* **2**, 128.

The spread of harmful autosomal recessive genes in human populations. *Ann. Eug.* **9**, 232.

(With P. Moshinsky) Inbreeding in Mendelian populations with special reference to human cousin marriage. *Ann. Eug.* **9**, 321.

The equilibrium between mutation and random extinction. *Ann. Eug.* **9**, 400.

Note on the preceding analysis of Mendelian segregation. *Biometrika,* **31**, 67.

Corrections to formulae in papers on the moments of χ^2. *Biometrika,* **31**, 220.

Sampling errors in the determination of bacterial or virus density by the dilution method. *J. Hyg.* **39**, 289.

(With W. Alexander, P. Duff, G. Ives & D. Renton) After-effects of exposure of men to carbon dioxide. *Lancet,* ii, 419.

1940 The mean and variance of χ^2, when used as a test of homogeneity, when expectations are small. *Biometrika,* **31**, 346.

The cumulants and moments of the binomial distribution, and the cumulants of χ^2 for a $(n \times 2)$ fold table. *Biometrika,* **31**, 392.

(With H. Gruneberg) Congenital hyperglycaemia in mice. *Nature, Lond.* **145**, 704.

Blood groups of anthropoids. *Nature, Lond.* **146**, 652.

The conflict between selection and mutation of harmful recessive genes. *Ann. Eug.* **10**, 417.

The estimation of recessive gene frequencies by inbreeding. *Proc. Ind. Acad. Sci.* **12**, 109.

The blood-group frequencies of European peoples and racial origins. *Human Biology*, **12**, 457.

Preface and notes to *Dialectics of Nature* (F. Engels translated and edited by C. Dutt). London: Lawrence & Wishart.

Science in Peace and War. London: Lawrence & Wishart.

Science in Everyday Life. New York: The Macmillan Co.

Keeping Cool and Other Essays. London: Chatto & Windus.

1941 The partial sex-linkage of recessive spastic paraplegia. *J. Genet.* **41**, 141.

The relative importance of principal and modifying genes in determining some human diseases. *J. Genet.* **41**, 149.

Can science be independent? *Nature, Lond.* **147**, 416.

(With E. M. Case) Tastes of oxygen and nitrogen at high pressures. *Nature, Lond.* **148**, 84.

The relation between science and ethics. *Nature, Lond.* **148**, 342.

Human life and death at high pressures. *Nature, Lond.* **148**, 458.

Science in the U.S.S.R. *Nature, Lond.* **148**, 598.

Number of primes and probability consideration. *Nature, Lond.* **148**, 694.

Physiological properties of some common gases at high pressures. *Chemical Products*, **4**, 83.

The faking of genetical results. *Eureka*, **6**, 8.

The fitting of binomial distributions. *Ann. Eug.* **11**, 179.

How to write a popular scientific article. *The Scientific Worker*, **13**, 122.

The cumulants of the distribution of the square of a variate. *Biometrika*, **32**, 199.

(With E. M. Case) Human physiology under high pressure. 1. Effects of nitrogen, carbon dioxide and cold. *J. Hyg.* **41**, 225.

The laws of Nature. *Rationalist Annual*, p. 35.

New Paths in Genetics. London: George Allen & Unwin.

1942 Moments of the distributions of powers and products of normal variates. *Biometrika*, **32**, 226.

The mode and median of a nearly normal distribution with given cumulants. *Biometrika*, **32**, 294.

Selection against heterozygosis in man. *Ann. Eug.* **11**, 333.

(With R. Poole) A new pedigree of recurrent bullouse eruption of the feet. *J. Hered.* **33**, 17.

The selective elimination of silver foxes in Eastern Canada. *J. Genet.* **44**, 296.

Civil defence against war gases. *Nature, Lond.* **150**, 769.

1943 Statistics of occupational mortality. *Camb. Univ. Medical Soc. Mag.* **20**, 38.

(With J. M. Rendel) Variation in the weights of hatched and unhatched ducks. *Biometrika*, **33**, 56.

James Prescott Joule and the unit of energy. *Nature, Lond.* **152**, 479.

1944 Mutation and the Rhesus reaction. *Nature, Lond.* **153**, 106.

Radioactivity and the origin of life in Milne's cosmology. *Nature, Lond.* **153**, 555.

(With U. Phillip, J. M. Rendel & H. Spurway) Genetics and karyology of *Drosophila subobscura. Nature, Lond.* **154**, 260.

Heredity, development and genetics. *Nature, Lond.* **154**, 429.

(With H. L. K. Whitehouse) Symmetrical and asymmetrical post-reduction in Ascomycetes. *Nature, Lond.* **154**, 704.

New deep-sea diving method: the case for helium. *Fairplay*, **163**, 740.

Reshaping plants and animals. In *Reshaping Man's Heritage.* (Ed. J. S. Huxley.) London: Allen & Unwin.

1945 A labour saving method of sampling. *Nature, Lond.* **155**, 49.

A quantum theory of the origin of the solar system. *Nature, Lond.* **155**, 133.

Inverse statistical variates. *Nature, Lond.* **155**, 453.
Cosmic rays and kinematical relativity. *Nature, Lond.* **156**, 266.
On a method of estimating frequencies. *Biometrika*, **33**, 222.
Moments of r and χ^2 for a fourfold table in the absence of association. *Biometrika*, **33**, 231.
Use of χ^2 as a test of homogeneity in a $(n \times 2)$-fold table when expectations are small. *Biometrika*, **33**, 234.
A new theory of the past. *Amer. Scientist*, **33**, 129.
Chance effects and the Gaussian distribution. *Phil. Mag.* (7), **36**, 184.

1946 The cumulants of the distribution of Fisher's "u_{11}" and "u_{21}" scores used in the detection and estimation of linkage in man. *Ann. Eug.* **13**, 122.
The interaction of nature and nurture. *Ann. Eug.* **13**, 197.
(With B. M. Gilchrist) Sex-linkage in *Culex molestus. Experimentia*, **11**, 372.
(With H. L. K. Whitehouse) Symmetrical and asymmetrical reduction in Ascomycetes. *J. Genet.* **47**, 208.
Auld Hornie, F.R.S. *Modern Quarterly*, p. 32.
A Banned Broadcast and Other Essays. London: Chatto & Windus.

1947 The mutation rate of the gene for haemophilia, and its segregation ratios in males and females. *Ann. Eug.* **13**, 262.
(With C. A. B. Smith) A new estimate of the linkage between the genes for colour-blindness and haemophilia in man. *Ann. Eug.* **14**, 10.
The dysgenic effect of induced recessive mutations. *Ann. Eug.* **14**, 35.
Effect of nuclear explosions. *Ann. Eug.* **14**, 35.
(With B. M. Gilchrist) Sex-linkage and sex determination in a mosquito *Culex molestus. Hereditas*, **33**, 175.
(With D. E. Lea) A mathematical theory of chromosomal rearrangements. *J. Genet.* **48**, 1.
Science Advances. London: George Allen & Unwin.
What is Life? New York: Boni & Gaer.

1948 The precision of observed values of small frequencies. *Biometrika*, **35**, 297.
A note on the median of a multivariate distribution. *Biometrika*, **35**, 414.
The theory of a cline. *J. Genet.* **48**, 277.
(With G. D. Snell) Methods for histocompatability of genes. *J. Genet.* **49**, 104.
The number of genotypes which can be formed with a given number of genes. *J. Genet.* **49**, 117.
Biology and Marxism. *Modern Quarterly* (NS), **3**, 2.
(With C. A. B. Smith) A simple exact test for birth order effect. *Ann. Eug.* **14**, 117.
Differences, *Mind*, **57** (NS), 227.
The formal genetics of man. *Proc. Roy. Soc. B*, **135**, 147.

1949 Parental and fraternal correlations for fitness. *Ann. Eug.* **14**, 288.
A test for homogeneity of records of familiar abnormalities. *Ann. Eug.* **14**, 339.
The association of characters as a result of inbreeding and linkage. *Ann. Eug.* **15**, 15.
Suggestions as to quantitative measurement of rates of evolution. *Evolution*, **3**, 51.
Some statistical problems arising in genetics. *J. Roy. Stat. Soc. B*, **11**, 14.
The rate of mutation of human genes. *Proc. 8th International Congress of Genetics. Hereditas* Suppl. p. 267.
A note on non-normal correlation. *Biometrika*, **34**, 467.
In defence of genetics. *Modern Quarterly* (NS), **4**, 194.
Human evolution: past and future. In *Genetics Paleontology and Evolution*. (Eds. G. L. Jepsen, E. Mayr & G. G. Simpson.) Princeton University Press, p. 405.
(With D. Dewar & C. M. Davies) *Is Evolution a Myth? A debate*. London: C. A. Watts & Co. & The Paternoster Press.
Disease and evolution. *La ricerca scientifica Suppl.* **19**, 68.

1951 La methode dans la génétique. *C.R. 10th Cong. Internat. Phil. Sci.* **6**, 34. Paris: Hermann.

La narcose par les gaz indifférents. *Mecanisme de la Narcose.* (Pub. C.N.R.S. Paris), p. 47.

The rate of evolution. *Rat. Ann.* p. 7.

The mathematics of biology. *Sci. J. Roy. Coll. Sci.* **22**, 11.

A class of efficient estimates of a parameter. *Bull. Internat. Stat. Inst.* **32**, 231.

The extraction of square roots. *Math. Gaz.* **35**, 89.

Everything has a History. London: George Allen & Unwin.

1952 The mechanical chess player. *Brit. J. Phil. Sci.* **3**, 189.

Variation. *New Biology,* **12**, 9.

Simple tests for bimodality and bitangentiality. *Ann. Eug.* **16**, 359.

Relations between biology and other sciences. *Sci. Culture,* **17**, 407.

The origin of language. *Rat. Ann.* p. 38.

1953 The genetics of some biochemical abnormalities. *Lectures on the Scientific Basis of Medicine,* **3**, 41.

Animal ritual and human language. *Diogenes (UNESCO),* **4**, 61.

(With H. Spurway) The comparative ethology of vertebrate breathing. I. Breathing in newts with a general survey. *Behaviour,* **6**, 8.

Foreword. "Evolution" *Symp. Soc. Expt. Biol.* **7**, 9.

The estimation of two parameters from a sample. *Sankhya,* **12**, 313.

Animal populations and their regulation. *New Biology,* **15**, 9.

On some statistical formulae. *Sci. Culture,* **18**, 598.

Some animal life-tables. *J. Inst. Actuaries,* **79**, 83.

Closing address. *I.U.B.S. Symp. on Genetics of Population,* p. 139.

1954 (With H. Spurway) A statistical analysis of communication in *Apis mellifera* and a comparison with communication in other animals. *Insectes soc.* **1**, 247.

A logical analysis of learning, conditioning and related processes. *Behaviour,* **6**, 4.

The measurement of natural selection. *Caryologia* (Turin), Suppl. **6**, 480.

Introducing Douglas Spalding. *Brit. J. Anim. Behaviour,* **2**, 1.

(With H. Spurway) A statistical analysis of some data on infra-red communication. *Brit. J. Anim. Behaviour,* **2**, 38.

The genetical determination of behaviour. *Brit. J. Anim. Behaviour,* **2**, 118.

A rationalist with a halo. *Rat. Ann.* p. 14.

The origins of life. *New Biology,* **16**, 12.

(With R. Capildeo) The mathematics of bird population growth and decline. *J. Anim. Ecol.* **23**, 215.

La signalisation animale. *L'Année Biologique,* **30**, 89.

Substitutes for χ^2. *Biometrika,* **42**, 265.

An exact test for randomness of mating. *J. Genet.* **52**, 631.

The statistics of evolution. In *Evolution as a Process,* p. 109. (Eds. J. S. Huxley, A. C. Hardy & E. B. Ford.) London: Allen & Unwin.

The *Biochemistry of Genetics.* London: George Allen & Unwin.

1955 Genetical effects of radiation from products of nuclear explosions. *Nature, Lond.* **176**, 115.

Origin of man. *Nature, Lond.* **176**, 169.

Educational problems of the colonial territories. *Nature, Lond.* **176**, 750.

Population genetics. *New Biology,* **18**, 34.

Some alternatives to sex. *New Biology,* **19**, 7.

A problem in the significance of small numbers. *Biometrika,* **42**, 266.

The rapid calculation of χ^2 as a test of homogeneity from a $2 \times n$ table. *Biometrika,* **42**, 519.

The maximisation of national income. *Sankhya,* **16**, 1.

Biometry. *Sankhya,* **16**, 207.

(With H. Spurway) The respiratory behaviour of the Indian climbing perch in various environments. *Brit. J. Anim. Behaviour,* **3**, 74.

A logical basis for genetics? *Brit. J. Phil. Science,* **6**, 245.

Natural selection. *Trans. Bose. Res. Inst. Calcutta,* **10**, 17.

The genetic effects of atomic bomb explosions. *Current Science,* **24**, 399.

The prospects of eugenics. *The Roy. Inst. of Gt. Brit.* **36**, 290.

Targets. *Math. Gaz.* **39**, 1.

The complete matrices for brother-sister and alternate parent-offspring mating involving one locus. *J. Genet.* **53**, 315.

Aristotle's account of bees' dances. *J. Hellenic Studies*, **75**, 24.

On the biochemistry of heterosis, and the stabilisation of polymorphism. *Proc. Roy. Soc. B*, **144**, 217.

Animal communication and the origin of human language. *Sci. Progr.* **171**, 385.

The biochemistry of human genetics. *Society of Biological Chemists, India, Silver Jubilee. Souvenir*, p. 21.

Suggestions for evolutionary studies in India. *Nat. Inst. of Sci. Ind. Bulletin No. 7, Symposium on Organic Evolution*, p. 25.

The calculation of mortality rates from ringing data. *Acta Congr. Int. Orn.* p. 454, Basel.

Introduction p. 14 and, Critique de la méthode statistique utilisée pour l'étude de la *pars stridens* alaire de *Locusta migratoria*. p. 102. In *Colloque sue l'acoustique des Orthoptères* (Ed. R. G. Busnel). Paris: Publ. Inst. Nat. Rech. Agronom.

Remaniement du patrimoine héréditaire humain, and Mecanismes biochimiques d'action des gènes. In *La Progénèse*, pp. 389 and 397. (Ed. R. Turpin.) Paris: Masson et Cie.

1956 The detection of antigens with an abnormal genetic determination. *J. Genet.* **54**, 54.

The conflict between inbreeding and selection. I. Self-fertilisation. *J. Genet.* **54**, 56.

The estimation of viabilities. *J. Genet.* **54**, 294.

The detection of autosomal lethals in mice induced by mutagenic agents. *J. Genet.* **54**, 327.

Almost unbiased estimates of functions of frequencies. *Sankhya*, **17**, 201.

The estimation and significance of the logarithm of a ratio of frequencies. *Ann. Human Gen.* **20**, 309.

Mutation in the sex linked recessive type of muscular dystrophy. A possible sex difference. *Ann. Human Gen.* **20**, 344.

The theory of selection for melanism in lepidoptera. *Pro. Roy. Soc. B*, **145**, 303.

The relation between density regulation and natural selection. *Proc. Roy. Soc. B*, **145**, 306.

Some reflections on non-violence. *Mankind*, **1**, 1.

(With H. Spurway) Abnormal breathing behaviour in a fish. *Brit. J. Anim. Behaviour*, **4**, 37.

The sources of some ethological notions. *Brit. J. Anim. Behaviour*, **4**, 162.

Die Bedeutung der Makromoleküle für Evolution und Differenzierung. In "Vergleichend Biochemische Fragen". *Colloquium Ges. Physiol, Chemie*, **6**, 165.

Natural selection in man. *Acta Genet.* **6**, 321.

The estimation of mutation rates produced by high energy events in mammals. *Current Sci.* **25**, 75.

(With S. M. Smith) The sampling distribution of a maximum likelihood estimate. *Biometrika*, **43**, 96.

The argument from animals to men. An examination of its validity for anthropology. *J. Roy. Anthropol. Inst.* **86**, 1.

Time in biology. *Sci. Progr.* **175**, 385.

(With H. Spurway) Imprinting and the evolution of instincts. *Nature, Lond.* **178**, 85.

The biometrical analysis of fossil populations. *Journal of the Paleontological Society of India* (Lucknow), **1**, 54.

Les aspects physico-chimiques des instincts. In *L'Instinct dans le Comportement des Animaux et de l'Homme*. Paris: Masson et Cie, p. 547.

Can a species concept be justified? In "The Species Concept in Paleontology". (Ed. P. C. Sylvester-Bradley.) *Syst. Assoc. Publ.* **2**, 95.

Radiation hazards. *Lancet*, i, 1066.

1957 The conditions for coadaptation in polymorphism for inversions. *J. Genet.* **55**, 218.

The cost of natural selection. *J. Genet.* **55**, 511.

(With T. C. Carter) The use of linked marker genes for detecting recessive autosomal lethals in the mouse. *J. Genet.* **55**, 596.

The prospects of eugenics. *New Biology*, **22**, 7.

Karl Pearson, 1857-1957. *Biometrika*, **44**, 303. (Also published in *New Biology*, **25**, 7.)

Aunt Jobisca, the bellman, and the hermit. *Rat. Ann.* p. 15.

The elementary theory of population growth. *J. Mad. Univ.* B. **27**, 237.

Graphical methods in enzyme chemistry. *Nature, Lond.* **179**, 832.

Methods for the detection and enumeration of mutations produced by irradiation in mice. *Proc. Int. Genetics Symp.* 1956 (Cytological Supplement).

Genesis of life. In *The Planet Earth*. (Ed. D. R. Bates.) London: Pergamon Press, p. 287.

The Unity and Diversity of Life. Publications Division, Government of India.

1958 Syadvada system of predication. *Sankhya*, **18**, 195.

The scope of biological statistics. *Sankhya*, **20**, 195.

(With S. K. Roy) A research project for some Indian schools. *Vigyan Shikshak*, **2**, 35.

Parthenogenesis. *Triangle (Basle)*, **3**, 142.

Sex determination in Metazoa. *Proc. Zool. Soc. Calcutta, Mukherjee Memorial*, **4**, 13.

Mathematics and jute breeding. *Jute and Gunny Review*, **10**, 3.

The present position of Darwinism. *J. Sci. Ind. Res.* (India), **17a**, 97.

The pre-Christian religions of Europe. *Bulletin Ramakrishna Mission Institute of Culture*, **9**, 129.

The statistical study of animal behaviour. *Trans. Bose Research Institute*, **22**, 201.

The genetic effects of quanta and particles of high energy. *Sci. Culture*, **24**, 16.

The theory of evolution before and after Bateson. *J. Genet.* **56**, 11.

(With H. Spurway) The quantitative study of animal behaviour in an approximately steady state. In *Memoriam Methodi Popov*, Bulgarian Academy of Sciences, p. 89.

1959 The scope of biological statistics. *Sankhya*, **20**, 195.

The analysis of heterogeneity. *Sankhya*, **21**, 209.

An Indian perspective of Darwin. *Centenn. Rev. Arts Sci. Mich. St. Univ.* **3**, 357.

Suggestions for research on coconuts. *Ind. Coconut J.* **12**, 1.

The non-violent scientific study of birds. *J. Bombay Nat. Hist. Soc.* **56**, 375.

Parthenogenese. *Naturwissenschaftliche Rundschau*, **12**, 453.

Natural selection. In *Darwin's Biological Work*. (Ed. P. R. Bell.) Cambridge Univ. Press, p. 101.

1960 The theory of natural selection today. In *Proc. Cent. Bicent. Cong. Biol.* (Ed. R. D. Purchon.) Singapore: Univ. Malaya Press, p. 1; also *Nature, Lond.* **183**, 710.

Pasteur and cosmic asymmetry. *Nature, Lond.* **185**, 87.

The scientific work of J. S. Haldane. *Nature, Lond.* **187**, 102.

"Dex" or "order of magnitude"? *Nature, Lond.* **187**, 879.

The interpretation of Carter's results on induction of recessive lethals in mice. *J. Genet.* **57**, 131.

More precise expressions for the cost of natural selection. *J. Genet.* **57**, 351.

Physiological problems at high pressure. *Aero Med. Soc. J.* (New Delhi), **5**, 1.

Genetics in relation to medicine. *Proc. Acad. Med. Sci.* (Andhra Pradesh), **1**, 216.

Suggestions for research on human physiology in India. *The Medico* (Gandhi Medical College, Hyderabad), **4**, 2.

On expecting the unexpected. *Rat. Ann.* p. 5.

The addition of random vectors. *Sankhya*, **22**, 213.

Blood grouping and human trisomy. *Current Sci.* **29**, 375.

The water hyacinth—an appeal for information. *J. Bombay Nat. Hist. Soc.* **57**, 243.

Mind in evolution. *Zool. Jahrb. Abt. Syst.* **88**, 117.

Physiological Variation and Evolution. Maharajah Sayajirao. Memorial Lecture, p. 1.

1961 Some simple systems of artificial selection. *J. Genet.* **57**, 345.
Evidence for heterosis in woodlice. *J. Genet.* **58**, 39.
(With S. D. Jayakar) An enumeration of some human relationships. *J. Genet.* **58**, 81.
Natural selection in a population with annual breeding but overlapping generations. *J. Genet.* **58**, 122.
The selection of double heterozygotes. *J. Genet.* **58**, 125.
Natural selection in man. *Prog. Med. Genet.* **1**, 27.
The scientific work of J. S. Haldane. *Penguin Science Survey* (2), p. 11.
(With S. D. Jayakar) A statistical analysis of some data on ant and wasp behaviour. *Att. IV Congresso U.I.E.I.S.—Pavia. Symposia Genetica et Biol. Ital.* **12**, 221.
(With K. R. Dronamraju) Inheritance of hairy pinnae. *Amer. J. Hum. Genet.* **14**, 102.
Simple approximations to the probability integral and $P(\chi^2, 1)$ when both are small. *Sankhya*, **23**, 9.
Evolution as a test for ethics. *Current Sci.* **30**, 214.
The dark religions. *Rat. Ann.* p. 35.
Conditions for stable polymorphism at an autosomal locus. *Nature, Lond.* **193**, 1108.

1962 Beyond agnosticism. *Rat. Ann.* p. 5.
Human needs. In *What the Human Race is Up To* (Ed. N. Mitchison), p. 395. London: Gollancz.

1963 Tests for sex-linked inheritance on population samples. *Ann. Hum. Genet.* **27**, 107.
(With S. D. Jayakar) The distribution of extremal and nearly extremal values in samples from a normal distribution. *Biometrika*, **50**, 89.
The design of experiments on mutation rates. *J. Genet.* **58**, 232.
(With S. D. Jayakar) Polymorphism due to selection of varying direction. *J. Genet.* **58**, 237.
(With S. D. Jayakar) The elimination of double dominants in large random mating populations. *J. Genet.* **58**, 243.
(With S. D. Jayakar) The solution of some equations occurring in population genetics. *J. Genet.* **58**, 291.
(With S. D. Jayakar) Polymorphism due to selection depending on the composition of a population. *J. Genet.* **58**, 318.
(With S. D. Jayakar) A new test of significance in sampling from finite populations, with application to human inbreeding. *J. Genet.* **58**, 402.
Life and mind as physical realities. In *Penguin Science Survey* (B), p. 224.
The concentration of rare recessive genes in the past and in modern times. In *The Genetics of Migrant and Isolate Populations.* (Ed. E. Goldschmidt.) Baltimore: Williams & Wilkins, p. 243.
Some lies about science. *Rat. Ann.* p. 32.
Biological possibilities for the human species in the next ten thousand years. In *Man and His Future.* (Ed. G. E. W. Wolstenholme.) London: J. & A. Churchill, p. 337.
A possible development of J. S. Haldane's views on the relation between quantum mechanics and biology. In *The Regulation of Human Respiration.* (Eds. D. J. C. Cunningham, B. B. Lloyd.) Oxford: Blackwell, p. 103.
(With H. Spurway) The regulation of breathing in a fish, *Anabas testudineus.* In *The Regulation of Human Respiration.* (Eds. D. J. C. Cunningham, B. B. Lloyd.) Oxford: Blackwell, p. 431.

1964 A defense of beanbag genetics. *Perspectives in Biology and Medicine*, **7**, 343.
The origin of lactation. *Rat. Ann.* p. 19.
(With S. D. Jayakar) Equilibria under natural selection at a sex-linked locus. *J. Genet.* **59**, 29.
The implications of genetics for human society. *Proc. 11th Inter. Congr. Genet.* xci.
The proper social application of the knowledge of human genetics. In *The Science of Science*, p. 150. (Eds. M. Goldsmith & A. Mackay.) London: Souvenir Press and Penguin Books (1966).

1965 (With S. D. Jayakar) The nature of human genetic loads. *J. Genet.* **59**, 143.

(With S. D. Jayakar) Selection for a single pair of allelomorphs with complete replacement. *J. Genet.* **59**, 171.

On being finite. *Rat. Ann.* p. 3.

(With A. K. Ray) The genetics of a common Indian digital anomaly. *Proc. Nat. Acad. Sci. Wash.* **53**, 1050.

The possible evolution of lactation. *Zool. Jahr. Syst. Bd.* **92**, 41.

Data needed for a blueprint of the first organism. In *The Origins of Pre-biological Systems*. (Ed. S. W. Fox.) New York: Academic Press, p. 11.

Biological research in developing countries. In *Man and Africa*. (Eds. G. E. W. Wolstenholme & M. O'Connor.) CIBA foundation symposium. London: J. & A. Churchill, p. 222.

Postscript 1984

The following items came to light after first publication of this book:

1932 Preface (pp. v-vl) to *Recent Advances in Cytology* by C. D. Darlington. London: J. & A. Churchill.

1933 (With John R. Baker) *Biology in Everyday Life* (six talks). London: Allen & Unwin.

1947 Life at high pressures. *Science News*, **4**, 9. (Ed. John Enogat.) Penguin Books.
Oxygen poisoning in man. Letter (Aug. 9th) in *British Medical Journal*, **2**, 226.

1952 A biologist looks at India, *Viswa-Bharati: Quarterly*, 276.

1958 The unity and diversity of life, Sardar Vallabhai Patel lectures, Delhi. Government Publications Division.

1966 An autobiography in brief. *Perspectives in Biology and Medicine*, **9**, 476. University of Chicago Press. J. B. S. Haldane's life in India, by K. P. Dronamraju. *Perspectives in Biology and Medicine*, **9**, 482.

1972 Introduction to *The Biology of Mental Defect* by L. S. Penrose. (Fourth edition.)

1976 *The Man with Two Memories*. London: The Merlin Press.

N. W. P.
R. W. C.

Index

281